Praise for *Tell Me My Story*

"For anyone doing healing or humanitarian work, this extraordinary and candid book should be required reading. It's a working prayer—helping you discover why you are on your path, and how to follow it with freedom, inner guidance, and self-acceptance.

—**Ellen Balis, Ed.D.**, Clinical Psychologist

"*Tell Me My Story* offers suggestions and practices for how people and organizations can shift their mindsets and create cultures of empathy. This book should be required reading for staff at institutions that serve communities around the world."

—**Deepa Iyer**, author of *Social Change Now:*
A Guide for Reflection and Connection

"*Tell Me My Story* is a profound guide for anyone navigating the complexities of service and shows how embracing our humanity can lead to transformative healing and change."

—**David Treleaven, PhD**, author of *Trauma-Sensitive*
Mindfulness: Practices for Safe and Transformative Healing

"Part memoir, part manifesto, *Tell Me My Story* is a must-read for humanitarian professionals. In this vital, beautifully written, and well-researched treatise, Dhabalia shines an important light on what it's like to serve in this capacity, and how to do it sustainably. Only by addressing the debilitating side effects of burnout, compassion fatigue, and vicarious trauma can humanitarian workers heal themselves while so generously serving others."

—**Jenny Blake**, Webby-nominated podcaster and
author of *Free Time, Pivot, and Life After College*

"*Tell Me My Story* is a must read —not only for those who dedicate their lives to helping others but for all who have a story in need of healing."

—**Angela Bailey**, Founder & CEO, Angela Bailey and
Associates and Former Chief Human Capital Officer
for the Department of Homeland Security

"*Tell Me My Story* is not just a book; it's a transformative experience that should be on the reading list of every advocate, helping professional, and compassionate leader. Dhabalia's words serve as a guiding light for those committed to making the world a better place while reminding us that we must fill our own cups before we can pour into the cups of those we seek to help. True service begins with understanding and nurturing ourselves."

—**Katrina Whitney**, Director, Central Washington University, Mindfulness Practitioner and Equity and Social Justice Advocate

"*Tell Me My Story* is a must-read book for all those who work in fields that expose them to the traumatic experiences of others (secondary trauma. [Dimple] Dhabalia's insights help us find an understanding of our own actions or reactions without guilt or judgment as she suggests a better way to live fully in the moment while acknowledging our trauma, rather than simply surviving and working "through it." This book should be read by every public service lawyer, given to each judicial officer who takes the bench, and distributed to the judicial and probation staff in every courthouse to create safe and caring workplaces."

—**The Hon. Elizabeth Weishaupl**, Mediator/Arbitrator/Special Appointed Neutral

"*Tell Me My Story* powerfully speaks to a broad group of people who are by nature and work invested in making our planet a more just, equitable, kind, and compassionate place, while suffering from caring at the expense of self. Through a compelling integration of her personal and professional experiences, Dimple Dhabalia offers a conceptual framework for readers to use in their own reflections and insights. *Tell Me My Story* will leave humanitarians feeling affirmed in their own experiences and the quest for well-being as they try to change the world."

—**Pat Vivian**, co-author, *Organizational Trauma and Healing*

"Anyone with a true heart for service should read this book as early in your career as possible. It will not only save you from unnecessary trauma and all that comes with it but also compassionately remind you that giving voice to our own humanity and stories is just as important as the vital services we deliver to the world and its people."

—**Kay Adams**, LCSW. author of *Bedside Witness: Stories of Hope, Healing, and Humanity*

"*Tell Me My Story* comes at a pivotal moment for government and other human-centered organizations. In the race for recruiting and retaining high-performing humanitarians who will continue to thrive and deliver on their mission, leaders can easily adopt the brilliant Manifesto Dhabalia has developed. This wonderful and honest book is useful reading for all levels of humanitarians looking to lead with their heart while protecting it."

—**Anne Baker**, Foreign Service Officer of the
United States of America, Retired

"A compelling mix of vulnerable storytelling and call-to-action, *Tell Me My Story* highlights challenges like vicarious trauma and burnout that many humanitarian aid workers experience, and the need for change in how staff are cared for in this high-stress field."

—**Lauren Williamson**, INGO Staff Care Professional,
and Seasoned Humanitarian Aid Worker

"A beautiful, thoughtfully written, important read for every humanitarian, helper, and idealist. *Tell Me My Story* shares powerful and poignant stories that illustrate the root of the current epic trends of compassion fatigue, overwhelm, moral injury, and burnout that plague helpers of all backgrounds. Adding in the complexities of immigration, race, class, and socio-economic status, Dhabalia highlights the importance of healing the unhelpful stories that stifle helpers and disrupt their quest to serve sustainably and thrive as they work to make a difference. This book inspires hope."

—**Yvonne Ator**, MD, MPH Coach, Advocate, and Founder
of Thriving Idealist and Thriving Physicians

"Well-researched, captivating, and exquisitely crafted, *Tell Me My Story* shows humanitarian leaders the way forward out of workplace trauma and into embracing the wholeness of people at work, reminding us along the way that humans are just as important as the work they do. Leaders and culture change agents, you need this book."

—**Jenn Whitmer**, International Keynote Speaker,
host of Joyosity™ podcast, and Joy-Bringer

"Through vulnerability and sharing her personal story, Dhabalia provides not only a refreshing way of looking at a career of service but also the specific steps to work through our own narratives and facilitate our own healing. This book has already helped me in my personal journey and I look forward to sharing its teachings with my colleagues."

—**Corinne LeBaron**, M.S.S., CEO embrella

"*Tell Me My Story* gives those working in nonprofit management the opportunity and guidance needed to rethink what it means for organizations to fulfill their Duty of Care responsibility. It provides practical, human-centered advice to assist organizations in creating and rewarding healthy practices for their teams."

—**Jennifer Owens**, President & CEO, Arlington Community Foundation

TELL ME
MY STORY

CHALLENGING THE NARRATIVE
OF SERVICE BEFORE SELF

Dimple D. Dhabalia

For Mom and Dad—thank you for teaching me about love, grace, service, and most importantly, what it means to be human. I miss you and love you both with all my heart.

&

For Kajal—my little sister, best friend, confidante, and the only person who knows all the other moments–big and small–not captured within the pages of this book. I'm grateful our souls found each other.

&

For all the humanitarians who have spent their lives putting service before self—I see you, I thank you, and I honor your humanity.

"Between the stimulus and response, there is a space. And in that space lies our freedom and power to choose our responses. In our response lies our growth and our freedom."

—Viktor Frankl

CONTENTS

AUTHOR'S NOTE

Sensitivity warning: We all have a window of tolerance for stress and trauma that narrows and widens in response to our life experiences. This is why a group of people exposed to the same stress or traumatic event in the workplace will all have different reactions. The same will be true of readers engaging with my story. Parts of my life story in the pages ahead depict experiences of violence and trauma. The dream sequence I share in the prologue, my uncle Yash's story in Chapter 1, and some of the other stories about domestic violence, displacement, othering, and mental health, may activate your own stress or trauma response.

As you read, I invite you to notice any thoughts or body sensations that appear and address them in ways that support you. Try to create some space between you and the story—take a deep breath, go for a walk, or take out a journal and dig deeper into the questions or feelings that have arisen. If you find yourself struggling with unanswered questions or vicariously experiencing my reactions in certain situations, do your best to hold them with curiosity and compassion. And if you feel absolutely overwhelmed, find a friend or a therapist to walk alongside you on this journey.

To help you check in with yourself as you read, I've placed an image of a hummingbird inside an Ensō circle throughout the book as a reminder to pause, breathe, and reflect.

There are many interpretations of the Ensō symbol, but I use it here to represent strength and togetherness, which reflects the duality of our independence as humans and interdependence on our colleagues, friends, and loved ones as we live and work. I've used the image of a hummingbird in my work for many years to symbolize the feeling of lightness and joy we can experience through self-care and rest.

Disclaimer: I am not a mental-health professional. The information about trauma and mental-health issues I share in this book comes from the many resources I cite in the Notes section at the end, as well as training programs I've been through and personal experiences.

I've taken great care with the stories I've shared here, ensuring that they communicate my perspective rather than telling other people's stories or making assumptions about their intentions or feelings. Both of my parents have passed away, and the stories that involve them are based on my experiences and conversations we had. I've done my best to share the stories as I remember them, with help from journals I've kept over the years, but I may remember some things differently than others do.

I chose to share stories from my former work as a government employee that I feel can assist other leaders in determining the healthiest and most productive ways to be human within systems that aren't designed to preserve the humanity of the people working within them. My intention isn't to call out individuals but rather to advocate for change across mission-driven, trauma-exposed sectors. My aim is to shed light on the organizational lack of awareness, lack of intention, and lack of policies that continues to impose untenable expectations on humanitarians and leads them to deprioritize their own health and well-being in the name of service and productivity.

In some cases, names and other identifying details have been changed at the request of the people involved or for my own personal reasons. Any stories about refugees I've interviewed or that are told from the perspective of a refugee are a compilation of multiple refugee stories or narratives to protect individuals' privacy and ensure that no story can be attributed to any particular refugee or put them in harm's way.

How to read this book: This book is about healing the stories we carry within us that can keep us stuck in painful and unhealthy patterns of behavior in our lives as humanitarians. Our stories are experienced as an inner monologue that's trying to make meaning of the stress, trauma, challenges, and adversities we encounter every day. The problem is, the stories we tell ourselves aren't absolute truth—they're subjective projections of our fears, expectations, hopes, desires, and assumptions. This means that when we encounter a stressful or traumatic event, or some other form of adversity, our brain activates our sympathetic nervous system and moves us through a pattern—thought, emotion, sensation, reaction—which over time becomes a habitual series of conditioned reactions.

The story-healing cycle I talk about in this book uses mindful awareness and self-compassion to help us recognize, accept, and break our patterns so we can regulate our nervous system and tap into our own agency with greater ease. This process allows us to choose an intentional response to the situation, rather than simply reacting. As you'll see through the moments of my life that I've shared in the pages ahead, our internal stories directly impact our quality of life. Healing our stories is fundamental to enhancing our mental, physical, emotional, relational, and spiritual health and well-being, and it's what allows us to continue showing up as the best versions of ourselves—for ourselves, for our loved ones, and for the people we serve.

Parts one through five of this book reflect the five steps—*shaping, surviving, seeing, shifting, sharing*—of the story-healing cycle using moments from my life that recount how I moved from pain, trauma, and simply trying to survive, to healing and thriving in my personal life and work. As you read, you'll witness the different pieces of my narrative in the same way I did: one scene, one feeling, one thought, one experience, one small connection at a time—in the fits and starts, ebbs and flows that are common when we move from trauma toward awareness and recovery.

Part six of this book is a manifesto committed to changing the status quo—first by doing the work to heal our own stories, and then by working with leaders and organizations to create a holistic duty of care that addresses the unique needs of humanitarians and creates the conditions needed to heal who we are as a collective in our organizations. This section includes concrete examples of actions that can be taken at the individual and organizational level to facilitate story-healing across the humanitarian sector.

Finally, I've crafted this book to challenge our individual and collective narratives about *service before self*. Think of it as an exercise in mindful awareness to help you begin to notice not only the patterns of your internal dialogue and subsequent physical and emotional reactions, but also how your stories influence your behaviors. Repeated descriptions of tears and deep breaths are intentional and meant to help you as the reader more easily see patterns of default mind-body reactions that it took me years to notice. However, you may find yourself irritated by my reactions, feeling confused about how one story connects with the next, and even frustrated or judgmental that it doesn't all quite make sense yet.

In those moments, I invite you to pause and reflect. I've also provided questions at the end of each part to help you begin to explore your own narrative through this framework and move toward healing your own stories.

PROLOGUE

Running barefoot on the dirt road, I found myself drenched in sweat, my hair and clothes matted against my body. To my left was the long stone wall—the one supposed to protect the people in the camp but which now stood smeared with babies' blood. All around me was the chaos that comes in the midst of armed aggression—people screaming, sprinting, and trying to hide, ignorant of the futility of their actions.

The sound of horses' hooves beating against the packed earth reverberated as the attackers moved swiftly, efficiently working their way back and forth across the length of the camp. Those wielding torches lit huts on fire as others with machetes went after the people.

Suddenly, one of them rode past me and spun around—jumping off his horse to stand in front of me, blade raised, eyes wild with rage. I froze, tears streaming down my dust-covered face. The man raised his machete, but just as I opened my mouth to scream, he ran through me as if I wasn't there.

I gasped for breath as I turned to see where he'd gone, eyes darting frantically to find him. I watched in horror as he descended upon a young family, a man shielding his wife and baby. I gasped as the sharp blade came down on the man's arm, cutting through flesh and bone with the ease of a knife through a ripe mango.

The attacker then turned to the woman. Clutching her child to her chest, she reached out her other hand, palm up, begging him to spare them as tears flowed down her taut, black cheeks. The man pushed her to the ground and pried the baby out of her arms, deaf to her screams. After throwing the shrieking newborn against the stone wall, he returned his attention to the woman.

I knew as well as she did what was about to happen. But unable to move or make a sound, I did nothing as the man unbuckled his belt.

I sat straight up in bed—heart racing, throat raw, face wet with tears, hair and body soaked in sweat.

Disoriented and terrified, I tried to catch my breath while my eyes adjusted to the dark room. Within a few seconds, the faint outlines of a credenza and TV at the foot of the bed took shape. Recognizing my surroundings, my body softened and my breathing slowed.

I'm in a hotel. I'm in Zambia for work. I'm safe.

I took a deep breath, wiped my tears with my hands, and threw back the covers. Swinging my legs over the side of the bed, my feet landed on the soft hotel slippers I'd taken off hours earlier before collapsing into bed. I looked at the sliding glass doors, where faint light from the street came through the sheer curtains. I'd opened the blackout drapes the house-keepers had pulled closed during their nightly turndown service as soon as I'd returned from dinner that evening. I never liked sleeping in a dark room.

The red numbers on the nightstand clock glowed 3:48. I had at least three hours before I needed to get up, but I didn't want to close my eyes. I didn't want to go back there again—to the land of machetes and dead babies. This was the third night in a row. I couldn't understand what was happening.

Sliding my feet into the slippers, I stood up, pulling my sweat-soaked nightgown away from my damp skin. Using the light from the street, I made my way to the bathroom where I abandoned the slippers at the threshold to feel the cool tile floor. I winced as the fluorescent bulb buzzed to life and flooded the room with a harsh and unnatural light.

I stared at my pallid reflection in the mirror, the face looking back at me puffy and imprinted with lines from the pillowcase. My shoulders slumped in exhaustion and defeat. My eyes, still shimmering with tears, beseeched me for an answer: *How did this happen?*

This was supposed to be like any other trip—fly to an exciting new part of the world, check into a nice hotel, get up early the next morning, head to the worksite, listen to stories of individuals and families who were claiming persecution and torture, come "home" each evening, drink, have dinner, maybe work out, and then go to bed and start over again the next day.

I let out a deep breath I hadn't noticed I'd been holding.

Even before my first day of work in Zambia, it was obvious this wasn't going to be like any other trip. Something was different—*I* was different. Unable to answer my own question, I lowered my gaze and shook my head, tears threatening again.

Flicking off the bathroom light, I padded barefoot back across the thick carpeting to the other side of the bed—the dry side—pulled back the duvet, and got under the covers. Lying against the soft pillows, one part of me willed sleep to come, while the other hoped it didn't.

What had changed? In the nearly six years I'd been doing this job, I hadn't altered my approach to interviewing refugees, and I'd never had a problem maintaining enough emotional distance to keep going.

Turning on my side, I pulled the covers up to my chin and stared at the sliding doors. This section of Lusaka seemed so much quieter than other places I'd stayed, places where the sounds of the city penetrated the walls of the hotel. There, the cars, ambulances, street hawkers, and occasional church bells or calls to prayers from the mosques had made the unfamiliar somehow seem familiar.

Right now I'd take loud sirens—anything to drown out my thoughts and these nightmares.

I lay motionless, lost in thought, unaware of time passing. When the sun peeked over the horizon, I dreaded the day ahead, knowing it was unlikely to be any better than yesterday or the day before.

Was this my new normal? My breath caught as the heaviness in my chest made its way up to form a lump in my throat and then burst out as sobs.

No. Nothing about this is normal. Something is definitely wrong.

INTRODUCTION

I f you're reading this book, you're likely a humanitarian.

Now before you decide this is not you and close this book forever, please let me explain.

The word *humanitarian* often evokes images of people wearing cargo pants and safari vests working in jungles, war zones, and the villages of developing nations. And yes, the people who do that work are humanitarians. But so are teachers, activists, caregivers, healthcare professionals, first responders, public servants, government workers, members of the clergy, journalists, international aid and development corps, and so many others working to alleviate pain and suffering in the world.

The mission-driven space in which I chose to work, interviewing refugees and asylum seekers, was at the crossroads of the government and humanitarian sectors. People working in any humanitarian position carry a deep sense of duty, responsibility, and commitment to the mission, and they tend to really love their work. They also armor themselves to the fullest extent possible, determined to push through at all costs, regardless of how that impacts their own well-being.

After almost two decades working alongside and leading other humanitarians, I believe those of us who choose to work in human-centered fields love the work and are compelled by a common desire to alleviate the suffering of other humans—even if it means bearing our own pain in silence and shame. But those same two decades of experience have shown me that service doesn't have to come at this cost. I know there is a better way, and I have seen it work.

By the time I set off for Zambia, I'd been interviewing refugees for a little over six years and was really good at my job. But the reality of what it meant to be "of service" had started to take its toll. I approached every interview the same way: welcome the applicant, explain the process, put them under oath, verify their application details—ticking off each item in red pen to confirm its accuracy, and then invite the applicant to share their story with me. As I listened, I asked questions to test the applicant's credibility and address any inconsistencies between their written statement and the story they recounted. For six years, I had listened to stories of fear, displacement, torture, and persecution, all while showing just enough empathy to make the applicant feel seen and heard. I'd taken pride in my ability to create a wall of professionalism between myself and the applicants.

It wasn't that I didn't care. It was a survival mechanism I had developed that allowed me to keep showing up to do the work.

But that all changed in Zambia.

There, for the first time in my career, I felt broken and full of shame. Looking back now, that shouldn't have been surprising. I worked in a culture where exhaustion was often worn as a badge of honor, and self-care was viewed as a luxury. At that time, the concept of mental health in general carried a stigma and wasn't something openly discussed in my—or really any other—workplace. In fact, when I'd started in my field, the only indication that listening to other people's trauma day in and day out might impact those of us doing the work came during the basic training course I attended soon after I'd started working as an asylum officer. There was an optional question-and-answer session with mental health professionals at the end of a long and emotionally draining training day, which had been designed to teach us the skills needed to interview survivors of torture with compassion, empathy, and care.

The after-hours session was a general discussion about what we should do to take care of ourselves, but it included no information about things like *vicarious trauma*, *secondary traumatic stress*, or *compassion fatigue*—which by then were commonly documented experiences of people working in mission-driven, trauma-exposed fields like mine. The whole session felt like an afterthought, further stigmatizing mental health in the workplace and implicitly sending the message that the well-being of the people we served was more important than our own.

It was a full ten years later, after my own firsthand experience of vicarious trauma in Zambia, that I finally sought answers to my questions: "*What is wrong with me? What can I do to get better? Am I the only one?*"

Making the Personal Professional

"Tell me your story."

These words were a key part of every interview I conducted with asylum seekers and refugees for over a decade of my career. They were an invitation for the individuals sitting across from me—some of the world's most vulnerable people—to have someone bear witness to their experiences of fear, displacement, persecution, torture, injustice, trauma, violence, and grief.

But never once in all those years did I stop to consider that the story I needed to witness most of all was my own.

Why would I want to?

My own life story was filled with experiences of domestic violence, mental illness, generational trauma, forced displacement, and instability. It wasn't all bad—there was a lot of love, too, which is why I'm here and able to share my story now—but the memories were painful and sad, and the associated emotions often felt overwhelming. So I worked hard to move past those moments and leave them behind. As far as I was concerned, they had nothing to do with my current life and work.

Except they did.

Seeing the Human in Humanitarian

Often, when asked why we choose these professions, humanitarians talk about feeling connected to a sense of purpose or a desire to be of service to humanity. But what if there's more? At the heart of the word *humanitarian* is *human*. What if the humanitarian path we've chosen is actually an invitation—to see and heal and love and embrace our own humanity through the stories of the people we're serving? What if the path is giving us powerful opportunities to reveal and heal our own wounds, and we just don't realize it?

And what if healing could happen at both the individual and organizational levels?

Most of us humanitarians go to work every day without realizing that our personal experiences of pain and trauma are not only scars we bear, but also the source of our superpowers. They allow us to sit with others in their darkest moments and embody empathy and compassion instead of ignorance and judgment. Our experiences give us the strength and motivation to show up day after day, year after year, to do work that is challenging, heartbreaking, messy, and mentally and physically exhausting. But with mindful awareness, compassion, and rest, it does not have to be permanently destructive.

When I set out to write this book, diving into the dark and murky depths of my own stories wasn't part of the plan. I envisioned a simple leadership book with three key objectives. First, to create awareness about the mission-driven occupational traumas and mental-health challenges in humanitarian work—the very real and often minimized "costs of caring." Second, to demonstrate the moral obligation I believe mission-driven organizations have to provide a duty of care for their staff. And finally, to make the case for why I believe the sacrifice often expected of people working in service of others is not only unnecessary, it's unsustainable, unhealthy, and may be fatal.

But as with most things in life, that was only what I saw on the surface— only part of the story.

As I wrote, what started as a leadership book turned into part memoir, part manifesto as I realized the healing power of sharing my story—first with myself and then with others. I saw in my own experiences the way our needs as humanitarians are often overlooked because we silently do our work, minimize our own trauma, and put off healing our wounds in order to continue serving others. For many years I didn't realize I could both acknowledge my pain *and* serve others at the same time, that being a humanitarian doesn't have to be—and really shouldn't be—one or the other.

As you read this book, I invite you to wonder, feel, and most importantly, to recognize that your choices can influence how your story progresses, both personally and professionally. As you follow my path and see the examples from my life, I hope you'll find resonance with your own experiences, even if they are different than mine. And I hope this will lead you to consider how your life and career path may have been shaped by more than meets the eye. Because integrating the story-healing process into our day-to-day lives is what ultimately brings healing change and ensures that we're living our lives to the fullest.

And that is my wish for each of us.

—Dimple Dhabalia, July 2023

PART ONE

SHAPING

SHAPING

The stories that shape us originate outside of ourselves and result in the fears, expectations, hopes, desires, and assumptions that create the lens through which we experience the world and our place in it.

This lens influences the stories we create to explain what's happening around us. Often starting in childhood, these *shaping* stories take root through the values and beliefs passed down from our parents or other caregivers about things like money, work ethic, safety and stability, duty, preserving family reputation, gender roles, cultural norms, and the importance of caring for others before ourselves.

We're also shaped by the implicit and explicit messages we receive from friends, teachers, neighbors, and religious leaders, as well as in the books we read and shows we watch. It's often through these encounters and messages that highlight our differences that we experience moments of othering, subtle acts of exclusion, and confusion about who we are—or need to be—in order to fit in and belong.

There are other times when our shaping stories are informed by circumstances and events we're not fully aware of or learn about later, like the trauma experienced by previous generations before we're born. Even without our awareness, these experiences burrow into our minds and bodies—the way the sadness and struggles of the people around us makes us feel isolated and alone, and the way our values have dark undersides of shame that creep up when we're not performing to family, cultural, or societal standards—influencing our thoughts, actions and beliefs from one moment to the next.

The *shaping* stories in Part One reflect the complexities of a few pivotal moments that became the catalyst for the conditioned reactions that influenced the choices I'd make, both personally and professionally, for decades to come.

1

THE HISTORY WE CARRY WITHIN US

(Generational Trauma)

Uganda—September 1972
(Yashvantrai Sheth's story as told to Dimple Dhabalia)

"Give it here!" yelled one of the porters, startling me out of my thoughts. I stared at him, confused. "You're going to Masaka, right?" I nodded. "Give it here, then!" He pointed at my bag.

I walked toward him, gripping the handle of my weathered, gray suitcase. It was only slightly bigger than a briefcase, but within its hard shell were the few possessions I had left, and the thought of losing any of them made my heart race. In addition to my clothing, there were farewell letters from the girls at the mines and a soft blue journal with my poetry and musings about life. My face flushed at the prospect of someone finding and going through my things, looking in on my innermost thoughts.

Nonetheless, I handed him my bag. He lifted it up to another porter who sat on the roof of the bus, using a thick blue rope to tie everything down on the large metal rack that ran almost the full length of the bus. Once I saw that my bag had been secured and the porter had moved on to the next one, I looked around the depot one last time. I was desperate to capture the image in my memory—the sights, the sounds, the smells of this place I had called home.

I felt heavy with the weight of unshed tears as I walked to the bus door and climbed the two stairs. The driver, a thin Ugandan man with a shiny round head and pockmarked cheeks, sat with his legs facing the door as he checked tickets. He pulled a dingy white handkerchief from his pocket and wiped beads of sweat from his forehead, then held out his hand. I gave him my ticket and watched him snip a hole in the corner and hand it back, looking past me as he yelled, "Next!"

He acted like he hadn't seen me, which was fine. Being invisible was better than the alternative.

I looked down the long aisle, my senses battered by the sights, sounds, and smells around me—a cacophony of babies crying and people yelling out the open windows to loved ones and friends who had come to see them off, the thick stench of body odor and exhaust fumes, looks of disdain and contempt as I took my first step and the faces on the bus turned away from the windows to focus on me.

My heart pounded.

My legs felt like lead as I moved forward. As I approached each row, people put their hands on the empty seats next to them, disbarring me of any notion that I was welcome. I was the lone Asian floating in a sea of Ugandans—*black* Ugandans, as Idi Amin had called them a few weeks earlier when he announced the expulsion of all Asians from Uganda within 90 days. I felt my throat catch.

I was Ugandan, too. I was born and raised here—it was the only home I'd ever known.

I took a breath and mustered all my energy to keep moving toward the back of the bus, where I finally saw an empty row of seats. I slumped down and slid across the black-leather-covered bench, getting as close to the window as possible and resting my elbow on the grimy window ledge. The thick springs pushed up against the backs of my thighs. Rubbing my eyes, I felt exhaustion in my bones. Just a few more hours and I'd be with my cousins.

I looked out the window at the hustle and bustle of life at the bus depot—hawkers selling snacks, porters securing luggage, and travelers heading out on journeys. It was like any other day, and yet as I watched life move forward around me, I felt strangely suspended in time. I couldn't put my finger on what I was feeling, but as I turned my attention back to the rows of bobbing heads in front of me, I felt the weight of the reality I'd been trying to avoid settle onto my shoulders.

I don't belong here anymore.

I took another breath, trying to push the thought away. On my body, I carried only a few Ugandan shillings, my Ugandan passport, and the letter from my uncle I'd received a couple of weeks earlier. Retrieving it from my pocket, I unfolded it again to find, in his flourishing script, the news about my family—and my fate—that had led me to get on this bus.

My dear Yashu,

It is with a heavy heart that I write to tell you the time has come for us to leave Uganda. It is no longer safe for us to be here, and you must come back to Kampala and make arrangements to leave soon.

Your brother Mansukh was on his way back to Uganda from India to help me get my family out. He took a ship from Mumbai to Mombasa and then boarded a train to Kampala. But when they approached the border, the train was stopped by Ugandan authorities, and he was detained at the border between Kenya and Uganda for six hours. It was only by the grace of God that our friend Maganbhai knew someone at the border and was able to step in and get him released. But the Ugandan border guards refused to return his passport. He has applied for refugee status with the United States or Canada and is awaiting news of where he will go.

I'm glad your father made the decision to shift your mother, younger siblings, and himself to our home in Rajkot. I know it's an adjustment since none of your younger brothers or sisters had ever been to India, but at least they will be safe there.

I've made the difficult decision to close up our home here in Kampala and take my family to England since we all have British passports and Ramesh is currently studying there. I'm leaving 60,000 shillings with Babubhai so you can make your travel arrangements once you arrive. Please settle all our accounts in the mines and hand everything over to Maganbhai as soon as possible.

May God bless you and keep you safe and allow us to meet again very soon.

Bapuji

I closed my eyes for a minute and let my breath out slowly. I'd be with my cousins in Masaka in a few hours. It was going to be fine.

I folded up the letter and put it back in my pocket. As the bus pulled out of the depot and onto the road, I looked out at the rocky hills of Mbarara and felt my chest tighten. I had lived here for the past eighteen months, overseeing our mining operations in the hills. Our family had mined tin since 1969, but in the past couple of years, we'd started mining columbite, titanium, and baller.

Regardless of skin color or ethnicity, in the mines, we were all the same—Ugandan. But that was no longer the case other places. Since Idi Amin's statement of expulsion, I had been hearing stories of the violence and torture he and black Ugandans, emboldened by his words, were inflicting on Asians and any local Ugandans who supported them. I knew my uncle was right, but I couldn't imagine any other place being home.

On my last day at the mines, I had walked around and thanked the local workers in Swahili and paid them their final wages. That evening, I had enjoyed one last meal of pillowy ugali with beans and plantains with the Ugandan miners who had become my family. We laughed and talked and smoked and drank local moonshine late into the night. Early the next morning, I gathered my belongings, kissed my girlfriend, Perry, the mine foreman's daughter, goodbye, and headed to the bus depot to travel to Masaka.

The rocking of the bus lulled me into a fitful sleep, but I jerked forward and out of my reverie as the bus came to a sudden stop. The hairs on the back of my neck stood on end as I looked out the window and saw a police checkpoint. We were just outside of Masaka and only eighty miles from Kampala. The passengers were silent as a Ugandan officer in a khaki uniform with a sash made of ammunition boarded the bus, his index finger resting on the trigger of the large gun strapped across his chest as he walked down the aisle.

"Identity documents—I want to see your identity documents!" he yelled.

Everyone rustled through their belongings, but the officer moved toward the back of the bus, not stopping to look at the cards held out by other passengers. He'd caught sight of me and, keeping me in his gaze, pushed his short, stocky body through the narrow aisle to where I sat.

As I reached into the pocket of my shirt to pull out my passport, he pointed a thick, round finger at me. "You! Put your hands up!" I slowly raised my hands until they were next to my face. "Get up! Come with me!" I sat motionless, frozen with fear. "Well, what are you waiting for?" he barked.

I held my breath and slid across the bench. Standing up, I walked toward the front of the bus, noticing the relief on the other passengers' faces as they avoided eye contact. I silently pleaded for someone to say something—anything—but was met with silence.

Stepping off the bus, I felt the tip of the officer's gun in the middle of my back, pushing me forward.

"Stop here! Get on your knees!" he demanded.

I dropped to one knee and then brought the second one down, my hands still in the air. It was midday, and the sun was high in the sky, but a breeze made me aware of the sweat dripping off my brow and down my back. I struggled to breathe as I held back tears.

"Close your eyes and pray to your God, because this is your final moment on this earth!"

I closed my eyes and prayed. Tears streamed down my face as I squeezed my eyes tighter, resigned to my fate. Time stopped as I waited for him to pull the trigger. A tinny buzz in my ears distorted the silence that hung in the air around me. As the hum grew louder, I heard a voice in the distance speaking in Swahili. "Sise apana taka damu! We do not want more blood!"

I opened my eyes and saw a Ugandan police commander striding over. He stopped in front of me and looked down for a moment before facing the officer.

"Let him go." He reached down to pull me up and looked me in the eyes, his own filled with compassion as he spoke. "We're going to let you go, but you must leave this country and never return. This is no longer your home. Do you understand me?"

Unable to speak, I nodded and shakily walked back to the bus, which was still there, as the police wanted every person on it to see what happened—a warning of what might happen to them if they supported an Asian. As I climbed the stairs, I wiped tears off my face with the heels of my hands. Again, the other passengers made no eye contact, but I noticed several of the Ugandan women crying silently. There was a metallic taste in my mouth as I returned to my seat. Still trembling from the encounter as the bus pulled back onto the road, I stared out the window without seeing anything for the rest of the journey.

If this is no longer my home, what is? What now?

Almost thirty years after that terrifying moment on the Ugandan bus, my uncle Yash told me his story over dinner as we sat safely ensconced in the dining room of his home in New Jersey. He'd survived the police checkpoint, but he'd had several more challenges to overcome before he was safe.

After stopping at his cousin's home in Masaka for a few days, Yash finally arrived in Kampala to find the city of his childhood in a state of chaos. People were lined up at embassies, seeking refuge in Canada, the United States, and the United Kingdom. Local Asian businessmen closed their shops and packed what they could, certain their exile would be short-lived and they would soon return to their homes and businesses and the life they had enjoyed in Kampala for generations.

Having heard that Asians with Ugandan passports were being targeted by Idi Amin's soldiers, Yash immediately burned his, rendering himself stateless. He then made his way to the American Red Cross office, obtained temporary travel documents, and was told that he would likely be sent to a refugee camp somewhere in Europe. When asked to pay 150 British pounds for the airplane ticket, he was grateful for the money his uncle had left him. After paying for his passage, he distributed the remaining money to neighbors and friends so they, too, could buy safe passage out of the country.

Despite following up frequently, Yash was unable to get the Red Cross to provide him with confirmation of his date of departure or a guaranteed seat on a flight out of Uganda before November 8, 1972, arrived—the deadline Idi Amin had set for all Asians to be out of the country. Early on the morning of Amin's deadline, Yash made his way to Kampala's Entebbe International Airport with hundreds of other Asians. He had only the money in his pocket and his small, gray suitcase containing all his belongings. Without a ticket in hand, all he could do was show up and hope to get on a flight before midnight.

At the airport, he was met with more chaos as families crowded into the departure hall. Those with tickets huddled in groups, waiting for their flights to be called. Those like Yash, without a confirmed departure, waited in lines, trying to secure a flight out before the deadline. After several hours, Yash was offered a handwritten ticket for a seat on an Alitalia flight. He took it, found a place to sit in the hall, and waited.

In addition to being Amin's deadline for the Asian expulsion, that November 8 also happened to be Diwali and Eid—the Hindu and Muslim new year celebrations. It was rare for the two holidays to fall on the same day. Usually one followed the other, and each community held grand celebrations in Kampala every year. But there was no celebration in Entebbe Airport that day, and the only wish people had for the new year was to get out of Uganda safely before midnight.

Around midday, the low hum of voices in the airport was interrupted by sirens in the distance. As they grew louder, people near the windows watched in horror as Amin's motorcade came into view. Word spread through the terminal as Yash sat in his chair, clutching his small suitcase, imagining the worst—that Amin, notorious for his changing moods, would move up the deadline and all those remaining in the airport would be "disappeared" by his military, never to be heard from again.

The motorcade stopped in front of the airport and six-foot-four Amin climbed out of his vehicle to walk briskly into the airport, flanked by his guards. Despite being filled beyond capacity, the airport fell nearly silent, the air thick with fear. After speaking with the guards near the door, Amin entered the departure hall and approached a short, balding Gujarati man sitting with his wife and children. The dictator stood, towering over him in silence for what seemed like an eternity before holding out his hand and smiling broadly. The man, holding his sleeping baby in one arm, shakily extended his other hand as Amin grabbed it and shook it vigorously.

"Happy Diwali!" Amin bellowed, still holding the man's hand and clapping him on the back. "Happy Diwali! Eid Mubarak!" he shouted jovially, walking around and shaking hands, wishing his fellow Ugandans—who would soon become refugees—a happy new year as though he were greeting friends at a party, not speaking to people he was expelling from the country because they were a different race.

Though the whole experience lasted only a few minutes, for Yash and probably many others in the hall that day, it was as if time had stopped and they were suspended in a surreal version of hell, where new year's greetings from a madman seemed almost normal. After Amin left, the crowd sat in stunned silence, likely fully aware of how narrowly they had escaped death.

A few minutes before midnight, on the very last flight out of Entebbe Airport, Yash buckled his seatbelt tight across his lap and prayed for the plane to take off. It was only after the pilot announced that they had cleared Ugandan airspace that my uncle finally allowed his body to relax and fall into the deep slumber of a man who hadn't slept in weeks. He woke up several hours later as the plane began its descent into Rome, where he was greeted by the Red Cross. The aid organization housed him and the other refugees on the flight in a hotel for one week as they worked out arrangements to send them on to various refugee camps.

My uncle was sent to a refugee camp in Bari, Italy. Two months later, at age 22, he arrived at New York's JFK International Airport to start his new life in America with $32 in his pocket.

Upon arrival, he was taken to the Latham Hotel with the other refugees who had been sent to New York. They had been sponsored by the American Fund for Czechoslovak Refugees (AFCR), which was formed in 1948 following the Communist coup in Czechoslovakia. Its purpose was to help refugees with their immediate needs and aid in their resettlement in and adjustment to their new homes.

The refugees were told to come to the AFCR offices the next morning to fill out Social Security paperwork and start looking for work. When they did, the volunteers helped them fill out the forms and discussed potential jobs. A week later, Yash and his three roommates were sent to the Mount Avery Lodge in the Pocono Mountains in Pennsylvania to be waiters, for which they'd receive $75 per month, plus room and board. They were each required to sign a promissory note agreeing to pay back the $17 it cost for a bow tie, shirt, two pairs of black slacks, and shoes—the required uniform at the lodge.

Having attended a school where all his courses were taught in English, Yash was proficient at reading and writing English. However, his primary speaking languages were Swahili and Gujarati. Trying to navigate a new country and a new job that required him to speak English was overwhelming and, after the first day in the Poconos, Yash and one of his roommates knew this wasn't the job for them and returned to New York City. They went back to the Latham Hotel, only to learn that they'd now have to pay for their room. When they went back to AFCR the next day to ask for a new job, the volunteer refused to assist them. Undeterred, Yash and his roommate headed to the offices of the United Nations High Commissioner for Refugees, took the elevator to the 58th floor, and asked for help. Ultimately, Yash found a new job at a textiles company a week later through one of his roommates. It was a better fit, as he spent his days packaging up cloth orders for shipping, rarely having to speak with anyone.

As he settled into life in New York, a world away from his beloved Uganda, Yash reconnected with his older brother, Mansukh, with the help of the Red Cross. They hadn't known what had happened to each other after going their separate ways in Kampala, but Mansukh had arrived as a refugee in Toronto. In early March of 1973, Yash received a letter from him. As he skimmed the news of the family and Mansukh's life in Toronto, one line especially filled his eyes with tears of joy and left him feeling hopeful for the first time in a long while.

New York—March 1973

I woke up early, anticipation in the air. With Mansukh's letter, I had learned that my family was well and my favorite sister would be arriving in the US today.

> *I wanted to let you know that Patu got married on January 5 and will be arriving at New York JFK Airport on March 24.*

How strange to think we had both started new lives on almost the same day—she'd gotten married just as I had arrived in the United States.

Patu was two years younger and the sister with whom I had been the closest. After everyone had to leave Kampala without me, nobody knew whether I'd made it out safely. Aerograms to India could take weeks or months, so even if my brother had notified my family that I was alive, the news might not have reached them yet.

I hurried out of bed and made my way down the hall to the communal bathroom, stepping over used needles and empty beer bottles in the hallway. The place was such a shithole, often frequented by prostitutes.

Though I often reminded myself that it was cheap and temporary, I was glad my family couldn't see me living like this.

I showered and dressed, putting on a long-sleeved shirt, a flannel shirt, and a jean jacket I had picked up at a local thrift store. I missed the tropical climate of Kampala—the lush, green hills, clear air, and people who greeted you on the street. New York felt cold and impersonal, lonely. After two months of living here, it still didn't feel like home, and I wondered if it ever would. I grabbed my keys and headed out the door to the 28th Street subway station. I shoved my hands into my pockets and tucked my chin into the collar of my coat, my breath catching as the brisk air hit my face. *This is almost April?*

I arrived at JFK at 8:30 in the morning with no information about the airline or arrival time for my sister's flight. But I didn't care if I had to wait all day—I just wanted to be there when she came through the doors.

When I'd arrived at JFK a couple of months earlier and pushed through the double doors, I had been greeted by a sea of people waiting for friends or loved ones and limousine drivers. They'd stood holding signs and flowers and balloons, leaning forward in anticipation every time the doors opened. When I'd looked up, I'd noticed a balcony where more people stood, just watching passengers coming in and out.

Remembering this, I made my way to the upper balcony. I'd be able to see her from there. The hours ticked by as I stood, watching each flight arrive and deliver a new group of people. With each swing of the large, beige doors, I hoped to see my sister. Finally, a little after 3:30 p.m., the doors swung open and I saw several Indian people coming through. She had to be in this group. I leaned forward and scanned the faces coming out.

And then I saw her. She wore a pale yellow sari with not a wrinkle or pleat out of place, despite the long journey. She had all the markings of a newly married woman. Her curly black hair was pulled back loosely, the slight left-side part filled with bright red vermillion powder. On each wrist she wore one gold bangle, and around her neck was a gold mangalsutra with tiny black beads. In the center of her forehead was a small, red bindi. The loose end of her sari wrapped around her small frame as she gracefully weaved her way through the crowd.

A wave of fear rose up through my body, and for a moment I considered turning around and leaving. What if she didn't recognize me? It had been over two years since we'd seen each other. What if her husband got upset that I'd just appeared? I'd known plenty of Indian men in Uganda who had been possessive of their wives. I didn't know anything about her husband.

I watched as she took in the scene around her, her face showing no emotion. She followed closely behind a man who seemed to be her husband, in his mid-twenties with long, black sideburns framing his round face. He stopped outside the doors and scanned the crowd, his face lighting up. I followed his gaze and saw two couples and a little girl standing off to the side with big smiles and outstretched arms.

As they made their way to his friends, I knew if I wanted to see her, I had to move quickly. I hurried to the stairway so I could catch them before they left the building. The whole group was still off to the side talking when I reached the ground floor. As I walked toward them, one of the women hugged my sister from the side and handed over a winter coat. Patu smiled and started to put it on. As she pivoted to reach the other sleeve, her eyes met mine and the coat fell to her side.

I was overcome with emotion, but I had never hugged any of my sisters. I stood there, unable to move and unsure of what to do next. Her husband, noticing her reaction, looked from her to me and back to her. His face showed his confusion. Patu stepped forward and whispered something to him. Her husband broke into a huge smile.

He walked over and extended his hand. "Yashu! So great to meet you! We had no idea you were here in New York! I'm Dilip—Priti's husband."

Priti? She'd been named Pratibha, meaning brilliance, at birth, but it was her nickname, Patu, that had stuck. Only now it seemed she was Priti, which meant love, but left me feeling uneasy. Still, I put my hand in his, and he shook it heartily, pulling me in for a hug.

"Priti, don't you want to say hi to Yashu?" Her husband turned and offered his hand to her.

She shyly accepted it and stepped forward. "I'm so glad you're okay. We didn't know if you had made it out of Kampala," she whispered, stealing a quick glance at me as her voice trailed off.

She had always been shy around other people, and now here, in front of her new husband and his friends, she looked like she wanted to melt into the floor. I shoved my hands into the pockets of my jean jacket and stood nervously, my glance fixed on my sister as Dilip introduced me.

"This is one of Priti's older brothers," he explained to the couples. "Their family had been in Kampala, but everyone except him left, and this is the first time she's seen him in almost—what has it been, two years?" he asked, looking at me. I nodded. "Well, I'm so happy to meet you. Where are you living?"

My stomach sank. "I live in Manhattan, in a small hotel with three room-mates," I mumbled.

Dilip smiled and nodded. "Wonderful. We have to get on the road soon to get to Boston, but give me your address and phone number so we can stay in touch."

Smiling and shaky, I wrote out my address and phone number and handed it to Dilip. He tore the edge off the paper and wrote his information on it before handing it back to me.

"Thank you for coming to greet us. I'm sure knowing you're nearby is go-ing to make Priti feel a lot better about living in America."

We stood awkwardly for a moment, and then I put my hands back in my pockets to contain the wave of emotion I was feeling. I looked at my sister again. "I'll see you soon, Patu." When she looked up, I saw that her eyes were wet with tears, too. I nodded at the others, then turned and walked away, wondering when I'd see her next.

A little over an hour later, as I lay on our beat-up old sofa at home, dozing and listening to BBC News on the radio, the sound of knocking startled me. I turned down the radio and opened the door, surprised to see Patu, Dilip, and their friends all smiling at me.

Now it was my turn to wish I could melt into the ground. "Um...come in," I stammered, stepping aside. Scanning the room strewn with newspapers and beer bottles, I cleared off a space on the sofa and invited them to sit down. "Can I get you some orange juice?" I asked. Aside from beer, it was all we had in our tiny fridge.

"Sure!" said Dilip. If he was at all shocked by what he had seen on the walk up or where he was now, he didn't show it. "Sorry to show up like this, but as we were leaving we thought, 'Who knows when we'll be back in New York? We should go and see him now.' So, we decided to just come."

"It's no problem, really," I said as I sank to a spot on the floor across from them.

"So this is where you live!" Dilip said cheerfully. I nodded and watched as Patu pulled her sari tighter around her shoulders, her eyes darting around the room. "You know, we live in Lowell, Massachusetts. It's really beautiful out there. Have you been to Boston?"

"No. I've only been in New York, and a day in the Poconos."

"Ah! The Poconos—also very beautiful," Dilip said as his friends nodded in agreement. "You know, if you'd like, you could come to Lowell and stay there. We have a lot of friends and a nice community, and it might be nice for the two of you to be in the same place since you've been apart for so many years. Unless of course you want to stay here," he added with a wink and a smile.

I felt my face flush. I couldn't even begin to imagine what they thought of me in that moment.

"Thank you," I said. "I've never been up there, and I'd love to come. I'll just need to think about it and figure out when would be best."

He nodded. "Sure, of course. You have our address and phone number now. You can take a bus or a train to get there. Just let us know when you're coming, and we'll be there to pick you up. I'm really sorry we can't stay longer, but we do need to get going. We still have a drive ahead of us before we get home."

As if on cue, they all stood up and walked to the door.

"Thank you for stopping by." I opened the door, feeling unusually formal.

"Of course—we're family! We look forward to seeing you in Lowell soon." Dilip smiled and patted me on the back.

"Take care of yourself, Yashu," Patu said quietly before turning and making her way back down the dingy hallway with the others.

I stood in the doorway, watching their silhouettes get smaller. *What are you doing? Is this really how you want your new life to start? In a dingy run-down hotel with no real friends or job prospects in sight?*

"Hey wait!" I yelled after them. They stopped and turned around. "I can be there next week." I felt a smile stretch its way across my face as a feeling of warmth spread through my body.

Maybe America could feel like home after all.

2

THE MOMENTS THAT SEPARATE US

(Othering and Identity Trauma)

I sat up in my bed and squealed with delight. There at the bottom of my Raggedy Ann and Andy comforter sat a pale pink Easter basket.

"Mom!" I yelled. "The Easter Bunny came!" I untangled myself from my sheets and moved to the foot of the bed.

The basket was piled high with shredded plastic grass in bright pinks and greens, which had been topped with a box of bright yellow marshmallow Peeps, a shiny brown milk chocolate bunny with pink ears and white teeth, and a colorful array of plastic eggs. I grabbed one, popped it open, and a handful of brightly colored jelly beans tumbled onto my comforter.

Before I could put one in my mouth, my mom appeared at my door. "Did you brush your teeth, Dimpu?" she asked, using my parents' pet name for me.

"No," I answered petulantly. "Why do I have to brush my teeth first? All of my friends brush their teeth *after* they eat." I sat, holding the jelly bean and looking at her from the corner of my eye to gauge her reaction.

"They also don't shower every day," she noted. "Do you really want to be a dirty child like them?" When I didn't answer right away, she shook her head. "Well, it doesn't matter. I'm not sending my children out into the world that way. Brush your teeth and take a shower, and then you can eat your candy."

"Fine," I replied with a dramatic sigh, hanging my head in defeat.

She smiled, suppressing a laugh. "Was there anything else in the basket?"

Moving the candy and eggs around, I found a note from the Easter Bunny and read it out loud:

> *Dear Dimple,*
>
> *Thanks for being a good girl.*
>
> *Love,*
> *Easter Bunny*

I was overjoyed! *The Easter Bunny knows who I am and that I'm a good girl!*

But my excitement was short-lived as my mom shared her interpretation of the note. "See? If you don't listen to me, the Easter Bunny won't think you're a good girl anymore and won't bring you anything next year." Her tone was matter-of-fact.

I definitely didn't want the Easter Bunny to think that. I flipped onto my belly, slid off the side of my bed, and hustled to the bathroom.

Showered, dressed, and ready for my candy, I jumped onto our scratchy yellow sofa with its textured orange and brown lines and folded my legs under me so I could look out the picture window. I looked past the evergreen bushes to the homes lining the cul-de-sac, wondering when my neighbors might be ready to play. Something shiny caught my eye. There, under one of the bushes in my front yard was a shimmering blue foil-wrapped Easter egg! And there was another one! And another!

I jumped off the sofa, grabbed my Easter basket from the dining table, and dumped its contents on the sofa. I ran to the door, stopped to put on my shoes, and yelled to my parents, "The Easter Bunny didn't just come to our house. He came to the whole neighborhood!"

I was outside before they could respond. I hopped off the first step onto the moat of little red rocks that surrounded our yard, and hopped a second time onto the grass before skipping to the large spruce tree in the middle of the yard. Dropping my basket at the trunk of the tree, I ran to the thick evergreen bushes where I'd spotted the glint of foil. There was the egg.

I squatted down and reached under the greenery, careful not to let the prickly needles get my fingers or arm.

Egg in hand, I walked back to my basket, running my fingers over the crumpled texture of the foil. Dropping it in, I looked up and saw my dad at the window, smiling and giving me a thumbs-up sign. I smiled and waved, then turned my attention back to the yard. There were eggs everywhere, and I moved from one to the next in the same pattern: find the egg, pick it up, feel it, walk back to the basket, drop it in, start over.

I was about to pick up my fourth egg when I heard a voice behind me. "What do you think you're doing, young lady?"

I turned and found Mrs. Collins, our neighbor who lived in the pale green house two doors away. She wore a dress with brown and white flowers and a bow at the neck, sheer nylon stockings, and brown wedge sandals. Her hair was the color and texture of dried wheat stalks and had been carefully sculpted into a tiny bun and sprayed into place. Her nails were cut short and painted with the same shade of raspberry pink that she wore on her lips.

"The Easter Bunny came!" I giggled with excitement and held up the egg.

"That may well be, but those eggs are not for you," she admonished, stepping over the rocks and walking toward me.

I stepped back just as my dad came outside. "Hello, Mrs. Collins. Such a beautiful day, isn't it?" he asked with a smile. When she didn't respond or look at him, he continued, "Is everything okay?"

She put her hands on her hips and looked from me to my dad. "No, everything is not okay. These eggs that your daughter is collecting without permission from anyone are for the children in the neighborhood."

My dad looked at her, his brow furrowing in confusion, deepening the scar on the soft brown skin of his forehead.

Before he could respond, she looked him in the eye and answered the unspoken question: "They're for the *Christian* children."

"I see," my dad said. He knelt down next to my basket and began removing the eggs, placing them on the ground.

"What are you doing?" I screamed. "I found those eggs. Why are you taking them out?"

He didn't respond, but with a pained look on his face, he turned away from Mrs. Collins, holding my basket in one hand and grabbing my little hand in the other. Having learned the hard way that tantrums were not something my dad would tolerate, I relented. Head hanging in defeat for the second time that morning, I walked across the yard with him, back across the little red rocks, and into the house.

Once inside, I looked out the screen door and watched Mrs. Collins put the eggs back in their hiding places.

When I started crying, my dad gently moved me away from the door and closed it. "Take off your shoes, beta," he said, using a common Gujarati term of endearment. "Come on. Let's go look at everything the Easter Bunny brought special for you to our house."

He smiled, but I wasn't interested in my basket anymore. I slipped out of my shoes, unable to understand what I had done and why I was being punished.

I returned to the sofa, my elbows resting on its back as I cupped my chin and stared out the window. I watched my neighbors emerge from their homes. The girls wore pastel dresses with lace, bows in their hair, and frilly ankle socks tucked into shiny, black Mary Jane shoes. The boys, hair parted and neatly combed, were in slacks and dress shirts with ties, one even wearing a bow tie.

As they gathered in the middle of the cul-de-sac, Mrs. Collins spoke to the group. The kids listened intently, and the parents smiled and took pictures. Then the kids fanned out and began running across yards and driveways, including mine—all the places we played hide-and-seek and tag—picking up the shimmering eggs and dropping them in their baskets as I watched through the window from inside.

It wasn't the first time someone had noticed I was different from my peers, and it wouldn't be the last. In fact, I was different from the very beginning.

My first moments in this world were traumatic—not just for me, but for my mom as well. She spent over twenty-four hours in labor, only to deliver my 9-pound-4-ounce body via an emergency cesarean section in the end. She lost a lot of blood and almost didn't survive. It would be another forty-eight hours before she'd finally get to see me, through the glass of the hospital nursery. The hospital had all the babies on their stomachs in clear plastic bassinets, and I was in the center of the group. According to my mom, when she peered in through the glass, I was the only one with my neck up, looking around the room, a full head of jet black hair tied up in a tiny pink ribbon—a little Indian Flintstones baby Pebbles.

I was born in the suburbs of Chicago to Indian parents who had settled in the United States with aspirations of a better life for their kids than what they had known in India and Uganda. My dad had traveled from Ahmedabad, India, to Lowell, Massachusetts, in 1970 to get his master's degree in chemical engineering. He was the first person in his family to leave India, and once he did, he never looked back.

He lived in an apartment with four other Indian graduate students, most of whom had been his friends growing up in India. As young bachelors, they had the energy to go to school, do shift work at a local manufacturing plant, and then head to Jack in the Box for 10-cent ground beef tacos—a small act of defiance by a group of boys from a country that considers cows sacred.

One by one, each of the boys returned to India on the pretext of visiting family, only to return to the little two-bedroom apartment in Lowell with a new wife in tow. By the time my dad's mother called him back to India, he knew what was expected of him, even though his heart now belonged to America. When he arrived in India in November of 1972, his mother had set up a "marriage tour" that would have him meet almost forty women before he finally met my mom in December.

My dad's version of this story was that he saw her and knew instantly that she was the one. My mom's take was a little different. She thought my dad seemed nice—a little chubby, but he had kind eyes and filled the room with his laughter. After their families met, my parents were given thirty minutes alone to talk, during which my dad told my mom that he lived in and loved America. And if they got married, they'd be living there.

Having only arrived from Kampala, Uganda, a year earlier, my mom didn't feel like India was her home. And even if she'd had any sentimentality for the place, she had been raised with the understanding that it was her life's work to get married, have children, and take care of the home and her family anywhere her husband chose for them. For her mother, that had been Uganda. For her, it looked like it was going to be America. After their half hour together, my mom agreed to marry my dad. One week later, they were engaged. And since they needed to start the immigration process, they went to the local registry office and registered their marriage two days after their engagement. The plan was always to have a proper Indian wedding, but my mom knew her family's finances were tight, so when my dad suggested they consider the registry wedding to be their actual ceremony, she agreed. One month later, they arrived at JFK airport in New York where my dad's friends were waiting to take them back to Lowell and where my mom saw her older brother Yash again for the first time in two and a half years.

When I was one, we moved from the outskirts of Chicago—where my dad had gotten a job after completing his masters—to Aurora, Colorado, a suburb of Denver. My dad had been offered a job with Samsonite luggage and had his choice of several locations. He was the least familiar with Denver, but he thought the mountains looked beautiful. He decided to move us there, despite the fact that his other two options had established Indian communities and would have kept my parents close to their friends.

My parents didn't know anyone in Denver, but one of my dad's colleagues at Samsonite was a Punjabi man my sister and I soon came to call Arun Uncle. Arun Uncle; his wife, Janet Auntie; and his sister, Guddi Auntie, welcomed us into their lives. Though their food and customs differed from those of my Gujarati parents, there were enough similarities to give my parents a sense of connection.

Within a year, my parents made a down payment on a brand-new house in Aurora and wanted to have a ceremony to bless it before we moved in. Arun Uncle suggested they visit the local Hare Krishna temple, where most of the Indian families gathered. The following Sunday, we went to the temple and my dad introduced himself to everyone. He got a few phone numbers, and one month later, my parents had a house-blessing ceremony with all the Indian families in town invited to join us.

Since my parents had no furniture yet, everyone sat on the floor, which was covered wall to wall in bright orange shag carpeting. My mom cooked all the food for the gathering, including pillowy soft gulab jamuns soaked in a sweet rosewater sugar syrup—something most of the Indians in Denver hadn't tasted since they'd left India. After the ceremony, the men spread newspapers across the floor of the empty concrete basement so everyone could sit together in a large circle to enjoy the feast my mom had prepared. My dad walked around popping gulab jamuns into each person's mouth. This simple act of familiarity left a deep impact on the community, so much so that when my dad passed away almost thirty years later, almost everyone from Denver who came to the funeral said they remembered this moment of connection he'd created that day.

My dad always said he only wanted daughters and was pleased when he ended up with two of them. His big dreams for my younger sister, Kajal, and me were etched into my brain long before she was around, as he led me in my nightly prayers, speaking one line at a time in Gujarati and having me repeat after him. It translated to something like this:

Dear God

Please make me good and wise.

Please let me be educated and successful.

Please give me common sense and values.

And please make me a doctor or engineer.

Love you!

My dad's vision of who he believed we were may have been clear, but my sister and I struggled to find clarity as we navigated the complicated terrain of being children of first-generation immigrants. While my parents wanted us to assimilate and be American, they also wanted Kajal and me to remain connected to our Hindu culture and Gujarati customs and language. When we were very young, my dad insisted we only speak Gujarati at home—no English. He knew that between the TV and going to school, we'd pick up English just fine.

Like so many other Indian parents, their goals were well-intentioned. But they did not always understand the social implications of their decisions, which often left us feeling like outsiders. Like the time my dad brought home a Superman lunch box for me as I was starting first grade. This resulted in excessive mocking by my classmates who insisted Superman was for boys. Or the time my Brownie troop planned to "kidnap" all the kids in their pajamas and surprise them with breakfast at McDonalds. My mom, horrified at the thought of sending her child out of the house unwashed and unkempt, woke me up extra early that Saturday morning. She was unbothered by the awkward exchange with the troop leader, who found me in a dress with my hair neatly twisted into two tight braids, instead of my pajamas.

I was also regularly reminded that I was different through subtle acts of exclusion, known as microaggressions. When I was seven, a classmate called me an "Indian giver" for changing my mind and taking back my favorite pencil, which she had convinced me to give her. Not understanding the term, I explained to my teacher in tears that the person had made fun of my culture. Instead of reprimanding the student, the teacher initially chuckled, and then told me in a stern voice that it wasn't nice to go back on my word before making me apologize to the classmate and turn over the pencil. There were also ongoing experiences, like being chosen last as a partner when we had to square dance in gym class, or every time my mom was asked by the school to come in and talk to the students about "being Indian," or in college when a sorority sister asked me if I was a "dot Indian or feather Indian." These experiences, and so many others, created an invisible wall between me and my classmates and led me to hide away parts of myself in an effort to fit in.

As a first-generation immigrant, unless you choose to let go of one culture or the other, it's difficult to feel a sense of belonging anywhere. You're reminded that you're not quite American every time people ask you where you're from. When you say, "Oh, I'm American," they respond with, "No, but where are you *really* from?" In India, people can identify a non-resident Indian—or NRI as they like to call us—just by looking us up and down. They don't even have to hear us talk. I once asked someone how they could tell I wasn't from there, and they said my feet gave it away—they weren't hardened by years of being exposed to the elements.

In my case, the split identity was deepened further because of our social circle. While all the Indians in Colorado knew each other in the 1970s and '80s, people still tended to create the closest connections with Indians who came from similar backgrounds. For us, this was a group of six or seven Gujarati families with whom we gathered every Friday, Saturday, and Sunday. While the homes where we met rotated, the routine of these events was predictable: Everyone showed up around 5 p.m. The men sat in the family room or backyard with beers, women huddled in the kitchen to cook and catch up, the younger kids ran through the house, and the older kids hung out, played games, and antagonized the younger kids.

When it came time to eat, the kids were tasked with spreading newspapers across the floor of the basement or other designated area, and then we'd sit down in a big circle. We were given Styrofoam plates with the little dividers, and then the dads would serve us food. We were expected to try everything, even if it was just one bite (food allergies weren't a consideration back then), and you couldn't get up until you were finished eating. We learned early on that crying, spilling a drink, or calling for mom was futile. Somehow feeding the kids had become the dads' domain, and they had nowhere to go and no issue staring you down until you gave in and cleaned your plate.

As kids growing up in this space, it was often hard to know where one culture ended and the other began. This was especially true with holidays, because we celebrated both Hindu occasions and Western ones like Thanksgiving, Christmas, and Easter, though more for the celebratory aspects of gathering than anything religious.

I loved fall when I got to dress up in my bright and colorful chaniya-cholis. I did this first in October for Navratri, the festival celebrating the Hindu goddess Durga. My dad and the other men would divide up the phone list of Indian families in town and personally invite all of them to come. Two weekends in a row we'd be up into the wee hours of the night, dancing traditional Gujarati folk dances in our bare feet on the hard floor of a rented gymnasium, until our legs gave out. In November, we'd celebrate Diwali, the Hindu new year, by gathering in a rented hall for a massive feast prepared by all the women. There would also be games for the kids like bobbing for apples and three-legged races. Winners were rewarded with calculators and protractors (every doctor and engineer needs one of those!) and little trophies engraved with the year.

But I also loved this time of year because it meant we were heading into the winter holidays and Christmas. Christmas was always special because it meant three days of gathering with our friends at one family's home, starting on Christmas Eve—all the kids and adults under one roof, playing games and eating food. The younger kids sang Christmas carols without understanding the religious foundation of the holiday or the lyrics we belted out with such glee.

On Christmas morning, we'd gather around the tree to open a mountain of presents from the different families—and Santa Claus, of course. After the presents were opened, the women would sneak out to Walgreens, the only store open on Christmas Day, and collect all the discounted perfume sets and other gift items that they'd then stockpile for trips back to India. Though the day after Christmas was always a bit of a letdown, as families headed home after lunch, we were buoyed by the knowledge that we'd gather and do it all over again for the Western new year a week later.

In some ways, kids like my sister and I had the best of both worlds, and yet, as we got older, it often felt like the best of no worlds. My parents and so many other immigrant parents made a noble attempt to both preserve and include. But the problem with this split identity is that the parents—especially those who emigrated in the '50s, '60s, and '70s to further their education—got stuck with one foot in the India they remembered leaving and the other in the America where they now lived. As the years passed and the traditions, fashions, foods, and even values in India changed and evolved, our parents' beliefs about what it meant to be Indian continued to reflect the India of their memories. So, over time they lost a sense of belonging in both India and America, and as their children, we struggled to find it.

I stood on the stone porch, brow furrowed, absentmindedly scratching a large mosquito bite on my arm. Something about the design we were drawing on the ground didn't seem right to me.

"Deem-pal!" I cringed at my cousin's raspy-voiced version of my name. "Deem-pal! You know you'll get in trouble if you keep scratching your arm. It will leave a scar and your mom will get so mad!"

I looked up to see her with her hands on her hips, head shaking like *she* was my mother. Parul was less than a year older than me, but she liked to remind me as often as possible that she was my motiben, or big sister, which didn't mean much to me since I didn't like anyone telling me what to do.

Before bringing my sister and me to India for four months, my mom had spoken with my kindergarten teachers. Since I could already read, they'd had no problem with her taking me out of school one month before summer vacation, or with me returning to start first grade a month late.

We had arrived in India with six very large suitcases, only three of which carried our clothes for the summer. The rest were filled with Indian expat gifts and necessities: jeans, the stockpiled perfume gift sets, makeup, chocolates, toys, and other gifts for friends and family, as well as boxes of Kraft macaroni and cheese, bottles of Ragu pasta sauce and spaghetti, and small canisters of Country Time Lemonade and Tang for my sister and me—also known as peace of mind for my mom over the long, hot months.

After our initial bout of jetlag, my sister and I fell into an easy rhythm with our cousins. Every morning, my aunt would open the wooden doors of the house, and they'd stay open until we all went to bed at night. My dad's sisters and other family friends would float in and out, sometimes bringing my sister and me gifts. A fresh cup of steaming hot chai would welcome each guest, regardless of the time of day or the heat wafting in from outside. After lunch, everyone took a nap during the hottest part of the day. When we'd wake up in the afternoon, my aunt and grandmother would "get fresh," which meant washing and re-powdering their faces, changing their saris, and reapplying vermillion in the part in their hair and on their foreheads in the form of a fresh round bindi. Then we'd head to the local produce cart to pick out vegetables for that night's dinner.

It was monsoon season, which meant oppressive heat, humidity, and plenty of mosquitos, but it also meant time gathered with family, sitting in candlelight as the storms raged outside and the electricity inevitably went out in the evenings. My dad's younger brother, Atul, who we referred to as kaka, the term for your father's brother, taught us how to play carrom, an Indian tabletop game where players flick flat, wooden, checker-like discs, attempting to knock them into the corner pockets of the board. On some nights, he'd boil a big pot of peanuts in saltwater and we'd shell them on the large front porch as he told stories that left everyone laughing until they cried. Sometimes my younger cousin Montu would do impressions of family members. How a four year old had both the timing and attention to detail to do this continues to be a mystery.

The joy we experienced that summer wasn't the norm for our family, and unfortunately, we didn't experience it again on any subsequent trips back to India.

About two months into our trip, I got the feeling I didn't belong here either, despite all of the fun we'd been having.

"Not like that!" I said sternly as I knocked the chalk out of Montu's hand. My cousins and I had been drawing with the big, fat chalk sticks we'd brought as gifts for them. When we'd arrived in India, my mom had entrusted me with the chalk and told me that as the oldest, it was my responsibility to make sure everyone got to use it and that all the chalk was put away at the end of the day. I took the responsibility seriously and knew I had to set a good example for the younger children.

"You have to hold it like this," I insisted, holding the chalk between my fingers like a pencil. Montu bobbed his head in agreement and copied what I did. "Good. Now make an outline first, and then you color it in," I instructed with the authority of a six-year-old sidewalk artist.

The first drop of rain fell just as I finished filling in a large, pink flower petal. First there was one drop, then two and three and four, and then, a downpour. I jumped up, grabbed all the chalk around me, and ran for cover near the doors.

"Kaji, Montu, Sachin, Parul—come on. Grab your chalk and get under the covering!" I yelled. They all ran over to where I was standing, and we frowned as our afternoon of hard work in various pastels dissolved and disappeared. Puddles of chalk-tinted water soon replaced our masterpieces, and to my child's eye, they were not nearly as beautiful as the flowers and butterflies we'd created. The smell of earth and water filled my nose, and the damp air, not having cooled very much, filled my lungs.

"Come on, Montu. Come on, Sachin. Let's go!" Parul yelled, grabbing my cousins by the hand and pulling them back out to the uncovered part of the porch where they jumped and danced around like little monkeys.

"What are you doing? Come back here right now!" I yelled. "You're going to get in trouble!" But they ignored me, and soon my sister, whose hand I'd been holding, broke out of my grasp and joined them.

I stood alone.

Not knowing what else to do, I took a step forward and felt the warm water cover my bare feet. Another step forward and I felt it on my hair. Unable to contain myself, I ran off the sheltered porch to where my cousins and sister played and began jumping too, as though each drop of water was electricity, giving me a jolt.

It was raining so hard that streams of water ran down my head and over my face like a veil. And it was through this veil that I saw them—the children of the maids and cooks and other servants in the community running past our gate.

"Where are they going?" I asked my cousins as I climbed up on a stone bench to look over the walls that encircled our patio.

"Who cares?" Parul said. She hopped off the bench into a large puddle.

I watched as the pack of kids, with their smooth brown skin in little shorts and button-down shirts, made their way up the slight hill. They laughed and squished their bare feet in the dirt-packed street that had turned to mud. I curled my own toes there on the bench, trying to imagine what the wet earth felt like, but I couldn't.

I marveled as a young boy with shiny, oil-slicked black hair ran toward the slope. He stretched out his arms and dove to the ground, sliding through the mud as if it were a Slip N Slide like my neighbors in Aurora set up on their front lawn for all the kids in the summers. The boy stood up at the bottom of the hill, completely covered in mud with only the white of his teeth visible. He laughed and yelled for one of his friends to go. One after another, they went screaming and laughing down the mudslide.

"Come on, we're going out there, too," I said to my cousins and sister.

Parul looked at me and then out at the kids. "Chee! We don't play with them. They are the untouchables."

"I don't know what that means," I replied. Undeterred, I pressed the issue. "I already told you we're going, so we're going. You have to do what I say because my parents said I'm the oldest and all of you have to listen to me."

"You're not the oldest. I'm the oldest," Parul corrected, unmoved by my argument. "If you really want to go, why don't you go by yourself? I'm not going to get in trouble over *their* kind." She curled her lips downward and furrowed her brow in distaste.

I shrugged, turned away, and went down the two stairs that led to the gate. I walked up to a group of the mud-covered children, who were tagging each other and running away as they waited for their turn to slide back down the hill. Though I spoke fluent Gujarati, I usually let my cousins do the talking and now was at a loss for what to do next. Kids started pointing at me, and I thought about turning around, but then one of the girls walked over.

"Hi. I'm Savita."

I looked at her tight braids and mud-caked clothes and knew I wanted nothing more than to slide down that hill. I looked toward the hill, and she led me to the top.

"Vishnu, show her how to slide down the hill," she told one of the boys standing off to the side. He obliged, followed by the others. When the last child had taken their third slide down the hill, Savita cleared them all away so I could have a turn.

I looked toward our patio to make sure my cousins and sister were watching. Then I started running and hit the ground, arms stretched out in front of me. "Aaaaahhhh!!!!!" I screamed as I slid down the muddy hill. At the bottom, I couldn't stop laughing.

Seeing that I hadn't melted upon touching one of the "untouchables," my cousins and sister quickly followed. Soon, they too were heading face-first down the mudslide.

I climbed back up the hill and played tag with the other kids, all of us covered in mud and waiting for our next trip down the slide. But before I could take my next turn, a hand grabbed my shoulder. I screamed in pain and turned to see my aunt standing over me.

"Shameful girl!" she yelled as water dripped from her oil-streaked hair down the front of her face, melting away the vermillion powder she wore in her part. For a second, I thought she was bleeding, but I quickly lost that thought to the stinging pain in my shoulder as she dug her fingers in.

"Why are you playing with these children and dragging all the young ones with you?" she demanded. Before I could answer, she pulled me toward our gate. "Come on, kids. Let's go!" Turning to Savita and the other kids, she chided, "You all should know better! Wait until your parents hear what you've done!"

I writhed in pain, still not understanding why my aunt was so angry.

After pulling me through the gate and up the steps, she pushed me into the house and toward the bathroom. "Now we will have to wash all of you to get *their* dirt off."

3

THE CHANGES THAT UPROOT US

(Forced Displacement)

The glowing red numbers on my clock radio read 2:43 a.m. I lay on my side, facing the open door, through which I could see a faint light coming from my parents' bedroom. In our home, the bedroom doors were never closed when we went to sleep. I'd always felt comforted hearing my dad snoring down the hall. But tonight, the sounds from that direction were filled with despair.

"Deepu, please!" My mom pleaded with my dad in Gujarati, using a pet name I'd only heard once before. "Please calm down and come to bed. Please."

She wasn't crying or yelling, but the urgency in her voice gave me a strange feeling in my stomach and made my heart beat faster. I turned away from the door, onto my other side, and pulled my pink bedspread over my head. Squeezing my eyes shut, I wished I could be anywhere but here. I opened them again and waited for them to adjust to the dark.

The outline of my sister came into view. Curled up under the covers next to me, her hands rested under her chin, her breath even. I wondered how she could sleep through this.

I curled up next to her and put my arm around her, gently resting my hand on her back. It was warm and reassuring, so I kept it there, feeling it rise and fall with her breath.

"No, no, no. Stop it!" I heard my dad wail.

I lifted my hand off my sister, slipped out of bed, and crept toward the light coming from my parents' room. Pressing myself against the wall in the hallway, I inched closer to their room until I could see my dad sitting on the edge of their bed, head in his hands, body rocking back and forth, crying.

My heart beat so hard I could hear it in my ears, and I was sure my parents would be able to hear it, too. As I turned back to my room, my dad jerked up and begin slapping the sides of his head. "Why won't it stop? Make it stop! I don't want to hear these voices anymore!" Behind him, my mom tried to soothe him, rubbing his back and pleading quietly with him. But it was as if he couldn't hear her.

The butterflies in my stomach started to make me queasy. I'd never seen my dad this way and couldn't understand what was happening. I needed to get out of here. I couldn't listen to this sound for one more second. I crept back to my room and crawled back into bed, pulling the covers over my head again and squeezing my eyes shut. When that didn't drown out the noise, I covered my ears with my hands and hummed the first song that came to mind.

The sounds of "Grand Old Flag" by George Cohan reverberated from my throat up to my nose and into my ears. I'd been practicing this song on my flute for weeks for our upcoming band recital, and it was the only thing I could think of. With each round, my humming got louder and louder until I couldn't hear any other sounds.

I had managed to escape from that space, so I just kept going. Minutes felt like hours until I felt a hand on my shoulder. It was gentle, but I knew it was my dad's. I pulled my hands away from my ears and heard his muffled voice through the covers.

"Dimpu beta, are you okay? What are you doing?" There was concern in his voice. When I pulled the covers off my head, he was kneeling next to my bed. "Are you okay? What are you doing?"

"I... I was trying to stop the noise from coming in," I stammered.

"What noise?" he asked, stroking my shoulder.

"The noise of you crying and hitting yourself."

His hand froze and tears welled in his eyes. "You heard that?" His voice cracked. I nodded as tears streamed down his face. I could feel him trembling as he laid his cheek on my mattress, his hand still on my shoulder, and whispered, "I'm so sorry, beta. I'm so sorry."

Gently, I laid my hand on his head, my tears puddling on my pillow. I wished with all my might that I could find a way to help him.

When I was in the second grade, my parents bought a grocery store in downtown Denver. Just as they closed on the deal, my dad had a seizure and ended up in the hospital. An allergic reaction to the dye he was given for a CT scan shut down his kidneys, almost killing him and keeping him in the hospital for almost two months on dialysis. My mom, only twenty-seven years old, was now solely responsible for two young daughters, a brand-new business, and a husband who needed to heal. Fortunately, the community showed up to provide support. The men took turns at the hospital to help her make medical decisions. The women took turns spending the nights with my sister and me so we wouldn't be alone. One of our family friends even threw the birthday party my mom had planned for me rather than canceling it. The power of community in the healing process was something I experienced at the tender age of seven.

Once he had recovered, my dad started working at our grocery store, too. He and my mom worked it out so she went in early to open, and my dad went later in the afternoon and stayed to close up while she came home to make dinner. A few years later, my dad learned that the building that housed our grocery store was for sale. Though the thought of taking out a quarter-of-a-million-dollar loan scared my mom, my dad was a visionary. The rundown neighborhood was behind the state capitol building and, in the long run, would be a good investment.

Soon after, he faced one of the biggest professional setbacks he'd ever encountered when the parent company of the grocery store chain my dad had bought into declared bankruptcy. By the time the news came, he'd spent over a year overseeing construction of the new store and was only one month from the scheduled grand opening. Though he had done nothing wrong, he saw this as a personal failure, and it crushed him. He was never quite the same, and my mom constantly worried about his health, doing what she could to shield him from too much stress.

By the time I got to the fifth grade, my dad was exhibiting signs of depression and paranoia. He broke off ties with the friends who had been our second family for years, leaving us isolated and walking on eggshells around him. Because mental-health issues weren't as well documented or openly discussed as they are today, there was a lot of shame and fear surrounding this. And we couldn't talk about it with anyone. All we knew was that he had really high highs filled with little sleep and a steady stream of new ideas and paranoia, and very low lows filled with self-judgment, fear, and feelings of failure.

When I was in the sixth grade, a couple of months after the "Grand Old Flag" night—and after moving us from Aurora to Chicago and back to Aurora within two weeks—my dad decided the best business opportunities awaited him in southern California. So we packed up once again and headed west. And just as I found a rhythm in my new school in Diamond Bar, California, things took a turn for the worse at home.

One Sunday afternoon, our family was playing gin rummy after lunch. It had been a relatively good day, and we were enjoying the game when my mom, laughing, put her final card face down, indicating she had won. My sister and I threw our cards down, shaking our heads and laughing in mock disbelief at her good fortune. But the moment took a terrifying turn as my dad reached over and clapped my mom as hard as he could on her back, sending her reeling forward in pain. My sister and I froze as my mom's eyes filled with tears. When he realized what he had done, he tried to play it off as a joke—he was just trying to congratulate her with a pat on the back—but we all knew what had happened.

That day, things shifted. My dad's already heavy hand, made heavier by his ruby-stoned class ring, came down on my mom's body with more frequency. We never knew what would set him off, and the more we tried to find patterns to avoid the chaos, the more erratic he became.

One day, after a particularly violent night and worried that he'd return home any minute, my mom came into my room and asked me to call my uncles in Canada from the payphone on the other side of the apartment complex. She didn't know what else to do. My dad's childhood friends who lived in California, with whom we'd spent time since our arrival, had cut ties with us after my dad had a particularly scary manic episode on Christmas Day. We were isolated and had nobody left to help us.

I went to the payphone, called one of my uncles, and told him what was happening. By the next day, all three of my mom's brothers had arrived and told my dad they were taking my mom, my sister, and me with them.

We left with them to go to the airport for our flight to Toronto, my dad following us in his car. As this was pre-9/11, and my dad walked with us to the gate where we waited to board. He sat down with Kajal, who was now ten, and held her hand. Having always been close to my dad, when the time came to board, she refused to get on the plane. My mom—knowing that if we went back now, he'd be more violent than ever—made the difficult choice to board the plane without my sister. The flight was agonizing as I wondered how we'd survive this. My mom cried the entire way, despite my attempts to comfort and console her. She knew my dad would never hurt my sister, but she also knew she couldn't live somewhere without both her children. Within a week, we were back in Diamond Bar, where the cycle began all over again.

A few months later, toward the end of my eighth-grade year, my mom decided we had to leave once and for all. She again made the arrangements with my uncles, but this time we left when my dad was out of the house. The three of us made it to the airport, boarded the flight, and headed off to Toronto again, determined to finally find a place of safety.

"What are you doing?" my mom asked quietly. I looked up and saw her standing in the doorway, one hand on the door frame. Her skin, which had always been flawless, now betrayed her exhaustion and the challenges she was navigating. Life had dulled her usual glow and darkened the circles around her eyes.

"Just reading," I answered, trying to keep my voice light. We had been in Toronto for less than a week, staying at my mom's oldest brother's home. I'd been to this house many times throughout my childhood, yet it was hard to feel settled. I folded the corner of the page I'd been reading, something I had found on a shelf in the basement. I was sad to be missing my eighth-grade graduation that week, and I really wanted my own books. But we were safe, and that was most important.

My mom came over to the top bunk bed where I was sitting. "He knows we're here."

I felt my stomach tighten. "What do you mean? How did he find out?" My voice cracked, and my eyes filled with tears. We couldn't go back there again. It would be even worse.

"There weren't many places we could go. He called your uncle yesterday and said he had booked a ticket and is coming. He suspects we're at this house, so we have to go. Today." There were no tears or pleading. There wasn't time for any of that. We had to get our things and leave soon, in case he showed up earlier than he'd said he would.

We packed with a heavy silence between us.

"Did you tell Kaji yet?" I asked.

"Not yet. It will be easier to tell her once we're ready to go," she replied softly. "Make sure to grab our toothbrushes from the bathroom."

We didn't have much to pack, as we'd left home with just a couple of suitcases. There hadn't been room for any of my books, but I had grabbed my journal at the last minute and shoved it into my backpack.

We piled into my uncle's blue-and-silver van and rode over to my mom's younger sister's house in silence. When we arrived, my aunt, who had been waiting at the glass screen door, welcomed us in. "Kaju-bon!" she called, using my sister's pet name. After pulling both of us to her side for a hug, she turned her attention to my mom. "You okay?"

My mom melted into her arms. "I'm okay," she replied.

"I put you all in Kavita's bedroom."

My mom just nodded and motioned for me to take one of the bags as she picked up the other, dragging it to the back of the house.

The next twenty-four hours were excruciating as we went through the motions of a normal day. An unspoken acknowledgment hung in the air, though, reminding everyone that nothing about this day was normal. My mom's family was gentle and soft-spoken. An unexpected act of violence in the heat of the moment toward his youngest child had scared my grandfather so badly that he'd never raised his voice or his hand against anyone in the family again. The family had escaped life in the clutches of one of the most ruthless dictators in the world, and yet they were totally unequipped for the physical, emotional, and tangential impacts of the violence in our own family.

The phone rang at 2:30 the next afternoon.

My mom spoke into the receiver as I looked on. "No," she insisted after a few moments, looking at me with tired eyes.

I could tell it was my uncle's voice, but I couldn't make out his words. "What's he saying?" I whispered. She held her hand up and shook her head.

A couple of hours later, my sister and I were back in the van, headed to the family snack shop to see our dad. I had begged and pleaded with my mom to not make us go, afraid of how my dad might react since we had chosen to leave. She had tried to reassure me that my dad wouldn't hurt us. While that may have been true, my sister and I both knew he would not be satisfied until he actually saw my mom. I sat in the van, gripping the seatbelt tightly, my stomach tied up in knots of uncertainty.

When we arrived, my mom was right. Dad was calm and satisfied for the moment with seeing my sister and me. But I was right, too. Reuniting with us wasn't enough to placate him for long, and he remained adamant about seeing my mom. Within a week, she'd relented and reconciled with him, leaving my sister and me in Canada with my aunts and uncles as she returned to California with him on her own for almost a year. At the end of my freshman year of high school, my sister and I left the peace and stability of Toronto and returned to California and into one of the most turbulent phases of my dad's mental-health crisis.

4

THE BELIEFS THAT SACRIFICE US

(Work Ethic)

I stared at the mountain of garlic heads on the table in front of me. In a few months, I'd be going to college. But instead of spending these last few months with my friends, getting ready to have a fun Friday night out, I was stuck here at home, about to resentfully peel several pounds of garlic.

I grabbed a large head off the pile and twisted it until the thin, papery skins loosened and I could access the cloves. "Do we really need all of this?"

If my mom heard the petulance in my voice, she ignored it. She looked up from the list she was making across the table. She'd gotten home 20 minutes earlier and was still dressed in her uniform—black pants and a white polo shirt, with hints of vanilla and sugar from the bakery where she worked perfuming the air around us.

After taking a large sip of the chai my grandmother had kept ready for her, she responded. "Yes. I know it's a lot, but we're cooking for five hundred people. We're definitely going to need all of it and maybe more." She returned to her list and continued making calculations and writing.

Feeding others had always been my mom's greatest joy, but as the years passed, it also became her greatest burden. In the kitchen she was an artist, and cooking was her medium. While my grandfather and great uncle had made a living through the traditional sweet and savory shop they owned in Uganda, my mom fed others to show her love and express her creativity. While growing up in Uganda, she was always on the lookout for new recipes and trends coming out of India and testing them out on her brothers and cousins. But in California and later in Colorado, catering became a necessity.

Our typical catering orders ranged from 50 to 200 people. This was the first time we'd be catering something this big. I could feel my mom's nervous energy, but instead of compassion in that moment, I felt contempt. I couldn't wait to get away from here and live my own life. I wanted to start over someplace where nobody knew my dad was locked up in a mental institution, and I didn't have to spend all my free time cooking for other people.

My mom paused to massage her right forearm, and I felt shame settle onto my shoulders. She'd been up since four that morning and had decorated cakes all day. She must be exhausted, but she was doing this to take care of us. I silently admonished myself for thinking only about what I wanted.

"Kaki, as soon as I'm done here, you and I can go out to the garage and start peeling and chopping vegetables. And I think we can make the puri dough before we go to bed so it's ready when we start rolling early tomorrow morning." My mom looked over at my grandmother who sat on the bench, her back against the wall, a small mountain of cilantro in front of her.

Kaki, meaning aunt in Gujarati (specifically your father's brother's wife), was my maternal grandmother. However, between my mom, her seven siblings, and all her cousins, more than twenty children had grown up together in a joint family in Uganda. There, my great uncle and his wife, as the heads of the family, had been reverentially referred to as Ba and Bapuji—the elder parents. My mom once told me that for the first few years of her life, she didn't actually know who her parents were. And since all her cousins referred to my grandparents as Kaka and Kaki, she did, too.

My grandmother nodded as she continued pulling and cleaning stalks, which she would soon turn into chutney by combining them with mint and green chilis. Seemingly unfazed by the challenge before us, she calmly replied, "I'll finish the chutney and then come out to help you. We should also soak the daal tonight so it will cook faster tomorrow morning."

My mom nodded and added that to her list, her body relaxing into the chair for a brief moment. Then with one final swig of her chai, she stood, selected knives from the drawer near the stove, and headed down the short flight of stairs to the garage. "Make sure when you're done with the garlic, you come out here to help me, beta," she called before closing the door behind her.

After peeling the garlic, I went out to the garage, where we had set up a makeshift kitchen with a commercial-grade propane stove and the extra-large pots and pans my parents had bought at a restaurant supply store in the months before we moved from California back to Colorado. In between peeling bags of potatoes and scoring pounds of baby eggplant, my other job was to do the dishes. It was nearly midnight when we finally went to bed, but rest wasn't really part of the plan. By the time I came down at 4:00 a.m., showered and ready to help, my mom and grandmother had already been up for an hour, working their way through the rest of my mom's list since the food had to be packed and ready for pickup by 10:00 a.m. that morning.

"You start rolling the puris so I can get the dhanshak going," my mom called over to me.

Accepting the thin, wooden rolling pin, I took her place in front of the round, wooden cutting board. Next to me, on top of an old milk crate, sat a large stainless steel bowl covered with a flat stainless steel lid. I lifted the lid and found a mound of whole wheat dough, much of which my grandmother had already pulled off in little pieces and rolled into balls, ready to be flattened and rolled out into disks with the pin.

As I found my stride and rolled as quickly as I could, my grandmother deftly lifted the puris I'd layered on a plate next to me, sliding them one after another into the hot oil before swirling them around and flipping them with a slotted spoon. As they ballooned into little round globes, she dropped them onto plates lined with paper towels. We worked in silence for a while, with only the sounds of hissing oil and my mom's spatula scraping the bottom of the pan echoing between us.

"How do you do this?" I asked my mom, pausing to rub my sore hands. Though my quick shower had taken the sleep from my eyes, my body was still exhausted. "You've been working on this catering order since Wednesday. You were up at four each morning, worked an eight-hour shift, came home, and barely had your tea before you started cooking for another six to eight hours each night. Aren't you tired?" I rolled my shoulders and neck as I watched her move gracefully from one large pot to the next.

"It's a privilege to be able to feed others. Plus, I don't do it alone. You and your sister help me, and this time Kaki flew out to help. I find the strength to go on because of all of you." She said this in her matter-of-fact tone, without looking up. "We do what we have to do."

I considered her words. The rest of us weren't going to work on our feet for eight hours before coming home to be on our feet for another eight. This was yet another reason I was determined to go to college and get a good job. *I don't ever want to work like this again*, I thought to myself as I picked up the rolling pin.

During the decade when my dad experienced his really high highs and very low lows, my mom did her best to keep the family afloat while learning to take care of herself for the first time. The therapy sessions she went to before we left California had helped her understand that despite her best efforts, there were some things she simply couldn't control. With that in mind, she'd shifted her focus to what she could.

Once we moved back to Colorado, she took charge of the family finances, consolidated debts, and began the process of paying off the credit cards my dad had used for his numerous business ventures, none of which ever panned out. While my dad dealt with the debilitating side effects of the antidepressants he'd finally agreed to take, my mom prioritized our needs as a family above his needs as an individual and threw herself into work, rather than exclusively caring for him. She took the early shift at the bakery where she decorated cakes so she could be home by early afternoon, have some tea, start dinner, and begin prepping for weekend catering orders.

She also planned menus and oversaw the kitchen during large meditation retreats in our spiritual community—her seva, or selfless service. She leaned into her faith, regularly getting up at 4:00 a.m. to ensure she never missed her morning prayers before going to work, accepting that the hardships she now faced were simply her karma to bear, just as what my dad was experiencing was his.

She was strong and did what she had to do to keep moving forward with a quiet dignity. But from time to time, I caught glimpses of her internal conflict, despite her tough exterior—like one afternoon a few months after my dad was sent away.

I was sitting at the kitchen table reading the paper when my mom came home from her shift at the bakery. She put a pot of water on the stove for her chai and, with a ceramic mug in hand, opened the fridge to get some milk. In the process, she knocked over a glass one of us had left in the fridge. Juice dribbled down the shelves of the fridge and onto the floor, and before I could get to the sink to grab a towel, I heard a guttural moan. Mom threw her mug to the floor in anger and crumpled to the yellow linoleum, sobbing. With my stomach in knots, I stepped over pieces of shattered mug and spilled juice, knelt down, and put my arms around her. She leaned into me and wept. Rare moments like these were reminders that just underneath, she was still human.

At 9:00 that morning, the customer who was hosting the wedding with five hundred guests called and asked if my mom could deliver the food instead of them having to pick it up. Since we were a home-based operation working with minimal time, delivering the food had never been a part of the service we offered, and she politely declined. When they continued to insist and told her they were worried they wouldn't know how to set everything up, she compromised and offered to have me follow them back to the venue to help set up, but she told them they'd still need to send someone to pick up the food.

The customers arrived forty-five minutes late to pick up their order, and by the time we'd packed up their van, it was almost 11:30 a.m. Though the food was for a lunch reception scheduled to start at noon, the certainty of the event occurring on "Indian Standard Time" meant that we made it to the venue, got the food set up, and still had almost an hour before the ceremony ended and people arrived to eat.

When I got back home, almost four hours later, it was close to 3:00 p.m. The garage had been cleaned, the stove folded up and stored, and all the pots and pans washed and stacked. If I hadn't experienced it, I couldn't have imagined that we'd just finished cooking a full Indian meal for five hundred people in that space.

I walked into the family room and found my mom sitting in the corner seat of the brown sectional, her legs stretched out in front of her, a cup of tea in her hand and bowl of crunchy chakri next to her. My sister and cousin were stretched out on the floor, a pile of Uno cards between them.

"You're home," my mom said with a tired smile. "Come here and sit down." She patted the cushion next to her. "Are you hungry, beta? You haven't eaten all day." Her eyes were concerned as she watched me cross the room and plop down next to her.

"I'm exhausted!" I declared, closing my eyes. A few seconds later, I opened them and saw my grandmother enter with a laundry basket.

She dumped the rumpled clothes on the sofa and pushed them aside so she could sit down. As she began folding laundry, she looked up and asked, "Which one of you girls is cooking dinner tonight?"

My sister, cousin, and I all stared wide-eyed as my grandmother grinned and my mom shook her head and started laughing.

"We're a houseful of women who just finished cooking for five hundred people," she said with a smile. "I think we've earned some pizza."

This catering life was exhausting and often grueling on our bodies, but it was also where we spent the most time laughing, sharing stories, and being together. Despite my frequent frustration, in time I came to understand the power of food as a connector of people. But by following my mom's lead, I also learned to embody the adage of service before self.

The stories that shaped me were born in situations outside of my control and became the subjective fears, expectations, hopes, desires, and assumptions that created the lens through which I saw and experienced the world. Each of these experiences—and many others not shared here—imprinted on my mind and body, shaping the person I would become and influencing how I showed up in my relationships and work for decades, for better and for worse. My shaping stories include generational trauma, othering and exclusion, split identity, violence and mental-health-related challenges, lack of stability, and the importance of both hard work and service to others.

Do any of these resonate with you?

- What events or circumstances in your life or in your family's history have created the stories that have shaped your experiences?
- How do these *shaping* stories impact who you are and the roles you play? Personally? Professionally?

PART TWO

SURVIVING

SURVIVING

Our *surviving* stories are influenced by the hardships, tragedies, and traumas of our *shaping* stories and experiences—they're the result of stories we tell ourselves to make meaning of the challenging and painful experiences we encounter as we move through life.

When we bump up against thoughts, beliefs, values, and perspectives different from our own, our brain initially views these new perspectives as threats and activates our sympathetic nervous system. *Surviving* stories are experienced as nervous-system reactions, which are designed to keep us safe when we're in danger. The problem is, our brain can't differentiate between real threats and perceived threats—or threats to our bodies versus threats to our identity or ego—meaning that our sympathetic nervous system can stay activated for much longer than it should be.

There are a total of five nervous-system reactions. In addition to *fight* or *flight*, there are *freeze*, *fix*, and *fake*.

- *Fight* shows up as blame, criticism, judgment, or even violence. All of these can be turned in, toward ourselves, or out toward others.
- *Flight* is about escaping a situation, physically or mentally. This reaction often leads to numbing our feelings and emotions through addictions and is also the reaction that makes it difficult for us to connect meaningfully with others.
- *Freeze* means feeling stuck, unable to make a choice or move forward out of fear.
- *Fix* is an intense desire to change ourselves or our circumstances and comes from a place of feeling unworthy of love and belonging as we are.
- *Fake* is a need for control that often pushes people to hide themselves behind a mask of perfectionism and prevents them from showing vulnerability.

The vignettes shared in Part Two highlight each of these nervous-system reactions and examples of the circumstances in which they've showed up in my day-to-day life.

5

ANYWHERE BUT HERE

(Flight)

"Beta, are you awake?" my mom asked from the doorway of my bedroom in Aurora, Colorado.

"Yes." Unable to sleep, I'd been listening to the sounds of her getting ready and praying. I looked up from my bed and saw her sad expression.

"Drive carefully today, and tell him I love him."

"He knows, but I'll remind him," I assured her before she set off for work.

I squinted at the clock on my nightstand. The red numbers looked blurred at the edges. *4:38 a.m.* It was still too early to get up. Maybe I could sleep a little more. I definitely needed it. I'd been up late with three of my sorority sisters, who were now camped out in the family room two floors below me. But thoughts kept swirling around in my mind, holding sleep at bay. *I should have known better. I've never gotten to live a normal life. Why did I think this time would be any different?* I pulled the sheet up to my chin. It was still dark outside, but I could hear birds chirping with the arrival of morning.

We'd moved back to Aurora in the summer of 1991. Things had been relatively good for the first year, until my dad had gone off his medication. After that he'd once again fallen into deep bouts of depression followed by manic episodes. Wanting nothing more than to escape from that space, I was grateful to have found a college two states away. Weeks after my high school graduation in 1993, my dad had gotten violent again. This time we called the police and had him arrested.

Knowing he'd likely be released, we changed the locks on the house. We huddled together in fear when he arrived two days later, pounding on the door and demanding to be let in. When we refused, he made his way to a friend's home, hoping my mom would relent and let him come back. But this time she was different. She told him the only way he'd be allowed back into the house was if he agreed to take his medication, which he did a few days later.

Since then, he'd been doing relatively well. In fact, in December of 1994, when I had come home for Christmas after the first semester of my sophomore year of college, it felt like he was on a good path again. My parents had opened a coffee shop, and things seemed to be calmer. So when I learned that one of my college friends would be getting married in Colorado that July, I'd offered my home as a place to stay for friends who were also planning to attend.

Unfortunately, soon after I came home for the summer, my dad decided to stop taking his medication again. This time, when he pushed my mom down a short flight of stairs over a disagreement about pizza toppings, I was the one who called the police and asked them to arrest him. I was the one who testified against him in court and then sat terrified in the witness box, answering his questions as he cross-examined me because he had decided to defend himself. I was the one in the courtroom when the judge sentenced him to six months in the state mental health facility and watched as the bailiffs dragged him out of the courtroom, yelling and screaming at me.

And now, I was lying here in my bed, dreading the two-hour drive to Pueblo, Colorado, and feeling the anxiety that always came with not knowing which version of my dad awaited me. *I can do this.* It was the least I could do after leaving my mom and sister here to deal with him for so long while I was away at school. *I have to do this*, I told myself as I rolled over and sat up in my bed, forcing myself to meet the day.

It was just after 8:30 a.m. when I pulled into the parking lot of the Colorado Mental Health Institute. A deep sadness settled over me as I looked out at the yard surrounded by barbed wire fencing.

It looked like a prison.

However, the front of the administration building had a pale cream façade, dotted artistically with round-edged square cutouts. It seemed entirely in contrast to the locked-down space beside it, and it left me feeling even more ill at ease. Nonetheless, I followed a few others inside, navigated security, checked in, and waited for my name to be called.

A little after 9:00 a.m., a young man appeared in the doorway. Dressed in blue scrubs, he wore his hair cut short against his scalp. The whites of his almond-shaped brown eyes contrasted with his light brown skin, which was smooth across his face. When he called my name, I detected a hint of an accent that would become familiar several years later when I interviewed refugees from Ethiopia and Eritrea.

"Hi, I'm Dimple," I said, rising from my seat.

"I'm Joseph. Please follow me." His expression was flat as he pressed a button. I heard a buzzer, followed by the click of a lock. Pulling on the heavy metal door, he held it open for me to pass through.

Oh God. I covered my mouth and nose with my hand to avoid gagging. The stench of musty air, unwashed bodies, and what I could only imagine was fear hit me with an unexpected ferocity.

"Your first time?" Joseph asked. I nodded yes, trying to regain my composure. "You'll get used to the smell after a while." His reassuring words fell as flat as his expression.

After a while? I couldn't imagine ever getting used to this. How were people expected to live this way?

"Okay, you'll have thirty minutes with your..." His voice trailed off as he flipped open the folder in his hand. "...father. You'll be in a small visitors' room. I'll show you the panic button. Just press it if you need it."

Heat flushed through my torso and armpits as I wiped my palms on my shorts. I wished there was a panic button I could press as we walked the long corridors. I felt dozens of anonymous eyes watching us through the mirrors and cameras mounted at the corners of the hallways.

As we navigated through the maze, I was overcome by the familiar sensation of fear and a desire to escape. I had experienced it many times in California, where it had usually led me to hide for hours in the library. I could almost smell the kind librarian's perfume, the pages of my favorite Sweet Valley High books, and the leather of the beanbag chair I'd spent so many hours in. In the eighth grade, I'd learned that books were magic.

They allowed me to disappear from an often disappointing and scary reality into places filled with adventure, joy, and laughter. I loved immersing myself in worlds where I could hang out with the popular kids, travel to different cities, and get a glimpse of families in which parents danced with each other in the kitchen after dinner as the kids did homework in front of the fireplace. They were the worlds I longed for—the worlds of "anywhere but here." Between the library, the tennis team, student government, and very long bike rides, I had quite often managed to be anywhere but there in those early days in California.

"We're nearly there," Joseph said, pulling me out of my thoughts.

"How's he doing?" I asked.

He looked again at my dad's folder. "I just escort people, so I don't really know. But given the unit he's in and the room you're using, he probably hasn't been responding to the medication." His tone was detached, emotionless.

I supposed you'd have to be that way to work in a place like this. I squinted at the fluorescent light reflecting off the white-brick walls. My legs suddenly felt like lead, as if I were plodding through wet cement, and the distance between Joseph and me began to grow.

"Please, you must come now. We have to stay on schedule," he said tersely when he noticed I was no longer right behind him. He seemed oblivious to or unable to acknowledge the fear and distress I knew was on my face.

He stopped in front of a gray metal door with a window on it and pressed another button. Again, the sound of a buzzer was followed by the click of a lock before he stepped forward and held the door open for me. The room was small, barely four feet in all directions, with metal benches on two of the walls. My dad sat on one of the benches—hair disheveled, eyebrows knit together—staring at us.

My heart pounded when I realized he didn't recognize me. Scanning the walls, I tried to find the panic button Joseph had mentioned. Then I silently admonished myself. This was my dad, and he wasn't going to hurt me. I took a deep breath and shoved my hands into the pockets of my shorts.

"Here is the panic button." Joseph pointed to a silver panel with a black button in the center on the wall near the door. "I'll be right outside if you need something. Once you're done, knock on the window, and I'll take you back out. Any questions?" he asked as he stepped out.

I wondered if it would it matter if I did. He hadn't even acknowledged my dad. "No, I think I've got it."

With that, Joseph slammed the heavy metal door shut. I winced, my eyes still on my dad.

I sat down next to him on the metal bench and tentatively touched his shoulder. "Hi, Dad. It's me, Dimpu. How are you?"

He glared at me for a moment, and I held my breath, unsure what to do.

But then his eyebrows smoothed slightly as recognition broke through. Smiling, he patted my back and asked, "Did they tell you to come?"

"Did who tell me to come?" I shook my head.

"President Clinton. I talked to him and Hillary, and they were asking where I was. I told them I was here, but they said I need to be there to help them." His gaze moved to something only he could see in front of him.

I removed my hand from his shoulder as my stomach tightened and tears filled my eyes. A wave of compassion moved through my body, dissolving the anger I'd felt less than an hour ago. He was sick and clearly needed help, yet the people at the facility didn't even see him as a human being. But my compassion was quickly subdued by a resurgence of anger—first at him, then at myself.

Why can't you just take your fucking medicine? Stop it! What's wrong with you? Do you think he wants to be here? Nobody deserves to live like this. He's lost all his dignity. Maybe you could stop being so selfish and think about how he must be feeling.

I touched his shoulder again, and he looked at me.

"I'm so sorry, Dad. I'm so sorry," I whispered, feeling my tears fall.

He put up a finger, indicating that I should wait. "Why are you interrupting while I'm talking to him?" His eyebrows furrowed in anger before he turned away and began speaking to the empty space in front of him. "Sorry. I'm so glad you came to visit me. How can I help you?" he asked the air earnestly.

I followed his gaze, wishing I could see what he was seeing. When I reached for his hand, he turned toward me again. "Dad, who are you talking to?" My back and shoulders were tight as I waited for him to respond.

"What do you mean, who am I talking to? You don't recognize President Clinton?" He laughed in disbelief. "He came here to see me, so let me finish talking to him." He turned back to the empty space and continued his one-sided conversation with the air.

I felt my whole body shaking as tears streamed down my face. In that moment, it felt like we were both imprisoned here. *I'm sorry, Dad. I can't do this. I can't see you like this. It's too much.*

I stood up and walked to the door, looking back at my dad one last time. He hadn't noticed that I was no longer sitting with him. Wiping my face, I turned my back to the room, knocked on the door, and waited to be released.

6

BEING ENOUGH

(Fake)

"**M**s. Dhabalia! Please come in." Dr. Armstrong sat behind his desk. "Have a seat." He motioned to the two chairs on the other side of it.

"Thank you." I sat in the chair closest to the door and placed my backpack on the ground near my feet.

"How was it?" he asked as he leaned forward. "The thing with Clinton."

"It was amazing! But you're not going to believe what happened..." I leaned forward as well and smiled.

A couple of weeks earlier, Dr. Armstrong, one of my college professors, had called me to this same office to let me know President Clinton was making a campaign stop in Kansas City and that the reelection campaign was looking for volunteers. Though my Southern Baptist college tended to lean more conservative, Dr. Armstrong knew some of us on campus might take advantage of the opportunity.

"We were all told to show up at a hotel downtown to get our assignments," I told him. "When we got there, another volunteer pointed us to one of the smaller ballrooms where rows of chairs were set up. A few minutes after we found seats, six Secret Service agents burst through the doors yelling, 'Okay! Listen up, people! This is a meeting about the presidential motorcade!'" I shook my head. "They basically told us everyone in the room would be driving a car in the motorcade the next day."

Dr. Armstrong's eyes widened. Then he threw back his head, let out a loud guffaw, and clapped his hands together.

I laughed. "Exactly! Not what we were expecting. They gave us passes for the airport and car numbers and told us to show up at the airport in the morning at six a.m. So that's what I did. When I got there, I was grouped with other volunteers and then we were all taken out to the tarmac where two presidential limos, a line of minivans, and several police cars were waiting. Each van had a number on the windshield, and we were told to find our van and wait there."

Dr. Armstrong nodded along.

"About a half hour later, Air Force One landed, and President Clinton, his advisors, and the press all headed toward the motorcade. My van was filled with members of the press, and my job for the day was to drive them from one campaign stop to the next." I sat back in my chair. "Thank you again for letting me know about the opportunity. I'm so grateful!" I put my hand on my heart.

"I'm so glad it worked out," he said. "And now you have a great story to tell for many years to come!"

I nodded, though I wondered if I could pick up my backpack and say good-bye before we ventured into talk about the future. I wasn't ready to have that yet.

"I invited you here today because you're moving toward your last semester," Dr. Armstrong said. "I wanted to check in, see what's next for you after you graduate in the spring."

No such luck. My stomach dropped with a thud.

I had no idea what came next. And I still had months before graduation. Did we really have to talk about this now?

On cue, Dr. Armstrong continued. "I know we're still a ways out from graduation, but I like to have this conversation early. I want you to have time to consider your options and get things in place."

My heartbeat quickened. "Oh, wow, um...thank you," I stammered. "I wasn't really expecting to talk about this today." I laughed nervously, hoping once again to end the conversation.

But Dr. Armstrong pressed on. "I understand, and you don't need a full plan right now, but we should talk through some of your options."

I guess we're doing this. I silently coached myself to at least sound like I'd put some thought into my future and sat up straighter. "That sounds great. Thank you." The confidence in my voice was feigned.

"I remember you telling me you're interested in policy work. Is that still the case?" he probed.

Policy work. What did I even mean by that? I wondered. "Yes, that's still correct," I said. "I think with the education I've gotten through Oxbridge, policy work makes the most sense." I hoped he didn't ask for more detail.

When I'd arrived at William Jewell College, a Southern Baptist liberal arts school in Liberty, Missouri, three years earlier, I was one of only a dozen people to be admitted into an elite honors program called Oxbridge. The program was modeled on the British style of tutorial study, and we were required to declare our major at the end of our first semester of freshman year, after which we could not change it. Not loving math or science and knowing most Indians didn't regard English literature as a degree that would lead to a viable career in the future, I chose to pursue PPE—politics, philosophy, and economics—based on the British major of the same name. I had spent my junior year studying at Oxford University and now, having returned from abroad, I was busy working on a thesis project and preparing for the comprehensive exams I had to pass in order to graduate.

How was it that I'd made it through three and a half years of a rigorous educational system and still felt completely lost? With no clue about what I wanted to do?

I'd worked hard to convey confidence and ambition my whole life, but during my freshman year, a D on a moral philosophy paper, coupled with a discouraging comment from the professor, had seeded self-doubt about my capability. I'd spent the remainder of my college years questioning whether I was smart enough compared to the people around me.

Despite the accolades, encouragement, and high marks I got in other subjects, I never quite felt like I measured up. And this imposter-like feeling was only exacerbated when I spent time with classmates in my program and during my time at Oxford. Everyone around me seemed to be well-read, able to pick up nuances in the materials we covered, and quick to master all manner of details that often escaped me.

Given the cultural pressures, it had never occurred to me that pursuing a different field of study—something more artistic and creative, where I excelled—might have been a better fit. The destiny envisioned for me was a life better than what my parents had—more education, more money, more things. So pursuing a path that wasn't likely to guarantee material success simply wasn't an option for this daughter of first-generation immigrants.

I'd kept up a good façade, but behind my smile, I didn't know if I was everything everyone believed I was...or could be.

Dr. Armstrong's voice interrupted my shame spiral and the flush of body heat that accompanied it. "Well, I know Senator Ashcroft's office is looking for a new staffer," he said. "But I think your politics differ quite a bit, and you probably wouldn't enjoy working for him. However, there are plenty of other senators and congressmen. Working with them would be a great introduction to policy work. Have you thought about going to DC?"

"Definitely one day," I said. I could feel tingles of excitement and possibility trying to break through the armor of my insecurities.

I'd fallen in love with DC when I visited in high school. There was something about the history and knowing I was standing in places where America's founding fathers had stood. During that visit I had felt confident that Washington, DC, was where I'd be able to effect change. The fact that I wasn't yet sure what type of change I wanted to make hadn't bothered me then—I was sure I'd figure that out later. But somewhere along the way, that confidence and sense of adventure had given way to fear and a need to be in control.

As I sat across from Dr. Armstrong, unsure and insecure, I wondered if I had what it would take to find success in a place like Washington, DC. I was so awe-inspired by what it represented that I felt unworthy of working there.

"You might want to think about going out there right after graduation." He said this so matter-of-factly.

"Oh, well, you know, I'd really want to have a job and a place to live before I move there." My palms started to sweat at the thought of picking up and moving across the country without a concrete plan in place.

"DC is one of those places where even if you go without a job, you'll have no problem finding something and landing on your feet. There are plenty of us who have contacts we could put you in touch with, and I have no doubt you'd find something within a few months."

"That sounds so exciting," I replied, forcing a smile as my brain went into overdrive, wondering where I'd live and how I'd pay rent and feed myself. Going to DC without a job wasn't going to happen.

"Law school is another option with a PPE degree," Dr. Armstrong continued. "And a great foundation for policy work." My ears perked up at what sounded like an impressive next step. "But there's no harm in taking a little time and testing those waters first to make sure it's what you really want to do," he added.

Nope. I leaned forward in my chair and smiled. "It's funny you say that, because I've actually been thinking about law school. I think it would be much better to just go straight through and get all my schooling done. Then I'll be able to dive into my career."

Grateful to see Dr. Armstrong nodding in understanding, I reached for my backpack and wondered if I was trying to convince him or myself? Did I want to go to law school? It almost met my dad's expectations for me as a professional, and I did want to help people and go back to Washington, DC. But...was I smart enough? Ambitious enough? Committed enough to go down this path? The questions bubbled up slowly and then faded until there was only one question left that I couldn't ignore. *Am I enough?*

7

MAKE IT WORK

(Fix)

s we pulled into the driveway of Sahil's parents' house, confusion and fear churned in the pit of my stomach—a feeling I was all too familiar with after less than a year of marriage.

"I don't understand," I said, trying to keep my voice from shaking. "What do you mean we now have to pay half your parents' mortgage on this house?" I unbuckled my seatbelt and turned in my seat.

"It's our duty," Sahil mumbled, refusing to make eye contact with anything but the garage door on the other side of the windshield.

Duty. I rolled my eyes. This term was often thrown around in his family as a way to ensure that the younger generation understood their obligations to older family members.

Ignoring his explanation, I asked what was actually bothering me. "How long have you known?"

His silence confirmed what I'd already suspected: This wasn't new information. It was simply new to me.

"Why is this the first time I'm hearing about this?" My voice shifted in tandem with the anger I felt moving through my chest and into my face. "And today? Today of all days, when I just found out I got my dream job as an asylum officer! You choose to wait until today, as we pull into their driveway, to drop this on me?" My voice shook with indignation.

He squirmed in the leather seat of his Volvo. "I told you we'd have to take care of my parents one day." His tone was clipped, nostrils flaring.

"Yes, one day! Not today! And you never mentioned anything about paying the mortgage on a house we don't live in! Do you see how crazy this is?" The trembling spread through my body. "It's just like when you waited until a few days before our wedding to tell me about all your credit card debt!"

Sahil glared at me, and in a low and controlled voice said, "Well, it is what it is, so get over it." Then he opened the door, exited the car, and walked into his parents' house without looking back.

I stayed in my seat, seething and silently admonishing myself not to cry. This wasn't the first time he'd waited to drop a piece of news on me until the last minute. How many more times would it happen? How much more was I going to have to take?

After he'd told me about his debt, I'd plastered a smile on my face, even as the little voice inside my head got louder, yelling, "*Get out of this now! You're not married yet! Call it off!*" But I couldn't bear the shame calling off the wedding would have caused my parents, and me. And now I was here once again.

After a few moments, I took a deep breath and wiped my face. A heaviness filled my chest as I opened my door and made my way to the house, where my in-laws stood waiting for me, concern on their faces.

"What happened, beta?" my mother-in-law asked from the doorway. "He said you were still in the car and upset because of the mortgage payment."

Of course he did. I bent down to hug her hello and then followed her and my father-in-law into the foyer.

Bracing myself for the conversation, I took another deep breath and tried my hardest to keep my voice even. "I'm not upset about the mortgage payment—well, I mean, I am upset about it, but I'm more upset about the fact that this is the first time I've heard anything about it. Sahil never said a word to me before we got married or since I moved here after the wedding. The first time he mentioned it was as we pulled into your driveway a few minutes ago." I didn't hide my frustration as I headed to the kitchen. "I'm just trying to process it all and understand."

My in-laws followed me into the kitchen as I pulled out a chair and sat down at the table, which was already set for dinner. Nearby, my husband paced back and forth, nostrils flaring. He looked like a bull getting ready to charge, which I supposed made me the conquistador, figuring out the best way to avoid being gored.

"This arrangement has been in place for a long time," my mother-in-law said. "We made the down payment for this house several years ago, and the kids split the mortgage payments. Right before you were married, Sahil's sister agreed to take on the full payment until you found a job, since he would have to take care of all the expenses on his salary alone until then. As a member of this family, it is your duty to start contributing now that you have a job." She stated all of this as though it were fact.

Her statement landed like a punch to my gut. My breath caught in my throat for a moment before the heaviness in my chest moved down to my stomach, twisting it into tight knots. My heart pounded in my chest and ears. *Is this really be happening again?* Was I going to be trapped in this place and in his web of deception for the rest of my life? Indignation gripped my shoulders and the back of my neck with a furious intensity. Searching my mother-in-law's face for any signs of compassion, I found none. So this was my situation. I had no choice but to deal with it. *I have to find a way to fix this.*

I took a deep breath before responding. "I understand that I have a duty to all of you as a member of this family, and I will fulfill that duty," I began. "But as my husband, doesn't Sahil have a duty to be honest and forthright with me?"

"Of course he does," she answered in a snipped tone, her eyebrows arching.

"This is not the first time he's done this to me," I continued. "When we first met, I told him how much I loved to travel, and he told me he loved it, too. Then after our wedding, I found out he didn't even own a passport."

My mother-in-law rolled her eyes, crossed her arms, and stared at me. It seemed that was a weak example.

My father-in-law gently put his hand on my shoulder and spoke for the first time. "What Sahil did was wrong. He should have told you, and I'm sorry he didn't. But we're not in a position to make the payments. This was something everyone agreed to long ago," he explained.

I nodded in resignation and wondered what my parents would think if they knew the truth. They would be concerned. But I couldn't fail in this marriage. My grandmother's words from the morning of my wedding came rushing back: "*Once you're married, you represent not one, but two families—the one you came from and the one you go to. You have a duty to never let either one be looked down upon or shamed in any way.*"

I had to accept that this was my life and figure out how to make it work. There wasn't another choice. If we could set up a budget and cut some corners, with my new job, we might be able to get his debts paid off, pay half of his parents' mortgage, pay my student loans, and save some money for us to eventually buy our own place. I knew others had it a lot worse. So I'd find a way to fix this. I'd figure it out.

There was nothing more to say.

8

A THREAT FROM WITHIN

(Fight)

"How you doin', kiddo? It's good to see you." Dr. Safayan breezed into the small exam room. His tight gray curls were cut short, and his dimpled smile immediately put me at ease.

"I've been better," I said with a sigh. I'd come home to Virginia for Thanksgiving, having arrived from New Delhi, where I now lived while working for the US Embassy, just two days earlier.

Dr. Safayan had been my doctor since I'd moved to the Washington, DC, area in 2007. Three months after leaving my husband, I'd relocated to northern California to be closer to my sister, and I'd worked at the San Francisco Asylum Office for a little over a year while finalizing my divorce before getting a job at Asylum Headquarters in Washington, DC. Regardless of where in the world I was posted, though, I always came back to see Dr. Safayan.

"Well, let's get you back to being better again!" He flipped open my chart. "So, tell me what's been going on."

I took a deep breath and was overcome with emotion. "I—I'm sorry…" I stammered through the sobs.

"It's okay. Take your time," he said, handing me a box of tissues.

I grabbed one and wiped my eyes, carefully guiding the tissue under my eyeline to remove any black stains of mascara. Wiping my nose, I took another deep breath and started again.

"As you know, I've been in India for the past six months. Soon after I got there, I got really sick with a terrible cough I haven't been able to shake, and I've also been getting these weird rashes on my shins for months. I've been to the medical unit at the embassy several times, and they can't seem to figure it out. I've tried all kinds of ointments and such, and nothing is working. They just keep getting more itchy and painful."

Dr. Safayan nodded, taking it all in. "How are your stress levels?" he asked.

I looked at him and laughed, but got no smile in response. "Oh wait, you're serious?"

He raised his eyebrows and peered at me over the top of the glasses perched low on his nose.

"Well, they're not great," I confessed. "I'm responsible for running the largest overseas immigration office in the government, with a jurisdiction that spans eight countries, and I'm supposed to mentor, coach, and evaluate my staff. But as you've no doubt seen on the news, it's the height of the refugee crisis, so I've been traveling just about every month to Pakistan, which isn't exactly a garden spot. I'm gone for two weeks at a time, and then I return to an office filled with stacks of cases waiting for my review since nobody else is allowed to sign off on them. I have no social support because I started traveling within weeks of arriving in Delhi, so I didn't meet people and nobody really knows when I'm in town, so I don't get invited to functions very often. The pollution was terrible when I arrived, but now that it's getting cooler, it's even worse since people burn everything from trash to tires. I've had chronic sinus infections for years, and all of this has made those worse, too. And my boyfriend, Jay, is posted in Russia, so we can't really talk because it's pretty likely that a Russian operative is listening in, and we've only been able to see each other a couple of times. It's just...a lot," I finished, shifting my gaze to my bare feet and the bumpy red rashes climbing my legs.

Dr. Safayan took my hand in his and looked me in the eye. "That sounds absolutely exhausting."

Feeling seen for the first time in a long while, I felt my eyes fill with tears again.

He smiled and put my hand back in my lap before reaching for the tissue box again. "Okay. Let's take a look at your shins." He pulled on a pair of latex gloves and shifted his focus to my legs. After a few minutes, he rolled back his chair and pulled off the gloves.

"Remember when I told you a few years ago that you have Hashimoto's disease?" I nodded. "Well, Hashimoto's is an autoimmune disorder. Whereas hypothyroidism is a problem with your thyroid gland, Hashimoto's is a problem with your immune system. In Hashimoto's—as in all autoimmune diseases—the immune system gets confused and mistakenly attacks a part of your own body. When you're experiencing chronic stress, you're producing much higher levels of cortisol—you might know it as the stress hormone. While some cortisol is good, when you've got an excess, it further suppresses your immune system, which for you is already compromised because of the Hashimoto's." He paused to look at me a moment. "Your Hashimoto's diagnosis was your body telling you that you needed to make some changes. But you've now upped the stress levels, so the rashes are your body screaming at you to change."

I jumped into problem-solving mode. "Okay, so how do we fix this? Should we change the dosage of my thyroid medication?"

He looked up from my chart, where he'd been making some notes, and shook his head. "You're not getting it, Dimple. Unless something in your work is able to drastically change and reduce your stress, you have to come home now."

I stared at him blankly for a moment. "You mean curtail my assignment?"

He nodded.

"But I haven't even been there a full year! I can't leave. They paid a ton of money to send me there, and I've got at least another two and half years left, including a trip to Sri Lanka as soon as I get back."

Dr. Safayan held my gaze, eyes filled with compassion. "Well, it's your choice. You can come back now and focus on healing your body, or you might not come back at all."

"Come on, seriously?"

"I am dead serious. If you don't make some drastic changes soon, your body is going to keep upping the volume of its messages. And I promise, it won't be pleasant. Is this assignment really more important than your health?" he asked.

Of course I knew my health should come before everything else, and there were plenty of other jobs in my organization that were less stressful. But how could I possibly tell my bosses I needed to curtail my assignment and come home because the stress was literally killing me? They'd think I was weak and couldn't handle the work. Nobody would ever want to work with me again.

I looked at my doctor through tear-filled eyes. This should have been a no-brainer, and yet, the conflict I felt left me tired and afraid, unable to see a clear choice before me.

9

DEAL WITH IT LATER

(Freeze)

"Would you like a glass of champagne or some juice before we take off? I also have water, if you prefer." The flight attendant held a tray of stemmed glasses.

"I'll take some champagne, thanks." I pulled my hair into a loose bun at the nape of my neck.

She smiled and nodded, placing a small square napkin on the dark gray console before setting the glass on top of it. "Enjoy!"

I wish I could, I thought as I took a long sip, hoping it would tamp down the anxiety that had taken up residence in my stomach over the past couple of days. My mom had insisted I upgrade to business class on my return trip to India so I could get some rest, and I was already grateful I had listened.

Settling back in the seat, I closed my eyes, unable to silence the remnants of conversations still swirling in my mind or soothe the butterflies in my stomach.

> *"You're not getting it, Dimple. You can come home now or you may not come home at all."*

> *"Do you seriously have to think about talking to your bosses? This should be a no-brainer!"*

> *"Of course your health comes first. We're here to support you."*

"You tell us what you want. Do you want to take a few weeks to go home, work on a project in DC while you get better, and then go back to New Delhi?"

"It's your life and your career. You need to do whatever you think is best for you."

That last response had left me feeling the most uneasy. After everything we'd been through, that had been Jay's reply. We had been together on and off for five years and were finally in a place where we'd begun talking about the future. He was posted in Russia while I was in New Delhi, but we had both agreed that after these assignments, we would get married and take any future postings together—or we would settle in Washington, DC, where we could both easily find work.

Jay's words stung more than his initial silence had. I opened my eyes and took another long sip of the champagne.

Just three days before, still shaken by the news I'd received from my doctor earlier in the week, I'd returned from running errands and parked my mom's car in the driveway. I'd unbuckled my seatbelt, but instead of opening the door, I had reached for my cell phone. I'd tried to call Jay as soon as I'd left Dr. Safayan's office, but he hadn't picked up then or the three other times I'd tried to call after that. This wasn't entirely unusual, given where he was posted, but it was frustrating when I needed to talk about something important—like when I'd been on assignment in Pakistan a few months earlier and my grandfather had passed away. I'd called and texted him for hours, receiving no response for almost a day.

This time he'd finally picked up on the fourth ring, at which point I realized I'd been holding my breath. I'd told him about my conversation with Dr. Safayan, and when he didn't offer much of a response, I'd continued. *"I thought we could talk through the different options and how curtailing my assignment and coming back early could shift the plans we've been making,"* I'd explained. And then I'd waited, nervously running my fingers across the steering wheel and staring at my phone, which I'd placed on the dashboard. *"Hello?"* I'd said, wondering if we'd gotten cut off after far too many seconds had passed.

"I'm here," he'd said quietly. *"I just don't know what you're expecting me to say."*

My breath had caught. "*Seriously? How about, 'I'm so sorry!' or 'What can I do to support you?'*" My heart had raced as I'd felt him shutting down and pulling away. Like he always did.

I took another long sip of champagne as I recalled every excruciating detail.

"*I thought that since we're in a relationship and trying to build a future together, and this decision might impact what we do in the future, it would help for us to talk through it together. We're supposed to be partners...*" I'd added, trying to keep my voice from betraying the panic rising in my chest.

After a long pause, he'd said, "*It's your life and your career. You need to do whatever you think is best for you.*"

As I stared into my champagne glass, now nearly empty, I realized his response had surprised me because of how far we'd come. But it was not at all surprising in light of our history. We'd broken up four times over the course of our five years together, and I'd returned the engagement ring he'd given me twice. But after our last reconciliation, I thought we'd made real progress and found a good space. That made this hurt all the more. The indifference in his voice when I spoke to him this week had landed like a gut punch and left me with an uneasy feeling ever since.

I shook my head, as if doing so would somehow dislodge the memory, and turned to look out the window of the plane. It was a little after 5 p.m., and the sky was a deep shade of midnight blue, the last hints of the sun having just faded. The planes parked at the gates reflected against the glass of the brightly lit airport, morphing machines and people into a series of fluid images captured in each window pane.

This isn't how it's supposed to be. I was supposed to finish this assignment and then finally settle down and have a life with someone. But now everything was up in the air—my career, my relationship, my health, my reputation. I'd never left a job this way. And after being there such a short amount of time? People were going to think I was weak and unreliable, and I'd never get an international assignment again.

My throat tightened and my jaw clenched as tears prickled behind my eyes. I blinked them back and took another drink, finishing off the glass and looking around for the flight attendant. When I caught her eye, I held up the glass for another.

She smiled and nodded, returning a few minutes later.

"Here you go, Ms. Dhabalia. Can I get you anything else?" she asked.

"Nope, this is perfect," I assured her as we exchanged glasses.

As I raised my new drink to my lips, my thoughts turned to the future, and I felt exhausted all over again.

I'd be on a flight to Sri Lanka in three days. How many flights had I taken since moving to Delhi? Between all the work trips and the flights I'd taken with family to perform my maternal grandfather's last rites a few months earlier, it felt like I'd spent more time in the air than with my feet on the ground. After a minute I'd counted twenty-seven flights over the past eight months. I shook my head. No wonder I was exhausted.

I set my champagne on the console and pulled out the duty-free catalog. But after flipping through the pages, I shoved the magazine back into the seat pocket and let out a long exhale.

I should make a list. I had so much to do when I got back to Delhi, because I'd decided to curtail my assignment and return to Washington, DC. It was going to take a couple of months to tie up all the loose ends—then there was the packout. I hated the packing and unpacking, even when assisted by government-hired professionals. I had finally gotten my apartment set up the way I wanted it. And the office. I didn't even want to think about how much work had piled up in my office while I'd been in the US. And no way was I getting to any of it since I'd be prepping with the team for our trip to Sri Lanka just three days after I returned. The pressure in my chest intensified.

"Ladies and gentlemen, the pilot has informed us that we're ready to push back from the gate. Please make sure your seat belts are fastened and..."

I finished off the champagne and handed the glass to the flight attendant before buckling my seatbelt. *How will I tell my staff I'm leaving? How do I stay in a relationship where I don't feel supported? How will I ever get another overseas assignment? Will people lose respect for me?* The questions kept coming, one after the other, uncontrollable like an avalanche. My shoulders ached and my head throbbed from the weight of it all. Overwhelmed and unsure of where to start, I gave up. There was too much to think about in this moment.

Instead, I pressed the start button on the large screen in front of me. Movies, food, wine, and sleep, if it would come—that sounded a lot better than trying to make decisions or find answers to these questions right now. I'd deal with all of this later.

Our brain creates stories and explanations to help us survive the hardships, tragedies, and traumas of our lives. Our nervous system's initial reactions to the stories that shape us—fight, flight, freeze, fix, and fake—over time become our habitual approaches to dealing with new types of adversity and the moments when something in our world threatens us. Because we spend so much of our lives operating on autopilot, we may default to one or more of these reactions without realizing it.

Quite often we experience multiple reactions at the same time, or one after the other. For example, in chapter 7, my *fight* reaction led me to blame and judge my ex-husband and his mother, my *fake* reaction kept me from telling my parents anything was wrong, and my *fix* reaction helped me rationalize the situation so I didn't have to deal with the underlying issues in my marriage. In chapter 9, my *freeze* reaction was activated, overwhelming me with fear and preventing me from taking action or addressing the questions that came up, and my *flight* reaction helped me numb my emotions and escape through alcohol and movies.

- Can you remember a time when you experienced one of these reactions? Has it occurred more than once?
- Which of the five nervous-system reactions seems to be most common for you?
- Can you see any patterns around which reactions you default to in particular circumstances?
- How do those reactions show up in your body?

PART THREE

SEEING

SEEING

There are moments in life that disrupt or altogether destroy our usual autopilot state (meaning we're not particularly mindful or aware of what's happening within or around us) and offer a sudden opportunity to *see* the space that exists between what happens to us and our default survival reaction. *Seeing* is our newfound ability to observe the pattern—thought, emotion, sensation, reaction—we move through every time we encounter a stressful or traumatic event or some other form of adversity. The repetition of a particular pattern of behaviors, coupled with our lack of awareness, creates neural pathways in our brain—like tire tracks in the snow—that continue to deepen and eventually become our default reactions any time we're faced with the stressor that originally set the pattern in motion.

This part of the story-healing cycle isn't an action step. *Seeing* is a state of being that is cultivated over time—through intentional mindfulness practices or through life experiences that help us realize that our default thoughts, actions, or beliefs have kept us stuck in our pain or adversity. Such moments remove our lens of projection and create space where we can see our stories with more objectivity.

Cultivating the mindful awareness of seeing does not get rid of the thought-emotion-sensation-reaction pattern. That stays the same. But we can begin to understand that the stories we've created for particular situations are first experienced as thoughts, emotions, and sensations in our bodies, quickly followed by one or more sympathetic-nervous-system reactions—*fight, flight, freeze, fix,* or *fake.*

Our sympathetic nervous system was only meant to be activated for short periods of time, to protect us when we're in genuine danger by sending hormones like cortisol, adrenaline, and epinephrine through the body. But since our brain doesn't always understand the difference between real and perceived threats, our sympathetic nervous system is frequently activated when we're on autopilot, not really *seeing* what's happening around us. This makes us more reactive in stressful or traumatic situations, and over time can contribute to chronic health conditions and disease.

The habit of seeing is not a one-and-done, aha-moment-style solution. Mindful awareness is an intentional act that must be repeated many times before new neural pathways can be formed. But once they are, when we encounter a similar situation in the future, it becomes easier to notice each thought, emotion, sensation, and reaction—the resulting story—and to make the choice to pause, breathe, and reset our nervous system so we're no longer operating from a place of reaction. In this calmer space between what happened to us and our usual automatic reaction, we can instead choose a different response that will better serve us in that situation.

The vignettes in this section highlight disruptions commonly experienced by humanitarians, including burnout, moral injury, vicarious trauma, and compassion fatigue. Each of these was an instance that jolted me out of my autopilot state and into a place where I could finally begin to create awareness of my patterns in survival mode.

10

PAINFUL LESSONS

(Burnout)

Floating on my back, arms outstretched, I felt weightless as I bobbed in the oval swimming pool. Wispy white clouds danced by on the bright blue canvas of sky, and the sun warmed my face and body.

It felt weird—nowhere else to be, nobody looking for me, no emails waiting. My pulse quickened, and the familiar knots formed in my stomach. Why was I anxious? Most people would do anything for a vacation like this. Why couldn't I relax?

Closing my eyes, I watched reds, oranges, and yellows swirl together behind my eyelids. I inhaled deeply through my nose, feeling the air move through my lungs and chest and willing my body to surrender to the ebb and flow of the water before exhaling. With my ears just below the surface, the only thing I could hear clearly was the sound of my own breath, which soon slowed and moved gently in and out of my body.

Where have I heard this sound before? I tried to place it. A memory surfaced of taking the bar exam in Colorado and wearing earplugs for the first time. The sound of my breath, loud and echoing, had felt as foreign to my ears then as it did now.

When was the last time I'd paid attention to my breath...to *myself*?

The words my doctor had spoken weeks earlier reverberated under the water: "*You're not getting it, Dimple. You can come home now or you may not come home at all.*"

It should have been an easy decision, but it had taken me three days to put my needs before those of the organization I worked for and muster the courage to tell my boss what was going on with me. Focusing on my breath had long seemed like an unnecessary luxury I didn't have time for.

Contempt and anger at myself for letting things get to this point now hijacked my thoughts. My inner critic seemed louder here in the water. Frustrated by my inability to silence the internal chatter, I opened my eyes, flipped over, and swam to the edge of the pool, ready to get out and away from the self-judgment.

I found my mom sitting on the front porch of our hut, glasses perched on her nose, reading a book. She looked up and slipped her glasses off as she saw me approach, resting her book in her lap.

"How was your swim?" Her eyes told me she already knew the answer, the way moms do.

I dropped into the chair across from her, the heaviness in my chest growing. "It was okay. I was mostly just floating and looking up at the sky..." I wrapped a string from the towel around my finger. "But I couldn't relax."

My mom looked at me for a moment, her expression soft. "Well, that's understandable. You've been running for so long. It's hard to just stop."

"I guess, but that's kind of crazy. I used to be able to relax. When I lived in Greece, you guys made fun of me for it." My cheeks flushed with irritation.

If she heard a hint of prickliness in my voice, she ignored it. "Well, we're here now, and you need to rest." Picking up her book, she put her glasses back on. "It's almost noon. Go take a shower and we'll get some lunch before our afternoon treatments."

"Fine." I felt resigned as I dragged myself inside to get ready.

My mom and I had been in Kerala, in the southern part of India, for less than a week and had two more weeks of Panchakarma, traditional ayurvedic medicinal treatments, ahead of us. We had decided to stay in India for a few weeks after packing up my apartment to begin healing my mom's shoulder, which had been damaged by years of repetitive motion and no rest, and my lungs, which had been impacted by the severe pollution in India, as well as addressing the autoimmune issues my doctor had insisted were becoming life-threatening for me. It was an overdue act of self-care before starting my new role as a special assistant to the Refugee, Asylum and International Operations (RAIO) directorate, but it was off to a rough start as I struggled to slow down and rest or show myself any compassion.

Things continued to get worse. Later that night, I stood in front of the bathroom mirror looking at my face, which had reacted to the thick mud they'd applied during the day's treatment. "What if I look like this forever?" I wailed, staring at the red splotches on my cheeks. "It looks like it's spreading!" The redness and bumps were even more defined in the harsh glare of the fluorescent tube lighting above the mirror. I dipped my finger into the small pot of aloe vera gel the ayurvedic doctor had given me that afternoon and dabbed it on my face, feeling relief as the coolness soothed the heat of the rash.

My mom appeared at the doorway, pity in her eyes. "It will clear up. It's just your body detoxing, like the doctor told you earlier today. Keep using the aloe vera and give it some time." Our eyes met in the mirror, and I saw a shadow of pain quickly replaced by a smile. "You're going to be fine. You need to try to rest."

I washed my hands and followed her into the bedroom. I flopped onto the bed, hopelessness wrapping around me like a blanket. "How am I supposed to rest when it feels like my face is burning off? I knew we shouldn't have done this. We should have just gone home after packing out in Delhi. Then I wouldn't be in the pain I'm in now. And what if this leaves scars all over my face?" I felt myself losing control of my emotions yet again, and my jaw clenched as the little voice in my head took over. *Get it together! Why are you so weak?*

I swept my hand across the end table in search of my work phone to Google my symptoms and find some answers. Feeling nothing on the smooth wood, panic fluttered in my belly for a moment. Then I remembered that I'd turned in my equipment in New Delhi before leaving my post. My personal phone didn't work here without WiFi.

No phone.

No tablet.

No computer.

For the first time in ten years, I was totally and completely disconnected.

I felt disoriented for a moment, quickly followed by an overwhelming powerlessness.

"What happened? Why are you crying now?" my mom asked from her bed.

I shook my head. "I don't know. I'm frustrated. I thought this would be fun and relaxing, and instead I'm anxious and in physical pain. And I have no way to reach out to friends or look up what's going on with me," I choked through my tears. "I feel guilty being here in this beautiful place, focusing on me, when I know other people are having to do the work I left behind." I moaned as the knots between my shoulders tightened. "I know it's stupid. I have no idea why I'm reacting like this. It all just feels hopeless."

Pain flashed across my mom's face. "I know this feels hard right now, but I want you and your sister to learn from my mistakes. I worked so hard my whole life, and for what? Now when I finally have time to do the things I want to do, I have problems with my shoulders and hands from all those years of working and never taking time to care for myself. For years, I didn't know how to rest, and I'm paying for it. I want you girls to take better care of yourselves." Her pleading tone uncorked more tears, and I reached for a tissue from the bedside table.

"This whole experience should be a wakeup call for you," she continued. "You have to take better care of yourself, and you're being given the opportunity to do that now. This may be a painful lesson, but it's a chance to make some changes. It's also an opportunity for us to spend time together and enjoy this beautiful space, to just rest and let our bodies heal. You have to make the choice to put yourself first. Can you do that?"

As she looked at me, it felt like she was staring into my soul. Yet the only words I could find were, "I don't know. I want to, but it's hard."

"I know. You've had years of doing things a certain way, and it takes time to change that. Just remember what your dad used to say: Be gentle with yourself." She got up from her bed and walked over to pat me on the head before going into the bathroom.

I knew she was right. I couldn't help others if I was sick, which meant I had to heal. But it was so complicated. Could I change? Was I even capable of that?

I closed my eyes and tried to focus on my breath, but an experience at work a couple of years before flashed before me—a stark reminder that change wasn't going to be easy. In fact, it was going to be excruciatingly hard.

In the summer of 2014, my colleagues and I had watched with horror as militants from the Islamic State in Iraq and Syria (ISIS) captured the city of Mosul in Iraq, declared a caliphate, and changed its name to the Islamic State (IS). Not only was IS seeking to destroy the secular, Shia-led government in Iraq, but it was enforcing its interpretation of Shariah law in areas under its control and demanding that Muslims and other jihadist groups declare allegiance to IS.

The stakes were particularly high for my team that summer because Mosul was only a little over 200 miles from the capital city of Baghdad, where we had multiple teams posted to interview refugees. Everything we were reading online indicated that after capturing most of northern Iraq, IS was planning on making its way south toward Baghdad.

This spot in the world had always been a high-threat posting for our teams, but the brutality of IS's treatment of westerners, especially US citizens, was particularly chilling and elevated our concern for the people we had on the ground. The proximity of Mosul to Baghdad, coupled with news of US-trained Iraqi soldiers laying down their arms and submitting to IS in northern Iraq, raised concerns about IS potentially capturing the airport, which would make it a lot more challenging to safely evacuate Americans and others from the country.

In my role as Branch Chief for Regional Operations in Washington, DC, I was responsible for overseeing the work of the regional desk officers who served as liaisons between the refugee adjudications teams on the ground and Refugee Affairs Division headquarters. While my stress levels were as high as they'd ever been, concerns about everyone involved in this work on the ground superseded any about myself and my well-being. My focus was on the team leaders trying to keep their staff safe and calm, the leaders across various US government agencies working to evacuate them, and my desk officers, who were working long hours to coordinate logistics and provide support to the refugee adjudications teams and their counterparts in other government agencies.

In an attempt to get my desk officers to rest, I stepped in to help fill the gap afterhours, which with the time difference meant I was often responding to time-sensitive questions and providing necessary information to team leaders in Baghdad in the middle of the night. I had also let the team leaders know they could contact me anytime, day or night, if they needed anything. It felt like the least I could do.

But it only took 48 hours for lack of sleep, coupled with the stress and fear of what was unfolding in front of us, to settle on my face.

"Have you slept at all? You look terrible!" My friend Anne stood in the doorway of my office.

"Um, thank you?" I laughed in response.

"You know what I mean." She walked into my office and sat down in one of the chairs at the little conference table. "You look tired." Her concern was genuine.

"Yeah, I'm exhausted. I haven't slept more than a few hours this week."

"I'm sorry. I know it's a lot." I could feel her empathy. "But you can't be effective if you're not getting any rest."

I knew she was right, but I felt guilty about resting while our people in Baghdad were trying to get out of the country alive. This particular situation may have been more extreme than most of the issues my team dealt with, or that staff on the ground usually encountered, but regardless of your role, our work as an organization was fast-paced, constantly evolving, and rarely easy. We were in the business of serving the world's most vulnerable people. And self-care was almost never part of the discussion.

"Take another picture." My mom giggled as she posed near the window of our hotel. We had finished our three weeks of Panchakarma in Kerala and were back in New Delhi for a couple of days. Having revived our bodies and minds, we had decided to complete the experience by shopping and getting our hair and nails done.

"Oh my gosh! You and your pictures!" I teased, faking exasperation.

We took a few more of each of us individually and then a few more together before collapsing onto the bed in a fit of laughter.

"Okay, what do you want to do now?" I turned and rested on my elbow, waiting for her answer. Instead, she smiled and stroked my cheek.

"I told you your face would be fine!"

Her knowing smile earned her a roll of my eyes and a smile. "You were right, as usual!" I flipped over onto my back, but I could feel her grinning at my sarcasm.

She had been right about so many things on this trip. By the end of the first week, the rash on my face had disappeared and my cheeks were smooth again. By the end of the second week, my lungs had cleared up, and I was traversing the winding stairs to the beach below us every morning without any coughing or shortness of breath. By the end of the third week, my habit of reaching for my phone had disappeared, and I found myself tuning in to my breath more often. I was more aware of my emotions and what I felt in my body. I felt more grounded and present around others and with myself. I had taken her advice of being gentle with myself, and my body had responded in kind.

That evening, after tucking my mom into a taxi to the airport, I made my way back up to the room, feeling physically and emotionally lighter than I had in a very long time. I smiled at the thought of another twenty-four hours with absolutely nothing to do.

Apparently I could change. Maybe when I arrived home and started my new role, I'd do things differently at work this time, too.

11

A CONFLICTED OATH

(Moral Injury)

"Hi, I have a reservation for tonight."

This was one of my favorite restaurants in Washington, DC. The petite woman at the hostess station wore a burgundy blouse, her long blond hair pulled back in a ponytail. She tapped the computer screen with a manicured finger, encircled by a thin silver ring. "Here you are. For eleven people, right?" she asked without looking away from the screen.

"Well actually, we're down to ten. I'm sorry about the last-minute change. I just heard from my friend on the way here."

"Okay, no problem. Follow me."

She led me through an obstacle course of tables and chairs to the back of the restaurant, where a long farmhouse table, the wood knotted and weathered from years of use, had been set up in front of a window. A white plate, silverware, cloth napkin, and water glass sat at each place, and small, blue metal canisters of olive oil were scattered across the middle of the table, awaiting the fresh bread that would come out after my guests arrived. I had selected a menu that included pan Catalan, patatas bravas, croquetas, gambas al ajillo, escalivada con queso, tortilla de patatas, puntillitas, and paella, all to be served family-style.

Setting my bag on a chair, I pulled out a stack of place cards and prints with the profile of a woman's face made out of the words "empowered women empower women." I walked around the table, setting one print and a place card on top of each plate. When the table was ready, I sat down and took a long sip of the wine a server had brought over a few minutes earlier.

Well, happy birthday to me. In truth, I was in no mood to celebrate. I couldn't believe I was about to host a dinner party when the future of the country was in question. Taking another sip of wine, I glanced at my phone. People would be arriving any minute, and I needed to find a way out of this funk. I'd always loved celebrating my birthday, but the butterflies of excitement and anticipation I normally felt had been replaced by an ominous cloud of unease that had been hanging over me for weeks. It had gotten worse over the past week and finally settled as a dark heaviness in the pit of my stomach just a few hours ago.

I'd returned from New Delhi ten months earlier in March 2016 and quickly settled into my new role as a special assistant to the associate director in the Refugee, Asylum and International Operations directorate. The urgency I'd experienced on the front lines in the field had been replaced by the frenetic and bombastic energy of working at headquarters. The work was initially challenging because it was new, but I'd soon fallen into a comfortable rhythm of work-life harmony. The yoga, meditation, and movement habits I'd created in Kerala made it easier to prioritize my health by eating nutritious food, drinking enough water, taking an actual lunch break, and moving my body by exercising and taking walks every day. I was reconnecting with friends and spending time with my family, all of which grounded me in a way I hadn't felt in years.

In addition to the things I was doing outside of work, I was also laying the groundwork for what would eventually become RAIO Thrive. I'd planted the seed of my idea for an in-house well-being and resilience program with my boss just before she was called to another part of DHS on a temporary assignment for almost a year. Unlike in the past, where I'd been looking for instant gratification, now I took my time and was intentional about envisioning what this program might entail.

During this period I was given the opportunity to attend a peer support and positive psychology training, which helped me begin narrowing in on the topics and interventions I wanted to bring to my workforce. Then, toward the end of the year, we'd received feedback from the Federal Employee Viewpoint Survey (FEVS) that indicated staff felt management needed to do more to promote work/life balance. As a result, our acting associate director created a new Work/Life Balance Committee and asked me to chair it, giving me the platform I needed to begin sharing my research. Instead of the my-way-or-the-highway approach I'd previously taken, this time I worked with committee members to determine how we could best serve the workforce.

Things were going well on all fronts, and I was moving forward. Then, on November 8, 2016, everything changed when Donald Trump was elected president. Overnight, the life of service I'd worn as a badge of honor was upended.

Over the next two months, I moved between a deep depression and feelings of disorientation. It felt like trying to walk across one of those bounce houses people put up at children's birthday parties. With each step, the ground beneath me shifted and swayed, leaving me perpetually off-balance and unsure how best to keep moving forward. Over time my anger blossomed into rage, and fear turned to numbness. In addition to having trouble sleeping, the crushing weight of a new type of anxiety had come to live permanently in my stomach and chest. I found myself breathing shallowly more often, instead of from my belly.

As I waited for my guests at the restaurant, I thought about how the past week—the new president's first full week in office—had felt like the longest week of my entire life, leaving me exhausted from a rollercoaster of emotions.

Nausea had flooded through me when Trump used his pen to sign away years of hard work and negotiations through the power of the executive order. I'd spent decades believing in the stability and superiority of American democracy as I'd traveled around the world to interview refugees. But now, for the first time in my life, I felt the same fear that so many of the applicants I'd interviewed had described in their home countries, where dictators and military regimes had worked to concentrate power in the hands of a few while taking away the rights of many. Helplessness and fear set in as the new president silenced federal employees and discredited the press. What would the long-term damage of his actions be for generations to come?

Anger swelled to new heights as I watched him sit behind the H.M.S. Resolute Desk in the Oval Office, surrounded by white men as he signed away women's rights, scientific research, and environmental studies. Numbness and defeat spread through my body as he froze raises for career public servants and instituted a government-wide hiring freeze, with an exception only for law enforcement.

But it was the order he had signed earlier today that felt most personal. I took another long sip of wine. I was the daughter of immigrants, and I'd dedicated almost fifteen years of my life to working in the service of refugees and asylum seekers. With one flick of a pen, everything had changed.

I took a long, deep breath, fully aware that my friends were about to walk in. Executive Order 13769, *Protecting the Nation from Foreign Terrorist Entry into the United States*, was already more commonly known as the Muslim Ban. It effectively barred all people from Iraq, Syria, Iran, Libya, Somalia, Sudan, and Yemen from entering the United States. It also banned entry indefinitely for those fleeing war-torn Syria and stopped the admission of all refugees to the United States for four months. How the hell were we supposed to protect the people who needed our help?

An hour later, I was surrounded by nine powerhouse women from different parts of my life. Though I was grateful everyone had shown up to celebrate with me, the mood at the table was somber, and a palpable fear hung in the air as we discussed what we were witnessing and what, if anything, we could do to voice our opposition.

I sat in the middle of the table, catching snippets of conversation around me, saying little and taking it all in. A few of the attorneys at the table were talking about volunteering to assist the ACLU in bringing injunctions against the ban, while a couple of government employees spoke in hushed tones about their outrage and feelings of helplessness.

I had intentionally seated a friend who worked in a senior position at the Department of Homeland Security next to me, knowing she'd have the latest information. She had just finished chatting with a couple of the attorneys on her side of the table when she lifted her wine glass and turned to me.

"Happy birthday," she said with a warm smile.

My heart sank, and I felt my chest getting heavy, a sure sign that tears were soon to follow. I picked up my glass and clinked it with hers before we both took a drink. "Thanks, but it really doesn't feel all that happy," I whispered, blinking back tears.

She tilted her head. "I know. It's been a shitshow at the Department."

"I can only imagine," I replied. "I'm supposed to travel to Toronto tomorrow and then on to Mexico for my cousin's wedding. I was born and raised in this country, but for the first time, I'm scared to leave for fear they may not let me back in." The weak laugh I mustered was unconvincing to both of us.

She nodded. "I totally understand your fear. Things are changing a mile a minute right now." She reached for the bread. "But don't worry. You'll be fine. Just go and have a good time. You have an American passport, and you'll be able to get back in."

"Honestly, it feels surreal that we're even having this conversation." I twisted the edge of my napkin between my fingers. "The worst part is, I didn't sign the order and I don't agree with it at all, but as a public servant, I'm going to be expected to enforce it. I have never felt this conflicted and...dirty...before."

"I know exactly how you feel. We've spent our life protecting people from these countries, and now it feels like our government is closing its doors to them. The fact that the refugee program is temporarily paused... Well, that isn't new. It's happened under other administrations when they reevaluate programs and look for inefficiencies."

It felt like she was trying to cling to some hope. "Yeah, but we both know it feels different this time," I told her. "We've known this was coming and have been waiting for the other shoe to drop all week. It's way more than just pausing to reevaluate existing programs, and it's more than just immigration."

The reality of the situation hung in the air between us for a few minutes as we continued to sip our drinks.

"I don't know if I can do this," I admitted. "How do I show up and enforce laws and policies that go against everything I believe in?"

"I know it's hard. But you know, people were upset when Obama created DACA by executive action. This time, it just happens to hit closer to home, about topics that are important to us," she reasoned.

I watched her dip another piece of bread in olive oil and pop it into her mouth. I hated to dispel her hope, but this story had been on my mind all week.

"I've been thinking a lot about the people I've interviewed," I told her. "One of the first refugees I interviewed in Nairobi in two thousand six was a young Ethiopian man—an outspoken proponent of democracy who had taken up the work after his father was killed. He had been arrested several times, beaten and tortured, and had given up his education to protest the treatment of his people by the Ethiopian government. Because of the work he and his father had done, his mother, older sister, and younger brother were kidnapped and disappeared. Things ultimately got so bad that he had no choice but to flee Ethiopia."

"Soon after," I continued, "his two remaining sisters fled when the Ethiopian government, unable to find him, targeted them instead. The three of them lived in exile in Kenya for a little while, but then they found out the Ethiopian government had tracked them down and was trying to make an example of their brother by bringing him back to Ethiopia. By the time I saw him, he had been in protective custody, not even able to see his sisters. The day I interviewed him was the first time he'd seen them in several months, and their reunion was so moving. Still, the prospect of having a free society where he and his people could celebrate their culture and beliefs was important enough to him that even the threat of death wouldn't stop him from fighting."

I pushed little pieces of potato around on my plate with my fork. "We've interviewed so many people like him—people who are the living embodiment of courage and service before self. I've already read about people or heard from friends in other government agencies who are taking a stand and resigning, refusing to serve in an administration they feel is morally reprehensible. I've been wondering lately if I have the courage to take a similar stand. And honestly, I'm not sure I do."

"I've been thinking about the same thing," my friend acknowledged. "But if we leave—if all the good public servants leave—what will happen then?"

I considered her question. "You know, until this conversation, I'd never thought about how most career public servants like us will eventually encounter an administration with which they disagree on various policies or procedures. I've worked for two administrations headed by different political parties, and as I'm thinking about it now, I definitely felt better about serving under one than the other." I stabbed an olive on my plate. "I suppose the people who opposed Obama and thought about quitting felt like they were the 'good public servants' who needed to stay and make sure things didn't go off the rails. But it just feels different this time. I may have disagreed with something in the past, but I never felt *morally opposed* to it."

"Yeah, I know what you mean. This is really challenging me to my core, and I've been hearing the same from so many others." She raised her glass. "You know what? These problems will be waiting for us tomorrow. How about we focus on celebrating you tonight?"

The next morning, nine days after the inauguration and the day after the Muslim Ban went into effect, I started my forty-third year on this earth at Washington National Airport. Sitting at my gate, a cup of Dunkin Donuts coffee in my hands, I waited for a flight to Toronto to begin celebrating my cousin Kavita's wedding. I had rolled my black, hard-sided bag covered in travel stickers over to a bank of seats facing the airport TV and listened as CNN reported what I already knew was coming: Refugees and others who had been en route to the United States and had arrived at ports of entry after the executive order was signed the day before had been detained and threatened with being sent back.

It was a cold but clear day as I boarded my flight and settled into my seat. I looked out the window and took a breath. There, set against the bright blue sky, was the US Capitol building and the Washington Monument. Emotions bubbled through me, when all I really wanted was not to feel at all. But a little voice in my head pushed through the noise and made sure I heard it loud and clear: *Well, what are you going to do about it?*

I had a duty to stand up and speak out, but I felt muzzled as a government employee—prohibited from expressing my opinion publicly about policies related to my work. I knew I was already walking a fine line with the articles I'd posted on social media and sharing my family's story of being refugees and immigrants. And I knew that if I crossed that line, I could be reprimanded or potentially lose my job. But at the moment, it felt like the bare minimum I could do.

Two of my cousins picked me up at the airport in Toronto. As soon as I got in the car, my younger cousin Ravi looked at me in the rearview mirror and said, "Yo! Your president is crazy! What the fuck is he doing?"

My face flushed as I rolled my eyes and gave a halfhearted laugh. "Don't even get me started." I reached into my bag for my phone. Powering it on, I saw the familiar red notification on my Facebook messenger app indicating I had a message. A colleague was asking me to send my phone number as she needed to speak with me. We had never directly worked together, but we worked in the same organization. I typed my number into the screen and hit send, and my phone rang a few minutes later.

I answered in the back of the car. "Hello?"

"Dimple, thank you for taking the time to speak with me." Her voice was quiet and tinged with fear.

"It's no problem. Is everything okay?" I asked. When my cousin glanced back at me in the rearview mirror, I smiled and waved to reassure him, but I could feel flutters of anxiety in my stomach as I waited for her to respond.

She hesitated for a moment. "I—well, I'm calling because I've been seeing your posts on social media about your family and your frustration with the new administration. I know you're angry right now, but I'm worried about you." Unsure how to respond, I stayed quiet. "You know my family is from Haiti. I was there in the lead up to the nineteen ninety-one coup, and I saw what happened to people on both sides who spoke up and protested. I know it's scary right now, but it's best to keep your head down and not attract any attention. I just wanted to tell you that."

Was this really happening? Was someone actually calling to warn me to stay quiet? I felt heat rush through my body. "Oh, wow—this was not what I was expecting. I'm really sorry you experienced that, and I'm grateful to you for sharing your story and for your concern. I really appreciate it." I paused for a moment, trying to find the right words. "I'm scared, too, but I also know I have to do something. I can't just stay quiet. But I promise I'll be careful," I added, my tone softer.

"I understand," she said. "I just felt like I had to say something, because if I didn't and something happened to you, I'd regret it. Also, happy birthday," she added almost as an afterthought before she said goodbye.

I ended the call and looked out the window at the skyscrapers of Toronto blurring by. A heaviness settled in my chest. She was right. I needed to be sensible. I was single and didn't have anyone to support me. Was it worth crossing the line if the outcome was losing my job and potentially being targeted in the future? Maybe these institutions I'd put so much faith in didn't actually represent what I thought they did. Would my actions really change anything?

I couldn't believe how idealistic I'd been and that it'd taken me this long to recognize that the country I'd proudly served for so many years wasn't as progressive as I'd believed. People I'd considered friends and allies had been hiding their true feelings about those who were different from them. Men like Trump could get into and hold positions of power, and our nation's capital was rife with corruption and immoral actions. I supposed the only difference now was that we had a president brazen enough to do it all openly.

"Everything okay?" my cousin asked.

"Yeah, it's fine. Everyone is just freaked out about what's happening in the US." I slipped my phone back into my bag.

He nodded thoughtfully. "You gonna keep working for the government?"

"I don't know. I guess for now. I'm not sure what else I'd do if I just quit. I have a mortgage, car payment—you know, life expenses. And this is so much bigger than me. I took an oath to serve the country regardless of who is in power," I explained, for my benefit as much as his.

He started to comment but then hesitated and changed the subject.

I was grateful to not talk about this anymore, and as he described the resort in Mexico we were all going to, my thoughts drifted to my first trip to Washington, DC, during my senior year of high school. It was on that trip that I'd first recognized the excited fluttering in my stomach as we walked the halls of Congress and read the messages of statesmanship and leadership on the various memorials to America's founding fathers.

I suppose that's when the choice of a career in service of others took root. I'd held this desire in my heart for as long as I could remember, even in the face of people like my ex-husband, who didn't understand the calling and was the first to try to silence it. I wondered what my moral tipping point was—or if I even had one. Was staying in my position taking a stand? It was something I could do—a silent act of defiance and resistance from within. I considered this rationale for a moment before my mind shifted to the applicant from Ethiopia and so many others I had interviewed over the years, to their not-so-silent acts of defiance and resistance.

And then the little voice inside me said the thing I hadn't wanted to admit: *Staying in your position isn't an act of courage. It's an act of fear, and you should be ashamed.*

12

MISSION-DRIVEN, NOT SUPERHUMAN

(Martyrdom Culture)

"Wow, it sounds like you all are doing some really impressive work related to employee engagement and well-being!" raved Jennifer, the associate director of the RAIO directorate, looking over the assembled group.

It was the spring of 2018, and we were gathered in a small, beige, windowless conference room. In the center was a standard, government-issued, walnut-colored, oval conference table with ten chairs around it. The space was packed, with people in every seat and more standing wherever they could find a spot. Additional chairs had been lined up against three walls of the room, above which hung framed, agency-branded posters highlighting various immigration stories and initiatives from over the years.

I looked at the eager faces, excited to have some time with the associate director, who was head of the RAIO directorate and also my boss. Her popularity with the staff often made me feel like a groupie traveling with a famous rock star.

The head of the local employee-engagement committee, who had just finished her presentation, beamed at the associate director's praise. "Thank you. That means so much coming from you. It's really a team effort, and we're so grateful that the leadership in our office has been so supportive." She looked over at her office director, who smiled. Shaking his head sheepishly, he stretched his arms out to the group, indicating that it had been their effort, as if he'd had nothing to do with it.

A few months earlier, I'd proposed a series of site visits to my boss as a way for her to get some time with field staff and share her vision for the directorate moving forward. I'd already been traveling to various offices to facilitate workshops about mental health and well-being, but there was still a disconnect I couldn't quite figure out—something preventing the information I was providing from having much of an impact.

Because of my background in coordinating official trips while I was posted abroad, I took on coordination of the site visits, which included working with the local offices to create an itinerary for the days we'd be visiting. Once all the details had been confirmed, I or one of my colleagues would generally accompany my boss on the trip. In my previous roles, I'd been leading teams and running offices; here I was an observer, listening in on various sessions, taking notes, and writing up a trip summary.

The previous associate director had taken a somewhat hands-off approach to managing the local field offices, which were spread out across the US. This management style had resulted in siloed processes and procedures in individual offices, which minimized organization-wide transparency and sometimes led to questions of fairness between offices. My boss, however, enjoyed meeting the staff because she genuinely believed that the people doing the work were the most knowledgeable about how to make things more efficient and improve operations. Many longer-reigning directors, who had enjoyed unfettered autonomy at their local offices in the past, weren't particularly excited about these site visits. But the staff generally welcomed them, particularly because of my boss's reputation for transparency and willingness to answer any question presented to her—not the norm for many local-office directors.

"Is there any way we can support you in these efforts?" my boss asked the committee chair.

"Well, it would be great if we could have some time built into the schedule for people to take advantage of the different programs and activities to help them manage their stress. People are interested and want to participate, but it's challenging, because at the end of the day, the workload remains the same and people don't feel like they can take thirty minutes to go for a walk or meditate or participate in some of the other activities we've offered."

The associate director nodded. "I know each office has its priorities and initiatives, so I would defer to your local director on this." She smiled and shifted her gaze to him.

He nodded. "We'd love to create time for these activities, but it's tough because the interview schedule is created in advance, so we're kind of limited on being able to accommodate things that pop up more organically." His tone was sympathetic, but bordered on patronizing. "We do try to plan some things in advance so we can adjust operations to celebrate things like World Refugee Day. But you know, at the end of the day, we all have to remember that we're here to work, so that's really the priority."

I felt my breath catch at his response, but my boss didn't immediately react. She paused and smiled.

"True, but these initiatives have value, too," she replied softly, looking him in the eyes a moment before turning her attention back to the assembled group. "Does anyone else have any suggestions?" When her question was met with silence, she thanked everyone for their work and ended the meeting.

I was outraged about what I had just witnessed, and I seethed silently as people began shuffling out of the room. This director's staff had spent the past half hour laying out all the different initiatives they'd been working on, and in one sentence, he'd minimized their efforts and told them all that the work was more of a priority than their well-being. My cheeks flushed with frustration, which quickly gave way to a wave of sadness as I noticed the disappointed looks on so many as they left the room.

Like so many other leaders in my organization, this local director had an office full of creative people who wanted to do the work *and* take care of themselves. But the lack of alignment between his words and actions prevented them from doing so. I knew those two things weren't mutually exclusive. I'd experienced it at the Attorney General's office, and I'd been living it since returning from New Delhi. His office could have served as the model of how self-care and service could exist together in the field. But instead, he had demoralized every human being in the room.

I felt the heaviness of futility settle over me. How were we supposed to change things when leaders either refused to acknowledge the occupational realities in our line of work, or simply said what they thought their staff wanted to hear without actually believing it?

"I'm so glad we decided to do this!"

A few weeks later, my friend Elizabeth smiled as the waiter poured us each a glass of pale pink Italian rosé.

We were tucked into one of the plush, peacock-green velvet booths at The Ministry, a little coffee and wine bar around the corner from my office near Union Station in Washington, DC.

"What have you been up to?" she asked, leaning back in the booth.

We had met at a facilitation training a couple of years earlier. Both certified executive leadership coaches, we'd since come together many times to bounce ideas off each other and talk through issues we were trying to navigate at work.

"It's been busy," I told her. "I just got back from a bunch of site visits with my boss. We traveled to several offices overseas and around the country." I reached for a bottle of sparkling water sitting on the table.

"You're so lucky you get to travel," Elizabeth mused. "How were the visits?"

"Well, not great. My biggest takeaways were that attrition is high, morale is low, and burnout seems to be running rampant. Honestly, I'm not even sure it's just burnout. I think we're dealing with so much more—compassion fatigue, vicarious trauma, moral injury."

Elizabeth cocked her head to the side. "Moral injury? I've never heard of that."

"It's a term originally applied to soldiers returning from combat who were struggling with the things they had done in the war. The symptoms are sometimes confused with PTSD and burnout, but it's different. In our work, I believe it's the whiplash we've experienced from the constantly changing policies and injunctions over the past few years and being told to enforce policies and procedures that conflict with our own personal morals. I started researching it last year when the new administration came into power because of the way I was feeling. Everyone keeps talking about burnout, but that's just one piece of it."

She nodded, considering what I had said.

I took a sip of water and continued. "It's just so frustrating. In office after office, the discussion revolved around productivity and meeting targets. We did get to learn about local-office innovations, but most of them were about making people more productive and able to meet the targets. Staff health and well-being is a collateral issue—viewed as a luxury rather than a necessity—so prioritizing your well-being is seen as a sign of weakness. It's like there's this belief that being mission-driven equates to being superhuman, and you're supposed to just push through. It ends up creating a culture of martyrdom."

Elizabeth leaned forward. "I never thought of it in those terms, but I know exactly what you mean. All of the NGOs I've worked for made no secret of the fact that if you couldn't handle the job, there were plenty of people who would be thrilled to step in and take over—a constant reminder that you were replaceable. I guess public service is the same, especially when you have a humanitarian mission."

"It really is." I shook my head. "The other thing I can't stop thinking about are the first-line supervisors in the local offices. We promote so many people based on their technical knowledge, with no thought about whether they have the self-awareness, compassion, empathy, or quite frankly, the capacity to lead people. And then, the only training new supervisors are provided is focused on the punitive aspects of managing a team: how to track policy violations and work with labor and employee relations to put people on performance-improvement plans. There's nothing about building trust and psychological safety, and basically nothing about how to connect on a human level." As my face flushed with anger, concern passed over Elizabeth's face.

I sat back, took a deep breath, and laughed. "I'm okay. I don't know why I get so worked up about this, but it really gets to me. It's part of why I wanted to get together tonight. I figured if anyone could understand, it would be you." I smoothed the napkin in my lap. "It feels like with each passing day, this system is asking people to serve others while not addressing their own needs—to shove down their emotions and set aside their needs in service of the mission. How is that sustainable?"

Elizabeth's smile was resigned. "It's not, but this is how it's been for so long. It's so deeply ingrained in these cultures. It feels overwhelming to think about where we'd even start to try to change it," she said, her brow furrowing.

I nodded. I didn't know how we could change things either. But things couldn't stay as they were. Something had to shift.

This way of thinking—that work takes precedence over everything else—is so deeply ingrained in humanitarian culture that even the staff who desperately needed these interventions murmured and balked when opportunities for self-care in the workplace presented themselves.

A few months earlier, I'd traveled to an asylum field office to facilitate a series of workshops about trauma and well-being, and I'd been confronted by a first-line supervisor. In a defiant tone, he'd told me that the whole thing was a waste of time. Before I could respond, the local-office director had pushed his chair back and apologized on behalf of the supervisor. I believe the gesture came from a good place, but it came off like a child being reprimanded publicly.

I knew firsthand how stressful it was to be a first-line supervisor in a bureaucracy where the work stops for nothing—not for mandatory training, not to learn and understand new policies and processes for creating "efficiencies" in the work that were often pushed down by headquarters, not even when you were sick or trying to take time off.

The nature of working in bureaucracies that operate in service of other human beings means humanitarians often go and go and go until they simply can't anymore. Having served as a staff member, a first-line supervisor, a mid-level manager, a senior manager, and a member of the executive leadership team, I understood the stressful realities of serving in the field. This knowledge made me even more determined to advocate for a duty of care grounded in social connection, and an integration of workforce mental-health and well-being policies into the fabric of our organizational culture.

What I hadn't been able to *see*, until I had the opportunity to shadow my boss, was that individuals would likely need an external force to slow them down as well. They needed policies in place that supported their ability to take care of themselves, *and* they needed leaders who stood up in rooms—not to keep everything moving smoothly, but to address the policies that held individuals hostage to the cycles of working, ignoring occupational traumas, and burning out.

We had to be aware of the obstacles in front of us before we could remove them and empower our staff to take care of themselves. Because one thing I knew for sure—the work was never going to stop.

13

THE WALLS BEGIN TO CRUMBLE

(Vicarious Trauma and Compassion Fatigue)

I looked out at the faces in front of me and took a deep breath. I'd gotten up to talk in front of people hundreds of times. Why did this feel different? *It will be fine*, I reminded myself as a hurricane of fear and anxiety swirled in my stomach.

I was seated on a stage in the space US Citizenship and Immigration Services used to conduct large gatherings—town halls, all-hands meetings, awards ceremonies. It was a long, narrow room encircled by television cameras that livestreamed whatever was happening at headquarters out to offices in the field.

Jennifer had placed her notes on the chair next to me, but she was busy shaking hands and talking with staff members before the town hall started. She was so calm and collected. I marveled at her grace in these high-stress situations.

"We're five minutes out, everyone! Five minutes out!" called the tech-support liaison coordinating the livestream.

I felt heat rise through my body, and little beads of sweat formed along my hairline. The normally frigid temperatures of the space were no match for my nerves. I fanned myself with my notes.

My boss walked over, picked up her papers, and sat down. "I'm so glad we're doing this!" she said. "I can't believe it's been almost two years since you came back from New Delhi and started advocating for it. And now here we are!" She smiled as she turned to her notes.

"This" was a new health and well-being program that addressed the occupational realities of the work we were doing in the Refugee, Asylum and International Operations directorate, or RAIO as we were more commonly known. Our directorate consisted of close to 3,000 staff members spread out across three operational divisions: the Refugee Affairs Division, which included the Refugee Corps that traveled around the world interviewing refugees for resettlement; the Asylum Division, which included staff of the various asylum offices spread out across the US; and International Operations, which consisted of international field offices located in a handful of embassies around the world. All of these field units had corresponding headquarters units where staff supported the field operations. At today's town hall, we'd finally be launching RAIO Thrive, the program I'd developed with a small committee, which would be available to all staff.

I nodded, even as my heart jumped to my throat. "I know. I'm excited, too. This is the first time I'll be sharing my story with so many people." I hoped my voice didn't betray the fear hovering just below the surface.

She looked over and smiled. "I know it's scary, but as a senior advisor, you're a leader in this organization, and I think your courage in sharing your experiences will help others know they're not alone and that these types of mental-health challenges don't have to hold you back. That's what you've been working toward this whole time."

I nodded. "Yup, you're right. It's going to be fine." I smiled and took a deep breath. "I'm sure hearing from you, at your level, is going to have a huge impact too."

"Okay, we're live in thirty seconds. Dimple, are you ready?" the tech liaison asked.

"I am." I stood, smoothed my dress, and walked to the podium. I took in another breath and looked out at the audience with a smile, as he checked my microphone. Then he stepped back and motioned for me to begin.

"Good afternoon, everyone. Welcome to today's town hall! For those of you who don't know me, my name is Dimple Dhabalia, and I'm the senior advisor to RAIO. It's an honor to be here talking with you all today."

I shared some housekeeping remarks as I looked around the room at the faces of my colleagues. My heart pounded, and my grip on the podium was a little too tight, the edges cutting into my hands. I relaxed my forehead, slowly inhaled, and launched into the remarks I'd prepared for the town hall.

"*Resilience* has become a real buzz word these days, with more sectors examining the interplay between stress, burnout, compassion fatigue, and in some cases, vicarious trauma. There's suddenly more discussion about how small changes in the workplace, aimed at building employee resilience, can have a positive impact on workplace performance and retention."

My voice sounded steady, so I stood straighter and owned my words with confidence.

"In the coming weeks, we will be launching a new initiative known as RAIO Thrive, with a mission of providing RAIO staff at all levels with traditional and innovative tools and resources to create a culture of resilience, support greater work/life harmony, and move from merely surviving to thriving. The Thrive committee will be rolling out a multifaceted program that will include a curated website, peer-support resources, collaboration with other DHS sister agencies, and our own workshops and training programs."

I paused for a moment, then forged ahead.

"This is simply our starting point. The long-term goal of the committee is to shift the culture at RAIO, removing some of the stigma associated with mental-health challenges, which are inherent in our line of work. We want to normalize practicing self-care and asking for help. We want to create a culture where we find ways to support one another and expand this program. But we need your help, and I hope you'll share your thoughts and ideas with us about what you'd like to see, learn, and experience. I'd like to finish my remarks by sharing the story of how this program came to be and why it's so important to me."

My heart pounded as the reality of what I was about to share set in. I paused and took a deep breath, looking over my assembled colleagues until I caught the eye of a friend, who smiled and gently nodded, urging me forward.

In the spring of 2010, my colleague Sonia and I were sent to Lusaka, Zambia, to interview refugees for resettlement to the US. With only two of us on this assignment, we had a full schedule and also had to review each other's cases to ensure we hadn't missed anything. Our days were extremely long, and physically and emotionally draining.

We generally arrived at the worksite with colleagues from support agencies first thing in the morning. The smell of smoke from the wood fires around the city was thick in the air, often burning my nose and throat as I hauled my laptop bag past the buses parked outside the hall of the local church where we were doing our interviews. We'd make our way past the line of applicants waiting to be checked in—smiling and nodding hello without actually making eye contact with anyone—and begin to set up for the day.

In this occupation, we were used to unusual work environments. In fact, it was rare to have an office and a desk when we were in the field. Lusaka was no different. The hall was large, with twenty-foot ceilings, tiled floors, and windows along the sides of the building. Because the mornings were cold, the waiting area for applicants and interpreters had been moved inside, along one wall of the hall close to the doors. Sonia and I were set up at white plastic patio tables and chairs on opposite sides at the far end of the hall.

In addition to the challenges that came with working with traumatized individuals, we were also experiencing racism from hotel staff and other locals around Lusaka. It was something Sonia said she'd been contending with more since she'd been posted in Kenya, but it was entirely new to me. Both first-generation children of Indian immigrants, who had been born and raised in the United States, we came face to face with the complicated relationship between Indians—or *Asians* as they're called throughout Africa—and Zambians.

The Indian community had originally been brought to the southern part of Africa as indentured servants to work on sugar plantations. When they were freed, many Indians moved to other parts of Africa, creating successful businesses, which stoked the fires of competition and resentment with local Africans. Many employees at our hotel saw us as Asians rather than Americans, and often dismissed us and our requests or questions. While this discrimination was fairly mild, it added a layer of stress to a trip that was already challenging for many other reasons.

We were there to interview the last of the 1994 Rwandan genocide survivors, Congolese applicants fleeing ongoing civil war and government-sanctioned violence, and protracted Burundians—individuals of Burundian ethnicity who had been born in refugee camps and then attacked there, making them refugees twice over.

We worked long hours, at workstations that were anything but ergonomic: laptops plugged into adapters connected to extension cords hanging precariously out of outlets that sparked. Not only did our bodies ache at the end of the day, the mental exhaustion was overwhelming. As we waded through horrific stories of persecution, torture, and violence, we spent a lot of energy trying to hear the applicants and interpreters over the perpetual echo in the large hall. We needed to concentrate to make sure we understood everything clearly, so we didn't inadvertently recommend approval for a persecutor or terrorist, which was stressful enough on its own, before adding in worry about whether the interpreter was accurately translating everything the applicant said.

But this is what we had signed up for. And we knew the people we were interviewing—people who had fled their homes, often with nothing more than the clothes on their backs—had it far worse than we did. Were we really going to complain about being tired or not being able to sleep because of nightmares? No. It wasn't an option. We pushed through because to do anything else—to ask that our own humanity be acknowledged—felt selfish in comparison.

This particular set of interviews included some of the worst stories I had heard in my six years of interviewing asylum seekers and refugees. During the genocide in Rwanda, government propaganda led Hutus across the country to massacre people of Tutsi ethnicity. Over the course of weeks, Hutu militiamen—drunk on fermented banana beer and raw meat—used machetes to kill friends, neighbors, and even family members, despite the fact that for generations before the propaganda, they had lived together peacefully in the same communities, their cultures largely intertwined in Rwandan society. The genocide was the culmination of decades of division and incitement of hatred towards the Tutsi by extremists in the country's leadership, which was controlled by members of the Hutu majority group. The Rwandan cases we were interviewing were primarily mixed Hutu/Tutsi couples, and the likelihood that the Hutu males had not participated in the genocide was very slim. The interviews were long, and the stress of balancing a desire to keep families intact while also ensuring that a persecutor wasn't admitted into the country weighed heavily on us.

The Congolese and Burundian cases were equally challenging. The type and severity of the torture inflicted by members of one Congolese group against another or by the government against its own people often left me feeling physically ill. The Congolese had opted to use rape as a tool of war, which meant nearly every Congolese woman we interviewed had her own story that needed to be explored. It was so prevalent that when a woman claimed she hadn't been raped, it left us questioning her credibility.

One of the Kenyan women on the regional support team had told us about a massacre at the Gatumba Refugee Camp where Congolese refugees, primarily women and children from the Banyamulenge tribe, were targeted by several Hutu armed groups. She recounted stories she'd heard about people being burned alive and babies thrown headfirst against stone walls.

I had heard similar stories over the past six years and never had a problem, but there was something about her level of familiarity with the massacre that felt more visceral than stories in the past.

My fourth case on the last day of two weeks of interviews was actually three separate cases, because they were siblings who no longer had any parent to anchor them. The oldest brother had taken care of his younger sister and brother after they'd witnessed their parents being killed by Mai Mai rebels in the Democratic Republic of Congo. The kids had managed to escape to safety on foot, fleeing with other refugees. Along the way, they had met a young Banyamulenge woman whose family had been massacred. She had been raped and left for dead but survived.

When the family of three found her on the road, they helped nurse her back to health and invited her to join them. She and the oldest brother had married after arriving at a refugee camp. The union had been born mostly out of a desire to protect the young woman, but they now spoke about how love had come later. By the time they got to me, they had shared their story at least two or three times with various aid officials and were emotionless as they sat here, numb from the trauma.

Seeing their vacant eyes and monotone voices, I had cried through the entire interview, embarrassed by my inability to contain my emotions as they explained once again why they'd had to flee their homeland. When we finished, the oldest brother looked at the interpreter and asked a question.

The interpreter turned to me sadly. "He's saying, 'So now we go to America?'"

I shook my head, partly in answer and partly to set aside the emotions that had overtaken me. I replied directly to the young refugee. "No, there are still a few things left to do, and then you will get a decision by letter, letting you know whether you have been approved."

As the interpreter translated my words, the stoic faces of all four applicants began to quiver, and then they burst into tears.

"Please, miss, please. You must help us. Please, we need to be somewhere safe where we can have a life. Please don't make us leave here today and go back to the camp."

As they pleaded tearfully, I kept trying to reassure them, knowing full well that rumors had a way of moving through the camps, and they'd likely heard that if I couldn't give them a decision today, they would be denied.

All applicants fourteen and older were fingerprinted and vetted through an extensive background- and security-check process. The youngest brother had just turned fourteen, triggering the procedure and requiring that he also be cleared before his case could be finalized, even though the checks for his siblings and sister-in-law had cleared. It was standard procedure, and though I had recommended that the family be approved pending clearance of the vetting process, we weren't allowed to share decision information with applicants.

"I'm so sorry I can't do more right now," I repeated over and over.

Realizing there was nothing more to be done, the oldest brother stood, a stoic expression returning to his tear-stained cheeks. His wife and siblings followed his lead, wiping their tears and all emotion from their faces as they stood.

"Please, don't worry. It's going to be okay," I tried to reassure them one last time.

The oldest brother nodded and, looking completely defeated, thanked me as he led his family away.

As I watched them walk out of the hall, my heart raced. Heat climbed from my torso up through my armpits, shoulders, and then to my head, making my face burn and my ears ring.

I had to get out of there.

As I walked toward the doors, a regional support staff member from Kenya called out to me. "We have an add-on baby. Can you take a look?"

I kept walking, not wanting anyone to see the tears that were threatening again. "I just need a minute. I'll be back and will take a look then," I said without turning, my tone harsher than I had intended.

I burst through the doors and into the smoky Lusaka air, breathing in large gulps, trying to fill my lungs. I walked around to the side of the building, bent forward, and put my hands on my knees.

"Dimple, are you okay?" One of the local staff had followed me and now approached tentatively.

I put up a hand to stop her and from my hunched position croaked, "I'm fine. I just need a minute."

"Okay," she whispered and quietly walked away.

After another minute, I stood up and laced my fingers behind my head, pacing back and forth on the dirt, taking long, deep breaths.

What is wrong with me? I have to get it together. Everyone is waiting for me. There isn't time for any of this.

I took one last breath, let my arms fall to my sides, and reentered the hall, feeling the weight of the world on my shoulders. I returned to my work, but I wasn't the same.

The slow buildup of my stress and exhaustion over time, coupled with the disturbing experiences I listened to for hours on end each day in Zambia, had finally broken something in me. Suddenly, the wall of professionalism I'd spent over six years building came crashing down. The survival mechanism that had allowed me to keep showing up to do the work was gone, and I felt myself in freefall.

I could no longer regulate my emotions during interviews, and for the first time, I found tears streaming down my face as applicants recounted their experiences of persecution. These moments left me feeling weak, ashamed, and worried about what the applicants and my colleagues would think of me, which then left me feeling isolated and disconnected. I was impatient and easily irritated with colleagues and with people we encountered outside of work.

Without any tools to mitigate my reactions, my survival mechanisms kicked in. By the time we got back to the hotel at the end of our workday, the only thing I wanted to do was head to the bar to forget, and find a way to reset so I could show up again the next day.

Compounding the problem, every time I closed my eyes, I saw images from the stories I'd heard that day. When sleep did come, it was fitful and for days on end included graphic nightmares that left me with intense guilt, because I couldn't do more to protect people, and shame because nobody around me seemed to be struggling at all.

This had never happened before. I'd always been able to leave the cases at the worksite when I was finished. But something had shifted; I just didn't know how to put words to it. So I tried to shake it off, chalking things up to a difficult assignment. I told myself it was nothing, that it would pass.

I pushed forward, assuming that when I returned to the safety and familiarity of my home in Greece, where I was based at the time, the symptoms I'd experienced in Zambia would go away and I'd feel like myself again. But that wasn't the case.

After several sleepless nights back home, with more nightmares, less patience with those around me, and unprovoked emotional outbursts, I was desperate to figure out what was going on. The Sunday after I returned to Athens, I carried my coffee and laptop to the balcony of my apartment, pulled up Google, and stared at the search bar.

I knew there was a term for my experience. Some kind of trauma... It took several moments for my memory to call it up: *vicarious trauma*. I was experiencing the symptoms of someone else's horror.

As I typed the words *vicarious trauma and humanitarians* into the search bar, I remembered a specific training I'd received for my first job out of law school at the Attorney General's office in Colorado. Our unit had worked on cases involving child abuse and neglect. My boss, Wade, understanding the impact this type of work could have on a person, had made us go through an annual vicarious-trauma training. At the time, I was a cocky new attorney who didn't understand why we needed it. But now, ten years later, sitting on a balcony in Athens, all the things I'd been experiencing since Zambia clicked into place. They were symptoms of vicarious trauma.

My search also directed me to links for articles and resources on something called *compassion fatigue*. It caught my eye because it was described as the "cost of caring" for others experiencing emotional pain. I spent the next two hours devouring article after article, trying to understand what was happening to me and, more importantly, how I could fix it. I came across a couple of websites that mentioned the impact mindfulness practices could have on someone working through vicarious trauma, compassion fatigue, and burnout. Several articles also talked about the value of talking to a therapist.

It became clear that what I'd been experiencing was common in the humanitarian sector.

A wave of relief washed over me as I closed the laptop and reached for my coffee. It was cold, but it didn't matter. As I took a sip, I felt grateful to finally put names to what I was experiencing and to know there wasn't anything wrong with me.

But my gratitude quickly morphed—first into frustration and then anger.

The work we were doing was known to affect mental *and* physical health. So why wasn't anyone talking about it? Preparing us for it? Helping us work through it? There was so much research about the mental-health implications of humanitarian work, yet I didn't feel safe bringing it up with anyone at work. I had no idea how it might impact my security clearance or future job prospects.

These experiences, coupled with the deep stigma associated with mental health, continued to leave me suffering in silence, leading me to believe I had to manage mental-health issues on my own if I didn't want to lose my job. And anyway, everyone else seemed to be doing just fine.

As I got to the end of my story about serving in Zambia, I noticed people in the audience nodding and leaning forward in their seats. My spine tingled. They were connecting with my experiences.

"Obviously things worked out for me, because I'm standing here today, sharing with all of you," I told them. "But it worked out because as I learned more about the painful realities of our work, I recognized the signs and symptoms in myself, and I made the decision to ask for help. Your story may not be so extreme. Perhaps you feel run down or impatient. Perhaps you're questioning your purpose or are no longer feeling connected. Maybe you feel tired all the time. Here's what I can tell you for certain: The mental-health challenges, traumas, and burnout common in our line of work don't recognize pay grade or job title. Any one of us can experience them. I've shared this personal story today for a few reasons." I could feel myself talking faster, the rush of momentum pushing me to utter words rarely heard in the humanitarian workplace.

"First, I want every person in this directorate to know that sharing our vulnerabilities with one another is not a sign of weakness. It takes great courage and reminds us that we're human, and humans struggle from time to time. Second, I want those of you who are struggling right now to know that you're not alone and that taking care of yourself and your needs is an incredibly important component of your own personal success and ultimately our collective success as a directorate. Finally, my hope is that by sharing this story today, I'm helping to start a new conversation that will begin to shift the culture within RAIO to one where building resilience, caring for our mental health, and fostering a sense of connection and belonging is a fundamental part of who we are. Thank you so much for your time and, on behalf of the RAIO Thrive committee, we look forward to serving you."

I smiled, waved, and went back to my seat, wiping sweat from my face as applause from my colleagues thundered in the background.

It was out there now, and there was no turning back. I took a deep breath as a wave of hope washed over me.

Seeing is a form of mindful awareness—the ability to notice what's happening as it happens—and the point in the story-healing cycle when our autopilot experience is disrupted. We finally begin to notice our conditioned survival reactions. Because many of us operate on autopilot much of the time, we can go for years without seeing the patterns in our behavior, or the way each element within the pattern connects to the others. We may notice individual aspects—"I feel angry" or "my shoulders feel really tight"—without understanding that the pain in our body is related to the thoughts and emotions that came first, which ultimately lead to the way we react soon after.

These moments of disruption force us to recognize that something has to change, such as when my doctor told me I had to slow down and manage my stress. Or when I realized in Zambia that numbing the pain of my work through alcohol and staying busy all the time wasn't effective, and I had to change something because I wasn't sleeping or able to manage my emotions while interviewing refugees. Without this awareness, we'll never be able to see our patterns well enough to break them, nor will we be able to make new choices that better support our health and well-being, and in turn, that of the people we serve.

Over time, I came to see my survival stories for what they really were—a jumble of thoughts, emotions, fears, and projections that were keeping me stuck in painful narratives. Each disruption was a blessing—though sometimes in disguise—that helped me realign my course and make different choices about how I wanted to respond to challenging situations.

- Can you recall a disruption to your autopilot experience? A time when burnout or compassion fatigue or moral injury or some other obstacle caused you to notice and evaluate your usual way of reacting?
- Did you notice the experience when it happened? Did you realize something needed to change?
- What might you do now to intentionally create more awareness of these experiences?

PART FOUR
SHIFTING

SHIFTING

While *seeing* is a state of being and the bridge from autopilot reaction to intentional response, *shifting* is moving forward and taking action. For many years, neuroscientists believed our brains stopped developing in our mid-twenties, which meant the neural pathways that formed our default reactions were permanent. But the principle of neuroplasticity, which refers to the plastic nature of the brain, has shown that our brains are flexible and continue to change throughout our lives, giving us the capacity to create new neural pathways that can better support us during moments of stress, crisis, and trauma.

Shifting is also the point at which we begin to see our own humanity, including our imperfections and flaws. For this reason, shifting our thoughts, actions, and beliefs requires that we couple our newfound self-awareness with self-compassion, which holds us accountable for being kind to ourselves, even as we make mistakes or backslide in our attempts to change and make new choices.

To be clear, this new space isn't about getting rid of our old *surviving* stories—made up of thoughts, reactions, and actions created by our *shaping* stories—but rather to change our relationship to them. Our *surviving* stories have protected us and helped us withstand every hardship, challenge, and trauma we've encountered up to now. They have helped make us who we are. *Shifting* allows us to accept the limitations of our stories and our imperfections, and to replace the survival lens we've been using with a new lens of self-compassion to break old patterns and lead us to healthier outcomes.

14

HELPING THE HELPERS

(Connection)

"**S**o you're going to sell jewelry now?" My mom seemed confused as she flipped through the brochure. "But you've already got a good job. Why would you want to do this?"

My shoulders tensed as I perceived judgment in her question. I got up from the little sofa in my bedroom where we'd been sitting next to each other and went to sit on my bed.

"It's more than selling jewelry," I said, trying not to sound defensive. "It's a mission-driven company that supports female artisans in developing nations. And it also helps people here in the US who want to adopt children from places like Africa and Asia but need help paying for the process. It's so expensive to adopt from abroad." I leaned forward and waited for her response. My heart sank as she momentarily closed her eyes and took a breath, as if considering her words carefully before speaking.

"That all sounds really good, beta," she said with an understanding smile. "But you already help people. Why do you want to take this on when your days are already so full with your actual job? Why don't you use your time away from work to do something for you?" Judgment faded into compassion as my mom looked back at me.

"Well, I don't feel like I really help people anymore. Now that I've moved into a senior-management role at RAIO, I'm far removed from the work that made me feel like I had a purpose. Honestly, I'm not sure I know what my purpose is anymore." Letting out a deep exhale, I laid back on my bed. I turned and looked at my mom as a heaviness settled into my chest.

Setting the brochure down, she looked over at me. "Is it really about your purpose, or is it about trying to fill up your time so you don't feel sad about your breakup?" Her tone was gentle and loving, but her question hit like a punch to my gut.

Are we really going here? My breath was shallow as anger shot through my body.

I bolted upright and wiped the tears from my cheeks. "I can't believe you think that's what this is about! I'm sharing with you that I'm trying to get back to a place where I can do some good and actually help people again, and you're telling me I'm depressed and just doing this so I don't have to feel my feelings?" Clenching my fists in my lap, I looked at the floor. "Why can't you ever just support me?"

"I do support you—always. But you've tried so many of these kinds of side projects, and they never seem to work out. I love you and want you to be happy, beta." I could hear pain beneath her words. "I don't think this is going to make you happy." Her gentle tone wasn't enough to comfort me.

Of course nothing had worked out. I was a creative person committed to the life of a "professional." It didn't fit; it never had. But what if she was right? Or what if I left my job and ended up like my dad—depressed and never able to finish anything? I couldn't complete any of the short stories I'd tried to write. At least my dad had had my mom to support him. I didn't have anyone. Why was I wasting my time?

I slid off my bed and walked to the door.

"Where are you going?" she called after me.

Ignoring her, I stomped down the stairs. *Anywhere but here.*

My mom was right. Selling jewelry was not how I was meant to help people. That became painfully clear when I arrived at the jewelry company's annual conference as one of only four women of color, surrounded by a sea of white, Christian women. The company prided itself in creating global entrepreneurs and spent the weekend making vague comments about its commitment to diversity without any specifics about what steps they were taking to make that happen. Their conservative Christian values, coupled with their liberal use of images of white women adopting black children framed by quotes from the Bible, normalized white saviorism while simultaneously undermining the stated desire to create a more diverse organization. Instead of a sense of belonging, the whole experience left me feeling uncomfortable, othered, and certain that this was not the right path for me.

I had to find something else. Six months later, I had another idea and called Sona, a childhood friend and brilliant marketing executive, for advice. She mentioned that her sister was in a similar position and working through some of the same questions. We decided to meet up in person for a week—a retreat of sorts to lay out our entrepreneurial visions. Within a couple of weeks, Sona, her sister, and my sister gathered in my home and took turns having one-on-one business-coaching sessions with Sona.

When it was my turn, she listened as I told her about my idea for Holistic Humanitarians and helped me clarify my why—why did I want to do this? Why was it important? As I shared my stories of compassion fatigue, vicarious trauma, burnout, and moral injury, I became more and more passionate about helping humanitarians learn how to take better care of themselves so they could continue doing the work and mitigate unnecessary suffering. No one should feel isolated and ashamed because they're dealing with a mental-health challenge, and everything I'd learned about recovering from trauma confirmed that compassionate connection with others was one of the most important pathways to recovery and resilience.

As human beings, we are hardwired for connection. It makes us feel safe, and feeling safe allows us to show up and focus, making us better at what we do. For me, one of the most powerful experiences of connection and compassion had come during a vulnerable moment of my adult life. I began to explain to Sona what had happened.

The summer before my dad passed away, I flew from my home in southern California to Princeton, New Jersey, where my parents lived, to visit him in another mental-health institution. My uncle Yash picked me up from the airport and as we weaved through the traffic, I didn't do much to hide my anger and judgment toward my mom and sister about their decision to attend a meditation retreat while my dad was institutionalized. My uncle, however, was far more compassionate, gently defending their decision to take care of themselves.

As we passed a large billboard advertising wedding venues, I smiled, thinking about my dad in his pale cream kurta, hands raised in the air as he danced with me at my wedding. Then, his laugh had filled up the room and he'd been the life of the party. Now, he floated in and out of reality yet again. A deep and heavy sadness settled into my stomach as I remembered visiting him at the mental-health facility in Colorado, almost 10 years earlier. I braced myself for a painful repeat.

But when I pulled up to the new facility the next day, it didn't have barbed wire around it. That immediately began to lift some of the heaviness I felt as I stepped out of the car and reached back in to grab two iced coffees. On a whim, I had ordered a butter pecan iced coffee from Dunkin Donuts for my dad. It was his favorite flavor, and though I wasn't sure they'd even let me take it in, it felt like a small gesture of kindness I could offer him.

Inside, the waiting room was a dull blue-gray color, but I was grateful that it felt more like a hospital and less like a prison. The woman behind the information desk smiled as I placed the coffees on the counter, her cheerful tone startling me and making me wonder for a moment if she could really be happy working here.

As I waited, I stared at a framed seascape photo next to me, thinking about my descent into New Jersey the day before when I'd seen the Statue of Liberty from the window of the plane, pale green with flecks of copper—a beacon of hope to so many immigrants, including my dad who had come to America in search of freedom and a better life. He had used his brilliant mind to get a student visa, travel halfway across the world, and build a new life—free of his family and their outdated ways of thinking—only to now be imprisoned within that same brilliant mind. I wondered if he'd ever be at peace. If any of us would be. Could be.

A pleasant, comforting nurse soon arrived and escorted me through a maze of identical hallways to my dad's room. And as she pushed open the door, she greeted him with a sing-songy, "Good morning, Mr. Dhabalia. You've got a visitor."

My heart broke open at the sight of my dad seated on the edge of the bed on the other side of the room, near the window. He wore khakis and a pale green and tan button-down shirt, his gray hair combed but in desperate need of a haircut. His eyebrows were bushy, and his eyelids hung heavy with drowsiness. All I could think was how helpless he looked.

The nurse explained that since he didn't have a roommate, it might be nicer for us to meet in his room. When she announced again, "It's your daughter—and she's brought you a little treat," my dad seemed confused.

Then, noticing me for the first time, he smiled, and I saw a faint light of recognition flash in his eyes. We whispered hellos, and when I didn't move, the nurse touched my shoulder, smiled, and reassured me that everything was alright before slipping out of the room.

Dad looked small and frail—a fragment of the massive presence he'd always been. An overwhelming desire to take away his pain and protect him dissolved into a feeling of helplessness as I stood in the doorway, unsure of what to do. I walked toward him, put the coffees on the window ledge, and leaned down to hug him, melting into his familiar embrace as his arms wrapped around me. Tears formed in the corners of my eyes. I didn't turn away from the pain I felt in that moment, instead staying present with him, even as his hands trembled when I offered him a coffee and his tongue, heavy from the effects of the antidepressants, slurred his words. I tried to blink back the tears, but I couldn't before my dad saw them.

His face softened as he reached out and stroked my cheek, apologizing for always making me cry and failing me.

I tried to reassure him that he hadn't failed, and when he apologized again, I sat next to him, put my arms around him, and held him as he cried. "You're not a failure, Dad. We know you loved us and wanted the best for us. All the other stuff, it wasn't your fault. It's okay. It's going to be okay."

"Can you forgive me?" he asked, turning to look me in the eyes.

I let go of him and rubbed his back. "Yes, Dad, I forgive you. I love you."

His eyes welled up again, and tears fell down his cheeks, but I didn't move to wipe them away.

"I love you, too, beta," he said shakily.

Suddenly feeling exhausted, I rested my head on his shoulder like I used to when I was a child, and he slowly put his arm around me. There, shoulder to shoulder, we sat together in silence as our tears continued to flow.

Something had shifted. These were no longer tears of anger, resentment, or sadness. They were cathartic and left me feeling changed.

Hopeful.

Here, in a space that so often dehumanizes people in desperate need, my dad—and I by extension—had rediscovered empathy, compassion, and connection. These three elements not only helped me let go of some of my anxiety about him being there, but I believe it created the conditions for us to connect with each other in a more deep and meaningful way than we had in more than twenty years—something I'd be so grateful for when he passed away just over seven months later.

Sona nodded without looking up and kept writing as she responded. "Okay, great! So it sounds like you want to help people connect to one another. Between life on the road, which can be isolating in a lot of ways, and the work itself, mental-health issues can be common. But you're saying connecting with others and talking about these things can help foster some sense of community and connection—maybe take away some of the shame. Does that sound right?"

I felt a tingle of excitement. "Yes! It's about finding connection and grounding, and feeling a sense of belonging no matter where you're posted and living," I continued.

"Okay. Say more about that."

"Well, my mom is always saying 'Aren't you tired of living out of a suitcase? Don't you want to settle down and create some roots?' But honestly, I feel the most connected when I'm out in the world—being tied down to any one place scares me more than anything. I know many others in my line of work who feel that way too," I explained.

"What does 'being rooted' mean to you?" Sona asked.

I considered her question for a minute. "I guess for me, being rooted is about connection—to the people, the food, the land—for the time that you're in a place. I don't have to live in any one place for that to happen. I travel a lot, so it's like I'm in the clouds and I carry my roots with me. I plant them wherever I go. Not sure if that makes sense." I laughed nervously.

"It makes perfect sense to me," Sona responded. With a sly smile, she continued, "How attached are you to the name Holistic Humanitarians? I think we might be able to find something that fits better. Rooted in the

Clouds? Roots in the Clouds—ooh, Roots in the Clouds—what do you think?"

"Yes!" I practically shouted, throwing both hands up in the air in triumph.

"Tell me a little about your vision," she said next. "You've said you want to help the helpers—how do you envision doing that?" She flipped her sketch pad open to a clean page and wrote *Roots in the Clouds* in large block letters across the top.

"I know this is going to sound weird, but I want to create a feeling of community and connection through food and storytelling."

Sona looked up and smiled. "I love it! Tell me more about this!"

"Well, food is such a connector. In my earliest memories of our families getting together every weekend, our connection always revolved around shared meals prepared together in community. As I got older and started getting out into the world, I saw similar experiences in the places I was visiting and working. I remember being in Ethiopia once to interview refugees, and when I came out of my interview room at lunch time, a group of refugee women from different places—Uganda, Congo, Eritrea, Somalia—were sharing a meal. These women, who had survived unimaginable horrors and losses in their respective homelands, were sharing what little food they had with one another, smiling and laughing like old friends, even though many of them had just met. Food was their common language, and sharing this meal created a sense of community in that moment." I sat back and waited for Sona to say something.

"I love this idea and can see you doing so many things with it."

Something about how she paused left me waiting for the other shoe to drop. There was always a *but*.

"But how does this relate to helping the helpers?"

My face flushed with embarrassment.

"I'm not saying it doesn't," she continued. "But we need to flesh that out a little more." She clicked the cap back on to her pen and stared at the ceiling, seeming deep in thought. "I think I'm noticing that your focus is on individuals rather than organizations. Why not focus on the organizations? You'll likely make a bigger impact if you go through them."

I nodded. "I know you're right, but I've been trying to do this at work, and while I have hope that organizations will eventually get there, at the moment, if people want to thrive and be healthy while working in a mission-driven space, we have to do it ourselves. I don't think the organizations are ready yet."

Sona nodded and sat up straight, ready to write again. "I get it. Then let's figure out how we help the helpers help themselves for now."

15

ONE SWITCHBACK AT A TIME

(Self-Compassion)

"**G**ood morning!" Joe, a Department of Homeland Security (DHS) colleague, greeted me enthusiastically in the lobby of our hotel. "How'd you sleep?" He slung his backpack over his shoulder and nodded for me to follow him to the front door.

I'd met Joe a year ago at a meeting hosted by the DHS Resilience Committee in Washington, DC. I'd been invited to attend because of the mindfulness work I was doing with RAIO. Joe worked for the US Coast Guard, another agency under the DHS umbrella. He was trained as a helicopter rescue pilot but had been temporarily assigned to work with the Resilience Committee chair to pilot a training program called Mindful Performance Enhancement, Awareness & Knowledge (*m*PEAK) across a handful of DHS agencies. Now we were part of a small group from various DHS agencies who had come to La Jolla, California, to begin the process of becoming *m*PEAK facilitators.

"I slept pretty well," I told him. "I'm excited to be here—feels good to be working on west coast time, too!" I laughed. Yet as soon as the words were out, I felt a heaviness, thick like molasses, spread through my chest. Tears filled my eyes.

Less than two months earlier, my mom had passed away unexpectedly. She'd spent eighteen days in the hospital, during which my sister and I had traded off sitting at her bedside to ensure one of us was with her at all times, even the last seven days when she was nonresponsive, no longer able to breathe on her own. After she passed, I'd found the invitation to this training waiting for me among hundreds of emails I'd ignored for close to a month—and just as I found myself at the beginning of a painful grief journey that left me feeling tender, raw, and unsure of how to be in this world without her.

I'd once read a description of grief as ebbing and flowing like waves in the ocean. In those early months after her death, the waves of grief came hard and fast, pulling me under until I felt like I couldn't breathe and leaving me spent. But every now and then there'd be a momentary reprieve. For a split-second, I'd forget she was gone and laugh or feel a lightness in my body like I used to. But then another wave would hit, and along with it deep feelings of guilt and shame. I believed that finding joy or excitement was somehow disloyal to her memory.

Sliding into the passenger seat, I buckled my seatbelt and sat back. "So, tell me a little more about what to expect." I needed to think about what was happening now, today, not dwell in the past. I turned my attention to the day ahead.

"I think there are going to be about ten of us from across different DHS agencies," Joe said. "And probably a couple of Navy Seals, too." He pulled onto the freeway and gave me a sideways grin. "The hope is that if all goes well here, we can use some of the funding to send this group through the full certification process so we can teach *m*PEAK internally at DHS."

"That's great to hear. I don't know a lot about the course yet, but I've only heard great things. I think being able to integrate *m*PEAK into the Thrive program I started building last year will really be helpful to our workforce. So this class is just for the ten of us?"

"No. Since DHS was only sending a small number, they decided to give us slots in an existing class. The course was originally created for the US Men's National BMX racing team, so it typically attracts high performers. We'll likely be in there with local law enforcement, elite athletes, and coaches."

"That's an interesting mix of people." I stared out the window, taking in the rolling green hills dotted with little houses that peered out from behind the buildings that lined the freeway. We traveled in silence for a few minutes, and then Joe pulled into the parking lot of a nondescript office park at UC San Diego's Center for Mindfulness. I looked up at the three-story building with dark windows as we collected our backpacks from the backseat.

As we headed for the doors, I shook my head and let out some nervous laughter. "So to sum up, we're about to enter a class that consists of members of the military, law enforcement, elite athletes, and me?"

He chuckled. "I suppose that's one way to look at it. Don't worry. It should be a lot of fun."

Maybe fun for you. Joe jumped out of helicopters and rescued people in the ocean for a living. Meanwhile I'd been sitting behind a desk, working late, and eating my way through my grief. I'd just had to buy new yoga pants because my other ones were feeling tight. I hadn't thought this through.

I walked toward the building, steeling myself for the worst. Just beneath the discomfort, however, was a flutter of hope. Not only did I hope to take something back to the Thrive program I'd helped start at RAIO, I was hopeful that this would help me process some of the overwhelming grief and the shift my emotional and behavioral patterns that I knew were getting in the way of my commitment to take care of myself.

I was doing better than I ever had, but I still had plenty of work to do if I wanted to continue being able to take care of others.

Almost a year earlier, on a Friday in the fall of 2018, I'd stood in my shower, silently imploring the hot water to loosen the knots I'd been carrying in my shoulders for months. It had been another long and frustrating week at work that had left me feeling discouraged and stuck. Hopeless, exhausted, overwhelmed, and in pain, I leaned forward and placed my hands against the white tiles in front of me, steadying myself as I tried to breathe.

I'd been a senior advisor to the RAIO associate director for two years, and it had been a year since I'd shared my story at the town hall where we'd launched RAIO Thrive. Despite my best efforts to model good self-care, I'd been stretched beyond my limits for months, and it was becoming clear to me that carrying my full load of senior-advisor duties while also trying to build out a cutting-edge mindfulness and well-being program within the government wasn't sustainable.

My requests for more help had resulted in the hiring of a second senior advisor; however, the person hired for the position came with her own agenda, which didn't actually include taking anything off my plate. The situation not only contributed to my stress, it left me questioning whether the leadership at RAIO was really committed to making workforce well-being a priority. Unlike the new senior advisor, who was skilled at maintaining boundaries around her time, my inability to hold my own boundaries meant I had taken on more tasks, projects, and responsibility, none of which were related to building Thrive. It all added up to frustration, resentment, and the all-too-familiar inklings of burnout. I'd felt them in New Delhi a couple of years earlier, and in the position I'd held before New Delhi, where I'd been working long hours with virtually no self-care.

What was different this time was me.

Even though I now understood the importance of taking care of myself, I'd fallen back into an old pattern, unable to keep the commitment to self-care I'd made when leaving India. I was taking on more work, even though I knew it was too much. But instead of falling into a shame cycle or believing I was failing, this time I tried to show myself some compassion for the backslide. I also knew I couldn't simply wait for something to change. I had to make the choice to change it.

I dried myself off and slipped into a robe, thinking about my options. A week earlier, the Refugee Affairs Division had announced that they had a sixty-day temporary assignment starting in late October. The position was with the senior management team, and while the thought of managing people didn't seem particularly exciting to me, I knew it would allow me to catch my breath and regroup as I figured out what to do next.

I arrived at work that day determined to get things moving, not wanting to wait another day.

I reported to the deputy director, Ted, but most final decisions were ultimately made by RAIO's associate director—Jennifer. She was one of the most forward-thinking and supportive managers when it came to professional-development opportunities. Even so, I felt guilty about even considering abandoning my current team and Thrive to pause and regroup. I also feared disappointing Jennifer in the process—one of the main reasons I chose not to approach her directly about the opportunity.

"Hey, do you have a minute?" I asked from the doorway of the deputy director's office. My heart beat fast at the thought of the request I was about to make.

Ted was standing at his computer with his back to the door, and as he turned and smiled, I felt myself begin to relax.

"Sure, come on in." He motioned for me to take a seat at the conference table in his office. After some initial niceties, he weaved his fingers together and leaned forward. "So, what's going on?"

My stomach lurched and guilt rushed through me. How could I do something for myself that would undoubtedly leave the team shorthanded and pause any further development of the Thrive program? I took a deep breath and reminded myself that I wasn't doing anything wrong. I was making this choice to give myself a little time and distance so I could figure out what was next. It was a perfectly reasonable request.

"Well, as you know, there's a temporary assignment at Refugee Affairs, and I wanted to talk with you about applying for it."

If Ted was surprised by this request, he didn't let on. Instead he nodded. "Remind me when it starts again?"

"Toward the end of the month. It's sixty days and goes through the end of the year."

He nodded thoughtfully. "I know you've been wanting to do some other things. If this feels like something you want to pursue, I'm happy to support you. I'll run it by the associate director and get back to you."

My stomach sank at the mention of our boss, but I smiled and nodded. "Sounds good. Thank you."

A few days later, the associate director popped her head into my office. "Hey, are you busy?" she asked.

"Always!" I laughed. "But this can wait. Come on in." My heart sped up as I anticipated what she wanted to talk about. "How's everything going?"

"Good! I wanted to stop by because I understand you want to go over to Refugee Affairs for a while."

I nodded, my stomach in knots. She was probably already disappointed in me and was going to say it wasn't a good time.

"Of course we're happy to support you," she said, still pleasant as ever as she sat down in one of the chairs near my whiteboard.

Wait, what did she just say?

"But I know you and how you work," she continued. "And I am sure they'll want to offer you something permanent at the end of your assignment. So, I wanted to say that while I think you should pursue the opportunity, once it's done, you should come back here. There's still a lot of good you can do here, especially with building out Thrive and developing the new leadership program you've been talking about."

She wants me to come back to build out Thrive and a new leadership program? This was definitely not what I'd been expecting.

The smile spread quickly across my face. "Thank you, Jennifer. I really appreciate you saying that. Honestly, I was starting to feel like Thrive wasn't a priority anymore since I keep getting assigned to other work and have been spread so thin. I worried my wanting to do this would disappoint you or that you were going to tell me it wasn't a good time for me to go."

"Well, it's never going to be a good time," she acknowledged. "But we'll manage. And you should know by now that you could never disappoint me!" She shook her head and laughed. "I meant what I said about you coming back. I'm sorry if it's felt like the work you started with Thrive isn't a priority. Keeping our workforce healthy is important, but other things are always going to come up, so we'll have to keep ensuring it stays a priority. You've already done so much with the weekly mindfulness sessions and resources you've been sharing. I'm sure with the positive psychology training, there's so much more you'll be able to do."

"It's no big deal," I deflected, looking away, uncomfortable with her praise.

"It *is* a big deal," she insisted. "And it's going to change how we do things. It's important."

I nodded and smiled at her emphatic tone. Buoyed by her reaction, I relaxed into my chair and considered what to say next. I knew I had to be honest with her. It was the only way things were really going to change.

"I love the idea of building out Thrive and creating a new leadership program, but I can't keep working the way I have been," I confessed. "It's too much, and I'm falling back into old patterns I promised myself I'd avoid after everything that happened in Zambia and India."

She nodded in understanding.

"If I do come back, I want to focus one-hundred percent of my time on all of this."

"Done," she said without missing a beat.

My eyes widened, and I felt butterflies in my stomach. Still not convinced this was really happening, I thought it might be best to clarify. "I mean no more traditional senior-advisor duties."

"Yup, got it," she replied.

"And I need a team of people," I added hopefully.

"Fine. They'll have to be temporary assignments for the time being. Will that work?" she asked.

"Um, yeah—yes, of course!!" I said, laughing and pressing my palms into my thighs to keep from clapping like a giddy child.

"Okay, great." Jennifer stood and extended her hand. "Let's shake on it. I have a good feeling about this!" She smiled again as I put my hand in hers.

So do I!

"I love that this course includes a hike!" Katrina enthused from the driver's seat. We were traveling together—along with John, an *m*PEAK classmate—in a car that was headed to the mountain I wasn't excited to see.

I had met Katrina on the first day of our *m*PEAK class, drawn in by her warmth. But that didn't make what I knew was coming over the next few hours any more appealing to me.

"I'm going to apologize to you both now," I began from the backseat. "The past couple of months since my mom died have been hard, and I'm not in the best shape of my life. You'll probably have to wait for me at the end." My tone was sheepish despite my best efforts to keep things light. I felt the heat of embarrassment rise up through my body, which grief and lack of movement had left soft and fleshy.

Katrina looked at me in the rearview mirror. "You take as long as you need. We've got plenty of time." Her genuine smile cooled the flush of shame.

John nodded in agreement. "Grief is hard no matter how much time has passed," he said softly. "It's like what we learned about self-compassion. You have to show yourself kindness as you navigate this time in your life."

My eyes filled with tears as gratitude filled my chest. "I'm so grateful I met you both."

A few minutes later, Katrina turned onto a side road where cars were parking for access to Cowles Mountain, the highest point of the Mission Trails region in San Diego. "We're here!" she exclaimed. "Now, we just need to find a place to park." As she looked for a spot, I looked out the window and felt my stomach drop. There, in front of me, was the tallest mountain I'd seen in a long while.

How the hell was I going to get up that thing? There was no way. Why had I agreed to do this?

Once we'd parked, I grabbed my water bottle and followed my new friends to meet our instructor, Pete. It was 7:00 a.m., but the air was already warm and only getting warmer as the morning progressed. As I stood with fellow classmates, I wished I'd taken Pete up on his offer to do a mindful walk on the beach if we didn't want to do the hike. But without a car, and worried about what others might think if I skipped the hike, I found myself at the base of a very tall mountain, already sweating after the short walk from the car, my stomach in knots about the humiliation I knew was coming when I couldn't reach the top.

"Okay, gather around, everyone," Pete called to the group. He was dressed in khaki shorts and wore a metal leg brace due to muscle atrophy from an injury sustained years earlier. "This is a silent hike. You are to do the hike on your own, with only your thoughts for company. The intention for today's exercise is to be mindful of our thoughts and the needs of our bodies. Some of you are going to be tempted to run up the mountain. Notice those thoughts, but stay present and hike. This isn't a race." He paused and looked around.

Run up the mountain? I couldn't even wrap my mind around the concept. I looked at the nodding heads around me and thought again that this was not likely to end well. I smiled at my classmates, even as I wanted to sink into the ground and disappear.

"For others, this will be a challenge," Pete continued. "Again, notice what stories are coming up. Notice any self-judgment, self-criticism, and comparison. Don't stop to judge or analyze your thoughts; just notice what's there and practice some self-compassion around them."

That was the second time self-compassion had come up today.

"I also want you to tune in to your body," he said. "What does it need from one step to the next? Can you push it a little farther, or should you pull back, if that's what's needed?" He paused again and looked around as people nodded their understanding. "Once you get to the top, I want you to spend at least five minutes savoring what you've accomplished, taking in the views, and just being present to the moment. Think about what's coming up for you before you head back down. We'll all meet back in the classroom at ten a.m. It should be plenty of time."

Three hours to climb that thing and get back down? My breath came fast and shallow as I considered the task ahead of me.

"Okay, have a great hike, everyone." With Pete's final words, the group set off.

The first part of the trail was a steep climb over uneven ground, with rocks jutting out to form craggy stairways along certain parts of the path. Fortunately, the earth below my feet felt solid as I slowly made my way up the initial ascent.

Who was I kidding? Shame washed over me as I looked at how far the rest of the class had already gone and as kids ran past me. Even the woman in our class who used braces to walk and had a support dog had already passed me. I felt myself spiraling. But, remembering the instruction to practice self-compassion, I took a deep breath and tried again.

It's been a rough couple of months. I took another step forward and tripped over a rock. I laughed out loud as I regained my balance, recalling how people tripping and falling always sent my mom into a fit of uncontrollable laughter. *Okay, stop deflecting the self-compassion.* I felt a lump of discomfort in my throat at the thought of saying something nice to myself. *Try again.* I took a deep breath. *Let's be honest. It's been a rough few years. Just be gentle with yourself.*

My eyes filled with tears as the phrase my dad used to say to my sister and me—when we were struggling and he was lucid—rang through my ears. I didn't wipe them away. Instead, I allowed them to flow and took another step forward, focusing on the stability of the packed earth below me, absorbing the shock of each step.

What do I need in this moment? I asked myself. Over the next half hour, I listened as my body told me what it needed. Often, I just needed to rest—permission to sit down. So I did. Sometimes it asked for water, and I obliged. With each step forward and each message from my body, my focus shifted away from comparison and self-judgment and on to the next stretch of the trail. As I approached what looked to be the summit, I came around a corner and my heart sank.

Behind the first peak was another much taller peak.

Are you serious?

It'd taken me a half hour just to get up this part of the trail, which was nothing compared to the rest of it. There was no way I could do this. I sat down on a rock and looked back at the part of the trail I had climbed. Overwhelming gratitude spread through my chest.

I looked at how far I'd come. I hadn't thought I could do any of this, but I had.

Then, as I turned and looked up at the next peak, I felt the weight of judgment descend on my shoulders again. Another deep breath and a long sip of water were all I could muster.

Okay, here's the deal, I told myself after a moment. *Maybe you can't do it. But maybe you can. Either way, you won't know until you try. Walk to the next switchback, and then if you want to turn around, that's fine.* I felt like a parent trying to cajole their obstinate child into eating broccoli or finishing math homework. Fortunately, it worked. I stood up and slowly began walking toward the next switchback. Then I spent the next hour replaying some version of this conversation in my mind as I moved from one switchback to the next, putting one foot in front of the other.

Something had shifted. The fact that I was barely halfway up as classmates were passing me on their way down didn't bother me anymore. I was enjoying the journey and no longer focused on the outcome. The heaviness that had accompanied me to the meeting point an hour earlier had lifted, and my body felt lighter with each switchback I conquered.

When I finally made it to the top of the mountain, I found a boulder to sit on and stared out at the land below me. My muscles burned, and my tank top was drenched in sweat, but I felt a giddy sensation in my chest. I took a deep breath and looked at the magnificent vista before me.

What am I feeling in this moment? I wondered, trying to name what I was experiencing. I closed my eyes and tuned inward. The first thing I felt was gratitude for my body, which had gotten me up to the top of the mountain, even though it had been trying to overcome a sinus infection before arriving in San Diego and hadn't worked out in months. The second was grief. Grief for the body I'd once had, which had been hard muscle, capable of ascending fourteen thousand feet like it was nothing. Grief for the loss of my mom, who would never get to experience this kind of beauty again and with whom I'd never get to savor little everyday moments of joy like this. Grief for all the things I had missed out on by telling myself I couldn't do them.

I thought about how strange it was to hold gratitude and grief together as I turned my face up to the sky, the colors of the sun swimming behind my eyelids. Lowering my face, I opened my eyes and stood. It was hard to believe this was the first time I'd really tried to figure out what I was feeling and the first time I'd let the answer, whatever it was, be okay. I turned slowly in a full circle, admiring the view from the top one last time.

I now understood why we'd done the hike. The mountain was a perfect metaphor for the challenges we encounter in our lives. I wondered how often I'd gotten close to something I really wanted and turned around because of my fear of failing or because I doubted my abilities and allowed my old, default patterns and reactions to take over. I took another breath and began walking back to the trailhead to start my descent, looking at all the switchbacks below me.

Imagine what might have been possible if I'd learned to take the challenges I encountered in life one switchback at a time from the beginning? It didn't matter. I now knew having an awareness of what was happening and showing myself some compassion would let me see things—and maybe do things—differently moving forward.

16

TAKING OFF THE MASK OF PERFECTIONISM

(Curiosity and Empathy)

There are a lot of great things about working in public service, but there is one problem with getting promoted in the government—especially in a hierarchical system where the path to promotion narrows considerably as you move into the higher positions: You will inevitably end up managing friends you've made along the way or colleagues who put in for the job you got—or in my case, both. This is not such a big deal if you're a leader who understands the importance of connection and collaboration. Unfortunately, in 2014, as a new manager who believed I had to prove I was worthy of the position, I'd found myself out of my depth and mimicking leaders from my past who I didn't exactly like and definitely did not respect.

I'd been promoted into a mid-level management position where I was responsible for overseeing a team of refugee officers as they prepared staff to travel around the world to conduct refugee-resettlement interviews. It was a major step forward in my career, and it should have been a time filled with excitement. But between my hard-charging leadership style and the resentment from a few people on the team who had competed with me for the position, what I remember most about the initial days of leading that team is how challenging it was. That period of my career is one of the only ones where I feel deep regret about how I went about working to create change. I told myself I was trying to collaborate with the team and wanted their input. But in reality, I knew my vision and expected everyone to get on board or move on, which a few of them did.

It wasn't entirely my fault though.

Most mission-driven organizations create metrics-driven cultures, and mine was no different. To be clear, metrics are not inherently bad. They serve a purpose by helping organizations determine whether their mission is being met. But when metrics become the primary driver for organizational decision-making, it creates a culture where numbers are valued more than the people doing the work, and perfectionism becomes the standard against which everyone is measured.

It wasn't like anyone ever told me I had to be perfect. But the message coming through was loud and clear—based on how our work was evaluated, the reputations of the people being promoted, and the ever-present reminder that mistakes in our work had a direct impact on the lives of the people we served.

Over time, I also began to realize that the ethos of care and protection embodied within our mission only applied to the people we served, not to those of us serving them. This, coupled with an emphasis on meeting organizational metrics above all else, created the perfect conditions for burnout, and it ensured that the staff doing the work never had a chance to thrive, because they were doing everything they could simply to survive.

As I moved up through the ranks, I noticed that awards and accolades were often tied to the creation of efficiencies and innovations that boosted metrics, with little to no value placed on projects and initiatives built to better working conditions for staff, which in turn would have improved metrics. For years, I had worked ever harder and longer hours and developed a reputation for being a meticulous and devoted team member. And in time, I was promoted to a supervisory role.

But becoming a supervisor meant more pressure and higher stakes. Now I was responsible for my work *and* my team's work. Fear of making a mistake that might negatively impact the people we served, or that would let my bosses down, became the driving force behind my actions. Like the obligation to pursue a career path that wouldn't disappoint my dad—created through the prayers I recited as a child—I now existed in a container where messages from the leaders above me reverberated against the walls.

Meeting metrics and completing projects were the priorities, and my worthiness was tied to public recognition for meeting those metrics.

As a result, the perfectionism that had masked my fear—and until my promotion had only impacted me—began developing tentacles that wrapped themselves around the people on my team. The transformation was swift, and before long, I no longer tolerated mistakes. My leadership style left people afraid to speak up, and any chances for innovation or collaboration were replaced by stagnation and competition. I felt threatened by others who brought new and different perspectives to the table, so I did what I could to squash them. I burned bridges and created an army of one, convinced it was better to do everything myself.

Though my team succeeded in revamping the entire pre-departure process for teams heading out on temporary assignments, the costs of that approach to success were immense. My actions left me feeling disconnected from most of my team, which meant we never fully came together as a cohesive unit. The more work I took on myself, the more team members resented me, and the more I resented them. Micromanaging them this way left me working twelve-to-fourteen-hour days, including weekends, forgoing any down time. This led to exhaustion, sickness, and eventually to the beginning stages of burnout, just as I accepted the position in New Delhi.

Three years later, in early 2019, when it became clear that the well-being initiative that had started as an additional duty after returning from New Delhi was now snowballing into a full-blown leadership and well-being program, I was once again faced with the inevitability of having to lead a team. This initially felt daunting, but a conversation with a good friend helped me recognize that my feelings about leadership were the result of thinking about leading as I had in the past.

But I didn't have to lead that way. I had a choice.

I was a different person. I had survived the consequences of the fear-based leadership that stems from perfectionism. And I knew I didn't want to ever experience them again. I also knew from my training as a leadership coach and the work I was doing in applied positive psychology that as human beings, we flourish when we feel a sense of agency, connection, and belonging. If I wanted to, I could be the type of leader who was attuned to the needs and experiences of the people on my team—the type of leader I could have used when I was struggling with vicarious trauma as an officer or burnout as a manager.

I had an opportunity to create a new, human-centered culture where every team member felt seen, heard, and valued—where perfectionism was not celebrated and where the culture eventually blossomed into a community in which people took care of each other.

And that's exactly what I did.

"Do you have any gum?" I turned to my sister, who was sitting at the makeshift desk next to me in the basement of my townhouse, which we had converted into a shared workspace at the start of COVID lockdown.

"Here you go." She tossed me the box.

Just as I opened it, my computer began ringing. One of my RAIO Thrive team members was calling. I put my headphones on with my free hand and accepted the call.

"Hi, Annie. How's it going?" I asked, popping a piece of gum into my mouth.

"Alright. How are you?" The heaviness in her voice caught my attention.

"I'm fine. Is everything okay?" I leaned forward and looked directly at her face on the monitor. Annie's long, red curls cascaded over her shoulders, which seemed to be hunched forward. Her forehead was creased as she looked back at me.

"Yeah, I guess. I just wanted to talk with you about the onboarding process." Her brow furrowed.

"Okay, sure. Tell me what's going on."

"I'm really frustrated that we haven't gotten the program off the ground. I feel like we've been working on this forever, and we're just in this holding pattern."

I nodded. I'd been here before. So many projects followed this trajectory. "I know how frustrating that can be," I responded.

"I feel like I should be able to do more—push it forward somehow. I feel like this reflects badly on me," she lamented.

Well, I'm the leader of this team. If it's going to reflect poorly on anyone, it will be me. My stomach fluttered with anxiety. *We're already past the deadline, and this new process feels like it's going to be so much longer and more drawn out, and out of our control. I wish I could just do this my way!*

I felt a familiar wave of resentment, though I hadn't experienced one in some time. Next came a realization: This conversation was hitting all of my perfectionist buttons. Annie and I were quite similar, so I was sure it hit hers as well. Perfectionism hadn't worked for me when I'd started as a mid-level manager in 2014, and encouraging it now wasn't going to help anything either. The ability to see my default reaction provided me with an opportunity to *shift* my behavior and do something different—something that would break the cycle of perfectionism and support each of us in the process.

"Okay, let me ask you this: What have you done on this project up to this point?"

I watched Annie on the screen in front of me as she considered my question. Resting her chin on her hands, she finally responded. "Well, I wrote the initial proposal and served as the project manager through the human-design process. I led the team through the various parts of that process to create the structure and content of the program. Once that ended, I proposed how many people we'd need to create the curriculum. And that's where we are." She sighed.

"Annie, I want to pause here for a moment so we can acknowledge everything you've done. It's a lot! You should be really proud of yourself for the headway you've made." I smiled as she seemed to soak in my words for a moment, and her face relaxed.

"I suppose," she said. "But I'd like to see this project completed. It's hard to see it just hanging out here this way."

I felt the warmth of compassion spread through my heart. *Oh, my sweet little high achiever. I remember being you once.*

"I get that," I told her. "But what's within your control right now?"

Annie rolled her eyes and laughed. "It always comes back to this question." She feigned irritation.

I nodded and laughed. "Yup, it always does!"

"Well, I've done everything I can," she said. "I guess the only thing in my control now is how much time I spend thinking about this." Her tone lightened a bit at the end.

"Exactly. We can always control how we respond. We've done everything we can to push this project forward. Had our team been able to do it ourselves, there might have been a different outcome. But maybe not. Bottom line, we didn't choose the course of action; it was chosen for us. I know, as a fellow high achiever, that you want to see things through because you know the impact this program could have on the culture of this organization. But when we get to a point where there are no other actions we can take, we can to choose to let go and have it remain unfinished. I know that's a tough thing to wrap our minds around, but sometimes that's how it is."

Annie nodded. "I just don't want people to think I dropped the ball on this."

"Don't worry about that," I reassured her. "You know I always have your back and would never throw you under the bus."

"Thank you for saying that. It makes me feel a lot better." She sat up a little straighter, a smile forming at the corners of her lips.

"Good! Anything else you want to talk about?"

"No, that's all. Thank you for taking the time to talk," she added before hanging up.

At one time I might have taken over the project and tried to do all the work myself, until I was exhausted and resentful. But I wasn't going to do that anymore. I didn't need to. I smiled, feeling proud of my new approach to leadership and self-care.

17

FROM SHATTERED TO SHARING

(Vulnerability)

"We have something new we'd like to offer to the workforce." I took a sip of coffee as the faces on the screen nodded. We were a few weeks into the pandemic lockdown, and the RAIO Thrive team's bi-weekly check-ins with the associate director and deputy associate director had gone virtual.

"They're called coffee chats," I continued. "Basically, they'd be small-group spaces where people can come together to talk about their anxiety around COVID, maybe even talk about grief, and learn some coping strategies. They don't all have to be serious. We just want to give people a place where they can connect with each other and talk about their fears and experiences." I took another long sip and watched the faces of the team over the rim of my mug as they considered my idea.

"I love it!" Jennifer, the associate director, exclaimed. Dressed in a T-shirt and baseball cap, she was the most informal I'd ever seen her.

I felt a wave of excitement pass through me.

"Who would run the sessions?" she asked. "And, how long would they be?"

"Well, we're aiming for about forty-five minutes, and we'll cap them at no more than twelve people per session. For now, we're thinking they should only be led by people on my team who know how to facilitate groups like this, and members of the senior leadership team—like asylum directors, you and the deputy, maybe even some of the headquarters senior leaders. This way people can have face time with all of you and continue to feel connected. We're in the process of putting together a facilitation guide, which we'll send out to all the offices by the end of the week, so managers in local offices can eventually host sessions as well. And we're setting up an online signup process."

"Sounds great. Just let me know what you need from us to get this up and running."

I nodded as I made some notes.

"Anything else?" she asked.

"That's all from me. Thanks!" I hung up feeling optimistic, yet weighted down by what lay ahead. With all of the losses from COVID, we were going to have to talk about grief. There was no running from it anymore.

The day after my mom's funeral, I came downstairs as the sun peeked over the horizon, bathing my dining room in the soft orange glow of early-morning light. For a split second, I expected to find my mom sitting at the dining room table, swiping through emails on her iPad, the smell of cardamom and ginger wafting up from tea brewing on the stove.

But she wasn't here. Nobody was. For the first time in weeks, my house was totally and completely silent.

Almost a week after she was admitted to the hospital, my mom's brother Yash and her sister Harsha drove down from Toronto to help my sister and me, giving us a little space to breathe and rest, though neither my sister nor I felt comfortable being away from the hospital for too long.

Within hours after Mom was intubated, most of our relatives from Toronto and other family friends began showing up, filling my and my sister's homes with the hubbub of daily life, praying with us in the waiting room, feeding us when it was time to eat, and gathering with us in Mom's tiny ICU room to witness her final breaths. Finally, they stood with my sister and me at a mortuary in Virginia as our mother's once-vibrant body was consumed by the cremation fire and reduced to the ashes we'd take with us to India a week later and pour into the same spot in the Narmada River where she'd poured my dad's ashes fourteen years earlier.

But the day after the funeral, all the activity and life that had been buzzing around me and in my home was gone. I was left alone to face the distinctive pain and loneliness that exists only in the silence of a deep and profound loss.

Though I'd experienced the loss of my dad years earlier, my grief for my mom felt different. It manifested as a physical pain in my heart and a hollowness in my chest, neither of which I had experienced when my dad had passed. I walked around in a fog, unable to follow simple conversations or focus on anything. I longed for one more conversation with her, one more meal, one more hug, one more, one more, one more.

I returned to the office two weeks after my mom died and just two days after returning from India. Still jetlagged and moving through a thick fog of grief, I felt like a totally different person. My whole world had been upended, and yet everything in the office looked exactly the same. I didn't know how to be there—to be anywhere, really—anymore, and most of the people around me weren't equipped to help. I felt pressure from within to turn my grief off like a light switch when I was around others, so I didn't make them uncomfortable.

On top of trying to get through a workday without breaking down, I was also facing the challenges of navigating the complicated bureaucracy of the probate system. My mom had been organized and made things as easy as possible for my sister and me, and yet the whole process was a strange kind of living hell. I was the trustee and executor of my mom's estate, and though my sister and I met on Sundays to tackle as much as we could together, the mountain of administrative tasks that could only be done by me often felt insurmountable.

Even though I'd been actively working to reroute my default reactions in different parts of my life, I realized very quickly that facing my grief was far too overwhelming. I wasn't ready. I'd have to deal with all the feelings and emotions later.

Using one of my newly developing skills of self-compassion, I allowed myself to default into my old pattern of finding solace in work—a pattern born of having no real coping strategies in place after my dad died and I'd ended my marriage. It was my *flight* response and my *fake* response showing up to protect me, doing anything they could to make me safe as I tried desperately to keep my head above water in a tumultuous sea of grief.

Unable to sleep or be in the unbearable silence of my home, I began going in to work around 7:00 a.m. and not leaving until 8:00 or 9:00 p.m. each evening. It was a welcome refuge from the reality that my mom, who had lived with me for close to two years before she died, would no longer greet me when I got home or sit down with me for dinner or go for a walk with me on the street behind our house. Once or twice a week, I made plans to meet friends for dinner or happy hour, and in those cases I only worked a ten- or eleven-hour day.

Though it was one of the hardest periods of my life, when I look back now, I'm grateful that things worked out as they did. Channeling my attention away from the grief and into my work not only helped me for a time, it allowed me to envision and build something that would be desperately needed just a few short months later.

During this period, I created an innovative, mindfulness-based leadership and well-being program—one of the first in the federal government—called the RAIO Daring Leaders Project (RDLP). The RDLP allowed me to bring a group of almost thirty leaders together to learn how to manage their own stress and deal with uncertainty, just days before the world locked down because of a pandemic. These leaders were then able to share these strategies with their own teams to create a sense of connection during a time when most people felt disconnected from their colleagues and anxious because of the uncertainty around COVID.

And, as fate would have it, this also allowed me to position myself as able to recognize, empathize, and hold space for the feelings of grief, isolation, overwhelm, anxiety, uncertainty, and anger that people in our workforce experienced, even as much of the organizational leadership chose to focus on productivity and numbers over people and emotions.

As counterintuitive as it sounds, consciously making the choice to focus my attention on my work was an act of self-compassion that eventually gave me the courage and strength to support my colleagues when the pandemic arrived and began ravaging lives around the world. Most importantly, though, turning the kindness I usually showed others toward myself gave me the time and space I needed until I was ready to process my grief in a healthier way.

It was inevitable that as the pandemic lockdown progressed from days to weeks to months, COVID would eventually reach the ranks of our workforce, either directly or vicariously through family members who had contracted the virus. During this first wave, the 24-hour news cycle was grim, sharing the growing death toll, the politicization of masking, and the news that health care facilities were running out of personal protective equipment, bed space, and ventilators.

My inner critic came to life, bringing all my fears to the surface. How could I be the resident expert on grief? I hadn't dealt with my own grief at all. Maybe I was an expert at shoving it down and spending all my time working, but what did I really think I was going to offer these people? Every time these thoughts came up, I'd take a deep breath and remind myself that what people needed most in this moment was connection and to feel seen. I knew how to do that.

These small, ongoing acts of self-compassion helped to quiet the thoughts. I also knew the only way to do this was to work through it. It was time to feel my grief, too—on a Zoom call.

I'd been facilitating coffee chats for a couple of weeks, but up to now they'd been focused on the anxiety and uncertainty of the pandemic. Realizing that people in our workplace were losing loved ones, I now knew we had to create a space for people to talk about their grief. Though I didn't know the details of their stories yet, I did know that each of the six colleagues staring back at me on the screen were, like me, grieving the loss of someone they'd loved.

"Grief is a complicated topic, and we only have forty-five minutes together today." I took a deep breath and dove in headfirst. "My mom passed away unexpectedly about nine months ago, and it shattered me." This was the first time I'd admitted this out loud to anyone, and my voice shook with emotion as the tears made their way up through my chest and to my eyes.

But if I was going to cry, there was no better place. This group would get it.

I wiped my eyes, took another deep breath, and continued. "We all deal with grief differently. My way has primarily been the shove-down-and-avoid method." I laughed and saw others smiling and laughing, too.

I felt my shoulders relax.

"There's no right or wrong way to deal with it. Your grief is your own and not something to compare with others'. One other thing I'd like to share is that for some of us, grief can feel incredibly isolating. My hope for our time together is that you walk away knowing you're not alone and feeling a connection to others who can relate to your experience. I also hope you find some compassion for yourself as you work through this process."

People nodded again, and relief washed over me. There was a purpose to this. It had meaning and was already making a difference. "With that, I'd like to open it up to the group. Would anyone like to share what brought you here today?"

18

CHOOSING A NEW
WAY TO SERVE

(Agency)

The map of my life during the four years leading up to the launch of the RDLP was filled with what I would describe as little moments of divine serendipity. I felt like the universe heard the voice in my head that said *there has to be a better way* and *we have to do better for our people* and provided the tools and knowledge I needed to create the *better* I and so many others around me were seeking.

I wrote a future vision statement for the RDLP as part of a proposal I presented to RAIO senior leadership in February 2019, almost a full year before the program officially launched and five months before my mom passed away. However, high turnover and low morale across the directorate, coupled with the fact that the program I was proposing focused on individual self-development, meant that many members of the senior leadership team didn't share my optimism or understanding about the impact this program could have on organizational culture.

Undeterred, I pushed forward. I believed the program would not only positively impact the leaders in the cohort, but would ultimately lead to positive ripple effects at all levels of the organization. My approach to leadership development, based in individual self-development, was unconventional. But the self-development work I'd done through leadership coaching, positive psychology, and *m*PEAK in the years leading up to February 2019 had taught me how to let go of old, outdated, perfectionism-based leadership tendencies and instead use a human-centered approach that had not only created psychological safety and connection within my own team, but had made me a better leader.

In the spring of 2021, I presented the outcomes from the RDLP pilot program during a virtual meeting with leaders across my organization. In just under one year, we'd seen aspects of the RDLP having an impact at the individual, team, and organizational levels. The ripple effects of leaders changing their perspectives and behaviors had had positive impacts on team performance, even during one of the most uncertain and challenging years we'd experienced. Leaders from the cohort, inspired by team performance, had begun taking on larger office-wide issues, which had led to a number of programmatic changes and new initiatives in local offices.

I was proud of what we had accomplished, but I had no way of knowing how the information I shared on the call was landing, since none of the leaders had turned on their cameras and I'd been speaking into the void. Their lack of engagement left me feeling indignant and frustrated. How could we create a culture of connection and belonging when we couldn't get the senior leaders in our organization to engage—or even allow me to see them while I was speaking?

As I finished my presentation, I noted that despite the positive results, we wouldn't be able to offer another RDLP until we had more staff on the team to assist with logistics and coordination. I explained that we'd asked for staff and were waiting to see if our request would be granted, but that the program couldn't move forward without permanent staff in place. I paused for a minute and waited to see if there were any questions. After a moment, one appeared in the chat.

Are you talking about asking for staff from the field again? We already have so much going on and really don't have staff to give you. We've already supported your programs at the cost of our own numbers.

"Thanks for the question," I said, trying to keep my voice calm. "I agree that bringing staff in from the field isn't ideal. But up until now, we've not only created and delivered a unique leadership program, we've been providing workshops, coffee chats, and other activities to support the workforce with a small staff made up of people here on temporary assignments. We'd like to keep the momentum going, but without a permanent staff, we can't. Are there any other questions?"

When nobody responded, I turned the meeting back over to the senior executive, muted myself, and sent a quick message to my team, thanking them again for all their hard work.

As the senior executive began moving through the meeting's agenda, responses appeared for the question in the chat about sending staff from the field to headquarters. Several people had attached thumbs up or heart emojis in support of the question, and a few others voiced their frustration at having to give up staff. Then another question popped up in the chat, and my heart momentarily sank into my stomach. Then anger began rising up through my body.

"We're losing staff to all these headquarters assignments and time during the day for coffee chats and workshops when people should be working. I don't understand why we continue to put money and resources toward these programs that don't contribute to meeting the mission."

Don't contribute to meeting the mission? I clenched my fists and felt the sting of criticism from my peers and leaders above me, which quickly morphed into resentment. It was because of the work my team had done during the early days of the pandemic that people could manage their anxiety and actually show up for work. It was our Furlough Survival Kit that had been passed around the whole agency and had helped people—not just in our directorate, but across the agency—understand their options during the looming furlough. If these leaders couldn't understand how having a happy and healthy workforce contributed to meeting the mission, I didn't know what else I could do. Frustration settled into my shoulders as I considered whether to respond.

But what was the point in responding? Not a single person on the call had disagreed with the comment or defended the work we were doing—not even the person leading the call, who'd gotten to experience the transformation of the leaders in the pilot cohort. I flipped off my camera and reached for a tissue to wipe my eyes. If the leaders in my organization couldn't see the value of our work or what my team and I had contributed to the mission after all we'd done over the past few years and through the pandemic—and after we'd received honors and recognition from the workforce—responding to this comment now wasn't going to change that.

I shook my head and let the tears stream down my cheeks.

I couldn't keep doing this. We expected people to take care of themselves when the truth was that their leaders and the organization also had a responsibility to ensure that the health and well-being of their staff was factored into the way we worked. I couldn't continue being the lone voice advocating for a duty of care for our staff.

I won't keep doing this.

I'd been up against a wall of resistance for such a long time, and even though I kept asking, I wasn't getting the right tools and support to chip away at it and bring it down. There was a need now. People were struggling and suffering, and we had to do better. Trying to do it from the inside wasn't working anymore, and I didn't have the patience to wait and hope that my organization would eventually get there. If I really believed the message I was trying to share, I had to have the courage to go out on my own. I would walk my talk and use my voice to create awareness and change.

It's time to go.

Once we see our default reactions, we can couple this newfound awareness with self-compassion and begin creating space between a stressful or traumatic event and our response. This shift from simply reacting to intentionally responding propels us toward agency, connection, curiosity, and vulnerability. The more we repeat this practice and create new neural pathways, the easier it becomes to break old patterns and begin healing the thoughts, emotions, reactions, and explanations that were keeping us stuck in painful or outdated narratives.

The stories I've shared in Part Four reflect moments in my life where I was able take my newfound awareness of my *surviving* reactions and use self-compassion to shift my mindset and make choices that supported finding a new path forward.

In this new, more-open space, I cultivated a feeling of connection to myself and my work, and I could offer myself compassion as I navigated through my grief to find hope again. I learned to use curiosity and empathy to embrace my own humanity and imperfection in order to be a more compassionate leader, and I leaned into vulnerability to foster trust and connection with my colleagues. And most importantly, as demonstrated in chapter 18, I could finally recognize the agency I had in my life and leadership and use it to choose a new path I believed would allow me to serve in a more humane and sustainable way.

Each choice helped me chip away at the mask of perfectionism I'd worn for so long and reconnect to my own humanity, ultimately allowing me to show up for others in the same way.

- What role has perfectionism played in your own life and how has it impacted the people around you?
- How might you shift one of your surviving stories or reactions using curiosity and self-compassion?
- Is there a new path you'd like to envision for yourself as you move forward? What obstacles can you *see* that are holding you back from pursuing it? What actions do you need to take to overcome those obstacles and *shift* to the new path?

PART FIVE

SHARING

SHARING

Part Five is the culmination of the story-healing cycle—the point at which we've moved through the journey of *shaping, surviving, seeing,* and *shifting.* It's only once we recognize and address the experiences that created our stories and led to our patterns that we can make new choices that will better serve us the next time we encounter a similar event or experience.

Sharing is the point in the story-healing cycle when we begin healing the brokenness within us and moving toward becoming whole. Sharing our stories with others fosters empathy and fulfills a primal human need for connection. It helps us experience a sense of common humanity and reminds us we're not alone in our suffering. The vulnerability we experience through sharing empowers us to write a better narrative—not only for ourselves, but for those we serve and lead.

19

BECOMING WHOLE

(Healing Through Story)

"Tell me your story."

I'd said those words to thousands of people over the years. And yet, the first time the invitation was extended to me, I felt my throat tighten and my heart race. I was gathered with a group of other writers, and as I looked at the wall in front of me, covered in Post-it notes of various hues, I wondered why I was reacting this way. I willed myself to speak, but no words came.

It's just a story. I tried to reason with myself as my eyes darted from one colorful square to the next. But it wasn't just a story. This patchwork quilt of Post-it notes was my life—it was *my* story. My stomach lurched. Each little square was a moment in time—the good, the bad, and everything in between. My body shuddered, my soul suddenly feeling naked and exposed at the thought of other people peering into a life that was so different from the one I had carefully curated for others to see over the years.

I took a deep breath, stepped back, and looked at the whole wall. This time, as my eyes moved from one square to the next, I saw past the individual stories and started to see new patterns emerging.

I turned and smiled at the assembled writers and pointed at the first Post-it.

"Okay, let's start at the beginning."

Seeing my life story laid out in this way—as a series of color-coded notes—made it easier to see how some stories had been written for me, while others I had written for myself. I could see the point at which I'd begun recognizing the impact of outdated narratives, and how using intention and compassion, I'd shifted old stories and created new ones that not only better served me, but allowed me to better serve others. This process also helped me to better understand what had led me to pursue a humanitarian path and, more importantly, why I continued doing this work long after I knew that serving others, the way I was doing it, was hurting me in the process.

Over the next six months, I kept looking at the various moments of my life and writing my story down. In the process of doing so, I noticed the themes of *shaping, surviving, seeing, shifting,* and *sharing* that form a cycle, which most of us experience throughout our lives.

In truth, I'd been teaching a similar framework for the past three years, but it had never occurred to me that the cycle existed in such a clear and profound way across the whole of my life story.

It took some time to understand that the best way I can serve people like me—mission-driven individuals working in service of humanity, often at a cost to their own health and well-being—is to share my story to help them connect to and heal their own. Why did it take so much time? Well, let's just say it hasn't been as simple as telling the story to a room full of other writers. Really committing to this last piece of sharing has forced me to look at moments I had carefully tucked away, consciously or unconsciously, in order to survive, and especially to serve. The hardest ones to engage with were the oldest of my origin story.

Here is my journey of moving through the story-healing cycle.

Shaping

My own early stories were shaped by generational trauma, displacement, instability, and personal experiences with violence and subtle acts of exclusion. Until writing this book, I couldn't fully see how those experiences not only shaped my identity but influenced every decision I made in my personal and professional life, including my choice to work in service of others.

Soon after passing the California bar exam in 2003, a few months after I got married, I was hired to work at a small private law firm in Anaheim that focused primarily on real estate cases. I knew from the first day that the work the firm was doing wasn't the right fit for me, but I took the job and then stayed with it out fear that I wouldn't be able to find something else and the pressure I felt to contribute financially to my household. I felt zero sense of purpose there, and I longed to feel connected to humanity in some way.

Since law school, I had repeatedly declared that I wanted to work on humanitarian and human-rights issues, but I didn't know what that might look like or why I was so drawn to this particular area of practice. Only after I got my job as an asylum officer did I begin connecting the dots.

On a trip to Princeton, NJ, for the holidays to visit my parents and my uncle Yash, about a year into my role as an asylum officer, I sat with my uncle in the living room, telling him about my job.

"It has been amazing. This is my dream job. It's everything I've been wanting to do since graduating from law school." My words tumbled out, propelled by excitement.

"So what exactly do you do?" my uncle asked as he took a long swig of his beer.

"I sit down with asylum seekers—people who have been persecuted because of their race, religion, nationality, social group, or political opinion and have somehow made their way to the United States. And I interview them. I ask about what happened in their country and why they can't go back. Then I research country conditions, and if the research supports what the applicant is telling me, I approve their application for asylum. Sometimes we also get the chance to go overseas and interview refugees—same kind of circumstances, but they haven't been able to get to the United States. I'm still pretty new, so I don't know when I'll get to go on one of those trips, but I think it would be amazing to be there on the ground."

My uncle nodded, head cocked to the side. He seemed deep in thought and then abruptly stood. "Wait here. I want to show you something." He went into his bedroom and re-emerged carrying a weathered gray, hard-sided suitcase. He set it down in front of me. "Open it," he instructed as he resumed his position on the sofa.

I slid off the sofa onto the soft beige carpet, unclasped the latches, and laid the bag open in front of me. Inside were various items that made up the story of my uncle's life: Blue journals with thin, onion-skin paper covered in his slanted writing laid against sleeves of old photographs, immigration documents, and letters. My uncle joined me on the floor and set his beer to the side. He reached for an envelope and pulled out a faded, handwritten Alitalia ticket dated January 4, 1973. It was the day he had arrived in the United States.

"What is all of this?" I asked, pushing papers around to see everything.

"This was the suitcase I left Uganda with. I was sent to a refugee camp in Italy while I waited for them to make a decision about my case. I kept everything from that time."

I stared at my uncle in disbelief. I noticed a slight smile appear at the corners of his mouth as he picked up one of the blue journals and flipped through it, getting lost in the memories from the past captured within its pages.

I knew my mom's family had lived in Uganda and that my mom, her parents, and her younger siblings had left before Idi Amin expelled all the Asians. But beyond those facts, nobody had ever talked to me about what had *actually* happened. It wasn't until that evening in December, sitting on the floor, surrounded by documents—the puzzle pieces of my uncle's life—that I realized a member of my family had been through the very refugee resettlement program for which I now worked. Without knowing that, something within me had been pulling me toward this work for years. After hearing his story, I felt a new kind of responsibility to do what I could to help legitimate refugees and asylum seekers the same way some other officer had once helped my uncle.

When I began interviewing refugees and asylum seekers for work, many of my personal life experiences were mirrored in aspects of the stories of persecution and harm the applicants shared with me, day in and day out. What I didn't realize at the time, though, was that as I sat with each applicant in their pain, the experience left me sitting in my own pain, too.

My heart broke over and over again as I listened to stories about othering and not fitting in, family violence, having to flee in the dead of night, and being persecuted by authoritarian governments and terrorist groups for reasons beyond their control. I thought I was maintaining distance through a wall of professionalism, but in truth, with each interview and each story witnessed, I relived experiences from my own life through the traumas of others, which were settling into my heart, mind, and body.

To be clear, a person doesn't have to have experienced violence or other forms of trauma in their own life to experience vicarious trauma. However, the shaping stories from my childhood, grounded in violence and trauma, certainly made me more susceptible to it.

My childhood circumstances wouldn't have fit the definition of persecution I used to adjudicate the asylum applicants' cases, because I wasn't being harmed due to a protected characteristic—race, religion, nationality, membership in a particular social group, or political opinion. But the generations that came before me had been. I carried that trauma in my DNA. My mom had carried fear and pain with her as she left the only home she'd ever known and awaited news of her missing brother. This led to me unconsciously experiencing the reverberations of refugee trauma. The experience of being othered by my neighbor at the tender age of three left me believing I was in some way unworthy or less than the white children in my neighborhood. It snuffed out the spark in my personality and put up an invisible wall that made it more difficult for me to truly connect with white peers for many years. It exacerbated the feelings of not belonging that already came with my split identity as a child of first-generation immigrants.

All of these experiences and so many others—along with the fear, violence, and trauma we experienced at the hands of a rogue actor that showed up in the form of my dad's mental illness—shaped my thoughts and beliefs about the world and my place in it. They left me with a desire to help other vulnerable people, ultimately leading me to a career working in service of other human beings. They allowed me to tap into a place of empathy in my work that I might not have been able to had I not had these experiences.

Surviving

The same events and experiences that shaped my view of the world and my place in it influenced the stories I *told* myself about how to navigate the challenging and painful experiences I encountered as I grew up. I was contending with instability and violence at home. Also, as the daughter of first-generation immigrants, I grappled with a lack of connection and belonging in my peer group. In addition, I shouldered the burden to do, be, and achieve all the things my parents had never had the opportunity to, and had as a result, dreamed of for me.

This led to *fight* stories that often faced inward, grounded in self-judgment, blame, and fear of not being good enough, smart enough, pretty enough, thin enough, funny enough, or worthy enough. These self-fulfilling prophecies validated my perceived shortcomings as a daughter, sister, officer, leader, and any other role that I took on. As my own worst critic, I didn't have the capacity to see myself as a leader, even though all the evidence in front of me—my career trajectory, the influence I had within RAIO, my ability to mobilize action, and praise from leaders who I looked up to—indicated otherwise.

Fear of how my actions might impact others often activated my *freeze* stories and left me working overtime to do what I thought would make others happy, in the process deprioritizing or completely ignoring my own needs. When my doctor told me I needed to leave New Delhi and come home for the sake of my health, the decision should have been a simple one. But it took three days of thinking and rethinking and polling the people around me before I could finally raise the issue with my managers, who were as supportive as a management team could possibly be in that situation. Despite their support, I still worried about the impact my curtailment would have on my colleagues, my long-term career prospects, and my standing in the eyes of leaders, mentors, and staff I admired and respected. My own health and well-being were repeatedly pushed to the bottom of my list of concerns.

My fear of vulnerability and what others might think of me often brought forward my *fix* stories, which came from a place of not wanting to burden others with problems or situations I believed were my own fault. The generational expectations for girls and women that many family members placed on me and other females shaped my stories of relationships and my roles in them. Although my mom stood up to my dad and took control of our lives once I was in high school, the impact of the early stories had left its mark. Those continue to be ones I am intentionally working to unlearn and rewrite to this day. These stories led me to believe that a broken engagement would make me unworthy of love, so despite everything in me telling me to walk away, I tried to *fix* the situation by marrying someone who had lied and withheld information before we ever said our vows. The cultural shame of a divorce led me to *fix* the situation by staying in an abusive marriage with a toxic family for three and a half years, at the end of which I was a shadow of the vibrant and powerful woman I had once been.

My fear of failure or disappointing others activated my *fake* stories, which regularly appeared throughout the course of my life—especially in relation to my career—as early as choosing to go to law school after college, rather than taking a chance and going to Washington, DC, without a job in hand. I have been a creative person my entire life, but instead of leaning into that and pursuing a career more aligned with my strengths and values, I went to law school, passed the bar exam in Colorado and California, and practiced law at a firm that sucked the life out of me—all to live up to a standard of success that had been set by others. When I got the job as an asylum officer, I felt myself come to life again. I felt connected to my purpose. And as I found ways for my creativity to break through the veil of professionalism I wore out in the world, I found moments of joy in my work, too.

While all of these survival mechanisms have showed up for me at different times in my life, my primary story of survival and the one that felt most familiar was always *flight*. It was a pattern inherited from my dad. His decision to move us from one place to the next when things weren't going right was his own survival story kicking into gear. As I got older, I noticed that any time I was scared, frustrated, embarrassed, or feeling shame about something, I felt a desire to escape. Sometimes escape meant pulling the covers over my head and humming to drown out the scary noises of my childhood; at other times it looked like hours in the library reading Sweet Valley High books so I didn't have to go home, never knowing which version of my dad would be waiting at the dinner table. As I got older, it showed up as fantasizing about walking away from my life, moving to the other side of the world, and creating a new identity—a new life where nobody knew me and I could start fresh and finally be happy.

Shaped and activated early in my childhood by my dad's mental illness, this *flight* response remained my most trusted survival instinct for decades. Combined with the work ethic I'd inherited from the women in my family, escaping into my work or food to avoid the realities in other parts of my life became a comfortable and familiar pattern, especially during times of adversity and challenge.

But here's the thing with survival stories—they're designed to help us survive in the moment, and they rarely lead to any kind of lasting satisfaction or happiness. More often than not, they keep us stuck in fear and isolation, unable to tap into the meaning and joy we so desperately seek.

Seeing

Years of living in survival mode without any long-term coping strategies or self-care practices left me vulnerable to taking on other people's trauma with my only outlet being to work more, drink more, travel more, eat more—anything to avoid reality. This made me more susceptible to a variety of occupational mental-health challenges like compassion fatigue, vicarious trauma, moral injury, and burnout.

The ability to *see* my own stories and less-than-mindful reactions started during my mindful performance training through the *m*PEAK course. With mindful awareness, I was able to begin seeing my *surviving* stories for what they were—a neurobiological jumble of thoughts, emotions, body sensations, perceptions, and reactions trying to manage different experiences in my life. Through this lens of increased objectivity, I began to learn that my stories—those that formed me and those I'd been telling myself—were neither good nor bad. They simply were.

Once I understood this, it became easier for me to separate the individual from the experience. I could differentiate myself from the traumas I had experienced, which in turn helped me separate other people from the traumas they had experienced or even caused for me. I saw my dad as separate from the mental illness that had plagued him for so many years. This perspective didn't excuse his actions, but it allowed me to connect to his humanity through a lens of compassion. I began to understand that by saying, "I am traumatized," the trauma had become a part of my identity. By saying instead, "I have experienced trauma," I could create space between me and my experiences. Separating myself from the story let me begin seeing each part of my past more clearly.

I experienced the power and clarity that comes in moments of silence while recuperating in Kerala, completely disconnected from the outside world for the first time in over a decade of leadership roles. Sitting in silence gave me the space to see my stories. With that clarity came a new level of awareness that allowed me to reassess my life and make the choice to prioritize my mental, physical, emotional, spiritual, and relational health and well-being over everything else—over cultures that prioritize productivity over their people, over suffering the consequences of taking in other people's pain in silence and shame, over living life in a constant state of survival and reaction.

When I started putting together a workshop for RAIO staff about navigating stress, crisis, and trauma, I was finally able to see that I (and so many others) had been experiencing moral injury since the outcome of the 2016 election. But I was the only one I knew putting a name to the experience and talking about it. Like many other public servants, I felt a deep sense of shame about staying in my position and being part of a government that was carrying out policies and processes fundamentally out of alignment with my core values and beliefs. I stayed out of a sense of duty to the public I served. The limits on public servants' ability to speak out or publicly share their opinions about laws and policies leaves them with the option of having to quit out of protest, if they have the means to do so, or suffer in silence. Being able to see my story of moral injury helped me identify my options and ultimately make the choice to leave the government in order to stay true to the values that drive me.

Losing my mom was one of the most painful experiences I'd ever endured. Pushing through the pain and finding my way to the center, I discovered pearls of wisdom about living in the present and finding the beauty of a life well lived in a world boiling over with uncertainty. Seeing my grief story in its entirety helped me recognize the familiar *flight* patterns of survival through work, which I'd relied on over the course of my life. This time, though, instead of defaulting into that pattern, I realized that consciously making the choice to distance myself from the grief for a while would give me the space I needed until I was ready to do the work to heal. In time, I began to see my grief story as a winding labyrinth of emotions— longing, sadness, and anger for all the moments that were forever lost, and also gratitude and joy for the memories sparked by particular sights, sounds, smells, and tastes, and for all the life I had yet to live.

In the white space between my emotions, the different stories that were impacting my health and well-being became visible like bursts of brightly colored paint on a fresh canvas. Grief, compassion fatigue, moral injury, vicarious trauma—these had been my default states of existence for so many years. I could finally see that my stories didn't emerge because I was weak or unable to handle the stress of the job; they emerged because I was human.

Shifting

At the heart of being human is imperfection. By embracing my own humanity, I could finally begin to let go of the shame that had shaped so many of my beliefs and choices for decades. Learning that I was more than the stories I had told myself gave me the courage to begin pulling at the frayed threads of the perfectionism, self-judgment, comparison, self-loathing, and lack of self-worth I had woven into my identity. Over time, I watched them unravel until they were nothing more than shapeless piles of yarn at my feet.

To be clear, this new space wasn't about getting rid of the old stories; they had, after all, protected me in the past. Rather it was about learning to see them with clarity and making choices that would allow me a lens of self-compassion to shift and create healthier new and meaningful stories.

But this required a great deal of *unlearning*.

In 2017, feeling disconnected from my purpose in life, I entered a new season of trying to connect to something bigger than myself. I explored different side hustles to provide me with purpose in a way my job in the government no longer did. And I found that most didn't feel like a good fit. Each time I tried and then discarded something new, a wave of shame washed over me. I felt my credibility waning, and feelings of being a fraud regularly surfaced as I invited friends and family to support my new projects and endeavors.

After reflection, I'm not surprised that I felt this way, given that I'd spent most of my life believing if I left my stable, government job to start my own business or lean into my creativity through writing or photography, I'd end up depressed like my dad—unable to finish anything I'd started. For over a year, each new thing I tried became a failure. And with each failure, I found myself deeper in a pessimistic story loop that wanted me to believe that being like my dad would never end well.

Being stuck in this story loop about my dad made it hard for me to see all the amazing qualities we shared. Aside from physical similarities, my dad and I were both smart, well-educated, caring, and trusting of others—almost too trusting at times, which got us both in trouble over the years. To the world, we appeared confident. We filled up any room we entered with our laugh and big personalities, and we shared a superpower that allowed us to connect with people we had just met, quickly turning strangers into friends. We were both visionaries, creatives, and often described as being "ahead of our time," which meant ideas we proposed or things we created sometimes weren't understood or appreciated by the people around us until years later.

But I'd never be able to appreciate these qualities and build on them if I didn't shift my story and get out of the loop I was stuck in.

Shifting my stories meant tapping into my own sense of agency. I had choice. I was no longer at the mercy of other people's stories or my survival stories. What others saw or what they believed wasn't important. I recognized the unique gift that my vision and creativity could offer to others. By seeing my stories through the lens of compassion, I was finally able to shift them and, in turn, expand them in new ways that didn't just serve me, but served the people around me, creating a number of unexpectedly beautiful ripple effects.

I became a better leader, choosing to move away from the domineering fear-and-perfectionism-based leadership style that had defined the way I was led and shift to a new style rooted in connection and humanity. I broke my old cycle of working to the point of burnout and replaced it with the understanding that prioritizing my own health and well-being wasn't selfish. Focus on my well-being was an act of radical responsibility that allowed me to show up and keep doing the important work that meant so much to me. It also helped me support my team in the process by modeling healthy boundaries and the importance of self-care. Letting go of perfectionism created space for me to ask for help and shut down once and for all the one-woman martyrdom show I'd been writing, producing, and starring in for so many years.

Watching my little team of people grow and flourish under my human-centered leadership approach confirmed my belief that connecting with team members on a human-to-human level built trust, created a sense of belonging, and led to happier and healthier teams—something I was able to share with twenty-four first- and second-line leaders across my organization right before the pandemic lockdown started. As a result of the leadership program I created, for the first time, we had concrete evidence demonstrating a difference in the resilience levels of the teams that were led by leaders who had gone through my program and those that were not.

I was devastated when members of the senior leadership team still couldn't understand how the work my team and I were doing contributed to the mission of our organization. However, this helped me realize that things weren't likely to change anytime soon. As a result of the shifts I'd created in my stories, I recognized that I had changed and subsequently outgrown the space. I was able to stand confidently in the knowledge that what I had created and offered was on the right track and that my organization would eventually catch up. In the meantime, I would walk away to support organizations that were ready to embark on a new way of meeting the mission.

Sharing

The first time I was asked to share my whole life story was at a writing retreat, and I was utterly terrified. Over the years, I'd shared different parts of my story with select people—close friends, extended family members, romantic partners—but those had been short, carefully curated snapshots of particular moments in time, without context from the broader picture. As I grew and evolved in my career and stepped more fully into my role as a leader, I felt a duty of care to my colleagues to share my personal experiences of vicarious trauma, compassion fatigue, moral injury, and burnout to normalize the experiences I was sure others in my organization had also had. I managed doing so during that RAIO Thrive town hall, but even that wasn't everything. That was the story of my work life.

And eventually, I realized even sharing all of that might not be enough. Yet the thought of sitting down and sharing *everything*—the good, the bad, and the messy middle that was thick and sticky like tar and kept me stuck in a place of shame—left me with a heavy feeling in the pit of my stomach.

Why do I need to share my whole story? I wondered. I just wanted to write a book about the occupational realities of working in mission-driven organizations and why I believed organizations owed a duty of care to their people that went beyond ensuring physical safety.

As I shared my Post-it note life story with the other writers, my mouth was dry, my palms were sweaty, and the words felt raw in my throat. Uncorking a lifetime of secrets and shame overwhelmed me, and I had to stop several times along the way to cry and let the unprocessed emotions out. I thought I was writing a story that would help others. What I came to understand was that in order to do that, I had to first write the story that would help me.

As with any act of vulnerability, feelings of shame, fear, and self-doubt almost immediately crept in. *How can I share such personal stories? What will people think of me? What will they think of my family?* It was one thing to share with a group of writers, but how would my family react? Stories of mental health and domestic violence weren't uncommon in the Indian community, but they were rarely shared openly. Would my family feel betrayed by me sharing the darkest moments of our life? What about my friends? My colleagues?

How were my childhood stories of violence and trauma going to help people understand my message that working in service of others should not require us to sacrifice ourselves? Why would they care? How would they see the connections?

The questions kept coming, and I kept writing.

In time, and as I've noted previously, I realized how the painful experiences and trauma of my early life had influenced my desire to serve others. I understood how my own stories of pain and trauma were mirrored in the stories of the refugees I served.

This is why I had to tell my full story. I had to share the stories that shaped me and helped me survive, because they'd led to my buy-in with the culture of service before self. These stories had created the conditions for my experiences of compassion fatigue, vicarious trauma, moral injury, and burnout. Healing requires vulnerability, and vulnerability requires courage. If I was going to help individuals and organizations change the narrative of service before self, I'd have to have the courage to be vulnerable so I could help others be vulnerable, too.

Over time, the heavy pit in my stomach was replaced by shivers of excitement, possibility, and hope that tingled their way up and down my spine.

What if sharing my story could help just one person believe their past didn't have to define their future? What if sharing could help remove the barriers that have kept so many workers trapped in the belief that being mission-driven equates to being superhuman, and that working in service of others means giving up parts of yourself? What if my story could help one leader let go of fear and perfectionism and shift to a human-centered approach—one where they and their teams experience health, happiness, and connection to each other? What if my story could help to positively influence the mission-driven sector as a whole, so that a duty of care toward staff mental health and well-being became the norm rather than the exception?

With each story I pulled out of my mind and put on paper, I felt a little piece of me crack open. I started to feel lighter and less encumbered by the weight I had carried with me for so many years. Through the process of writing, I grieved the person my dad might have been, had he not been shrouded in the shame of mental illness for most of his adult life, and I forgave him for all the harm his illness caused us early in our lives. I broke the old cycle of stories about my inability to flourish if I chose a new, less-structured path. I found new depths of compassion as I grieved my mom and experienced a deep sense of gratitude for the fierce way she protected my sister and me throughout our lives. I realized that the fact that people in my organization couldn't see the value in my work wasn't personal. I forgave myself for the way I had treated myself for so long and set intentions to do better moving forward.

Sharing the hardest parts of my life story helped me connect the dots and see how all the different pieces fit together. It helped me recognize how my stories had evolved and changed with time and experience, and that I didn't have to stay stuck in the old, painful story loops. I had a choice and could use the skills, awareness, and tools I'd collected along the way to write a new, more powerful narrative for myself and others in mission-driven fields.

And for the first time in my life, I really began to heal.

Sharing our stories is a fundamental part of the story-healing process because when our stories are witnessed by others, we fulfill a primal human need to connect, which makes us feel safe and allows us to begin the process of healing wounds that get in the way of flourishing. We often carry our pain and shame in silence. Sharing these experiences with others creates a feeling of common humanity, which reminds us that we're not alone in our experiences of suffering, or our experiences of joy.

The more we share our stories with others, the less power they have over us as the pain, shame, and stigma of experiences we've buried deep within us begin to fall away. The vulnerability we experience through sharing allows us to crack ourselves open and see ourselves more fully—the good, the bad, and everything in between—with less shame, judgment, and fear.

And it's from this place of curiosity, compassion, and non-judgment that we can connect to the best versions of ourselves. The versions that support us in our desire to be better partners, better parents, better siblings, better children, better leaders—better humans. With this ability to meaningfully connect to ourselves and the people around us, we're not only able to serve those in need, but we're able to care for ourselves and our needs, too.

- Think about a time when you shared a piece of your story with another person or group. How did you feel after sharing? How might your story have helped others in their own journeys?
- How might sharing stories in your workplace contribute to meeting your organization's mission?
- What are some ways you could integrate story-sharing into your organization?

PART SIX

A HUMANITARIAN MANIFESTO

SERVICE WITHOUT SACRIFICE: A HUMANITARIAN MANIFESTO

We are the teachers, the healers, the activists, the caregivers, the health-care professionals, the first responders, the public servants, the government workers, the clergy, the journalists, the international aid and development corps, and all who work to alleviate other people's pain and suffering, and to make the world better.

We are humanitarians.

Every day we serve the world's most vulnerable people, often under challenging and dire circumstances. Through our service, we're exposed to traumatic events and danger, regularly work long hours, experience high-stress and high-threat situations, and in some cases frequent, often back-to-back deployments in global fields.

In spite of all of this, we show up, day after day, ready to serve.

For generations we've been conditioned to believe that by choosing a career in the service of others, we agree to sacrifice our time, our relationships, our health and well-being—our humanity. We've been taught that the only way through the hardships, traumas, and exhaustion is to suck it up. Shove it down. Numb the pain. Be grateful that your life isn't as bad as theirs. Move on. Dismiss the desire for a better way. And we've been taught that to do anything different—to set boundaries, to prioritize self-care, to be less than perfect—is selfish.

Unprofessional.

In addition to what happens in our places of work, we too—like the people we serve—have navigated the challenges of a global pandemic. We too endure the traumas of social and racial inequities, subtle acts of exclusion, and war. We too care for loved ones, friends, and family members. We too manage chronic health conditions, feel pain, experience loneliness, and grieve our losses.

We too are human.

And yet, the organizations through which we serve often choose not to see our humanity. They choose not to acknowledge our trauma. They choose not to help us heal our pain. They choose not to respect or support our boundaries. They choose to turn a blind eye to our sacrifices of time, relationships, health, and well-being. They choose to celebrate perfectionism and to define resilience as the ability to meet organizational metrics.

They choose to dismiss our desire for a better way.

These choices, made by those who should be protecting us, have left us— humanitarians across mission-driven fields—languishing, exhausted, stressed out, burned out, traumatized, morally injured, depressed, and anxious. They've left us feeling unseen, disrespected, misunderstood, and undervalued. They've left us questioning whether we're tough enough, resilient enough, professional enough—good enough. They've left us feeling ashamed and selfish in our desire to want more—to want better. They've left us feeling invisible and alone, bearing our pain and shame in silence. They've left us without a sense of agency or belief in our ability to make choices that serve us, even as we serve others.

Carrying the weight of the pain, hardships, and traumas, we continue to serve.

We do so because the world needs people like us to show up, day after day, to do work most people cannot fathom. We choose to serve because of a deeply ingrained desire to give back. We choose to serve because doing so gives us a sense of purpose and connection to something bigger than ourselves in a world where so many feel disconnected and isolated. We choose to serve because caring for others is inherent to who we are, and to do anything different would leave us feeling unfulfilled and restless.

In addition to our choice to serve, using our newfound gifts of self-awareness and self-compassion, we now choose to remember that at the heart of the word *humanitarian* is *human*. We now choose to move forward with eyes wide open, secure in the knowledge that serving others does not require sacrificing ourselves. We now choose to believe that we deserve more, we deserve better, and we deserve to have our humanity acknowledged and protected. And while we'll choose to continue doing this work that lends our lives purpose and which we love, we will no longer do so by sacrificing our time, health, well-being, relationships—or our humanity— in the process.

We choose to serve without sacrificing ourselves.

To manifest this new choice, we commit to changing the status quo—first as individuals, and then by holding our leaders and organizations accountable for doing the same.

As individuals we commit to:

- Taking radical responsibility
- Embodying mindful awareness
- Redefining self-care
- Setting clear boundaries
- Becoming radically human leaders

As leaders in organizations, we commit to providing a holistic, human-centered duty of care to:

- Normalize and address occupational mental-health challenges and traumas
- Evolve from metrics-driven cultures into human-centered ones
- Support rest and recovery
- Foster shared purpose and commitment

Using this framework, we'll work together to rewrite the long-standing narrative of service before self and shift our collective expectations about what it means to be of service. We'll create awareness and compassion around our stories in order to heal them and move forward feeling happier and healthier, so we can continue showing up to do the important work this world needs us to do now more than ever.

This is our commitment to ourselves, and to the people we serve.

I intend this manifesto to (1) remind each of us that we must make the choice to prioritize our own health and well-being; (2) put mission-driven sectors on notice that they must do more—do better—to address the effect of occupational traumas and the resulting mental-health challenges inherent in humanitarian work; and (3) to advocate for a duty of care that makes the mental health and well-being of staff a cornerstone of all policies, processes, and procedures that organizations put in place to meet their mission.

That leaves us with this question: How?

Below I've expanded on each commitment identified in the manifesto and provided practical information and ideas to help individuals and organizations uphold their commitment to service without sacrifice.

FOR INDIVIDUALS: CHALLENGE YOUR OWN NARRATIVES

TAKE RADICAL RESPONSIBILITY

With greater awareness and more discussion about mental health and well-being coming out of the COVID-19 pandemic, I believe mission-driven organizations will begin to integrate workforce health and well-being into the fabric of their organizational cultures. However, this isn't likely to happen quickly, and expecting anything different sets us up as individuals for sadness, disillusionment, and frustration. This also leaves the primary responsibility for self-care with each of us.

I know from personal experience that our organizations aren't going to save us. And I don't mean for that to sound bleak. Instead, acknowledging this fact frees us to make choices that will let us flourish as we support our own health and heal our own trauma, even during times of adversity and challenge. Doing this requires us to practice *radical responsibility*—a commitment to ourselves and to the people around us to take ownership and responsibility for our own thoughts, behaviors, and the resulting outcomes. To be clear, radical responsibility doesn't let organizations off the hook, but it acknowledges that as individuals we have to make changes for ourselves before we can make them as an organization.

Radical responsibility consists of three key components: accountability, well-being, and mindset.

- *Accountability*: This means personal responsibility for the outcomes that arise from our thoughts, actions, behaviors, and beliefs. Because we often have a role in creating the problems we're experiencing, we also have an opportunity to be a part of any potential solutions. Personal accountability is about owning our mistakes, as well as apologizing and making amends when necessary. Taking accountability for ourselves leaves no room for blaming, shaming, or judging others.

- *Well-Being*: This is about acknowledging our humanity and remembering that the way we take care of ourselves is directly related to our capacity to care for others. When we take responsibility for our well-being, we ensure that we're setting and enforcing boundaries related to self-care practices, getting enough rest, what we're eating and drinking, and how we manage our stress. When we take responsibility for our well-being, we recognize that it's a non-negotiable for ensuring our success as people.

- *Mindset*: Our mindset has the capacity to make or break our health, well-being, and success as humanitarians. Imagine each moment of your life represented by a thin black line. At any moment, you're either operating from above the line or below the line. When you're above the line, you're using what's known as a growth mindset, which means you're curious, non-judgmental, and open to learning. When you're below the line, you're operating with a fixed mindset, which means you show up as defensive, judgmental, and determined to prove you're right, rather than wanting to adjust as needed to get it right.

Taken together, these three components create *radical responsibility*—a state of being where we show up with intentionality and awareness, regularly checking in with ourselves to ask whether we're operating from above or below the line, and making necessary adjustments to help us view situations with a growth mindset. Radical responsibility is about being accountable for the way we personally show up during times of adversity and the way we make ourselves part of the solution. It also serves as the foundation for every other commitment we make as individuals and as members of an organization. In cultures where blame, shame, and judgment are the norm, practicing radical responsibility and owning our mistakes, as well as apologizing and making amends when necessary, can feel challenging. But the ripple effects are powerful. Like anything else, the more we practice, the easier it becomes to embody this way of being.

And the easier it becomes for us, the easier becomes to support others in doing the same.

EMBODY MINDFUL AWARENESS

Through a regular mindfulness practice, you can develop mindful awareness, a foundational piece for rewriting our narratives. Mindful awareness is also a necessary first step for practicing self-compassion and regulating our emotions, especially during times of stress, crisis, and uncertainty. Operating in autopilot mode is similar to looking in a dirty mirror. Mindfulness practices like meditation or nature walking are tools that help us wipe the mirror clean so we can see ourselves and the things around us with greater clarity. Mindful awareness helps us notice what has activated our stress response and then tap into self-compassion to determine what self-care choices will best support us in a given situation, as well as which boundaries need to be set. Self-awareness, self-compassion, and self-regulation are all skills developed through a regular mindfulness practice.

In my work, I often encounter individuals who say mindfulness isn't for them because they can't turn off their thoughts or they don't have time to sit on a cushion for hours each day. These misconceptions are common, and they are just that—misconceptions. One of my favorite sayings from *m*PEAK is that the brain pumps thoughts like the heart pumps blood. Mindfulness isn't about turning off our thoughts, which would be impossible; rather it's about changing our relationship to them. I often explain this as an opportunity to notice, name, and navigate through moments of our lives.

- *Notice*: Mindful awareness allows us to notice patterns created by our *shaping* and *surviving* stories, notice the body sensations we experience when our stress reactions are activated, and notice what areas of our well-being have been impacted. In *m*PEAK we explain that this awareness is like switching from regular TV to high definition or from regular headphones to noise canceling. The programming remains the same, but we've got an added level of clarity and crispness. Cultivating awareness where it didn't before exist allows us to experience additional clarity in different parts of our life. As we begin to notice the different body sensations as they arise, we can more quickly tie them to the underlying emotion, making it easier to address the emotion rather than simply reacting.

- *Name*: As we begin tapping into our awareness, we can start diving below surface-level emotions and name what we're actually experiencing so we can identify the right response or self-care practice we need. For example, when I make a mistake in front of other people, I might get angry with myself. But with awareness I can dig a little deeper to recognize that below my anger is actually shame and embarrassment, and it's showing up in my body as a flushed face and butterflies in my stomach. The more we practice noticing and naming the emotions and corresponding body sensations, the easier it is to tend to the actual emotions we're experiencing.

- *Navigate*: Naming the underlying emotions allows us to navigate through the experience by tapping into choice—in this case, perhaps choosing to practice self-compassion to address the root emotions by reminding ourselves that we're human, that everyone makes mistakes and then by letting go, instead of berating ourselves for something we can't change. Breaking these patterns and creating new neural pathways that support us better during times of stress, crisis, and adversity requires us to use our awareness and compassion to make new choices—and not just once, but over and over again. For example, practicing breathwork in the midst of a crisis can help you regulate your nervous system in real time. But if you don't have a regular mindfulness practice that has helped you learn how to focus your attention, drown out the external noise, use your breath to activate your vagus nerve, and shift from fight-or-flight to rest-and-digest whenever you feel stress arising, it's unlikely that you'll default to this choice in the midst of a crisis. Your neural pathways will revert back to old survival-mode patterns until you've put in sufficient effort to build a new, healthier default pathway.

It's important to remember that all of this takes time and practice. We know going to the gym and lifting weights one time isn't going to give us beautifully sculpted muscles. Similarly, awareness, compassion, and self-care are all muscles that have to be built up with intention over time.

REDEFINE SELF-CARE

As humans, we intuitively know that we need to take care of ourselves. And this applies even more as humanitarians working in mission-driven organizations because the work we do directly impacts the well-being of other human beings. We've seen firsthand how a lack of care can leave people struggling, and how they flourish when their physical, emotional, spiritual, and relational needs are met. So yes, we believe, deeply, in the power of care.

Except, that is, when it comes to caring for ourselves.

With a never-ending to-to list, countless daily pressures in our work and home lives, and a desire to serve everyone else, our own well-being is rarely at the forefront of our minds, and self-care is usually the first thing to drop to the bottom of the list—if not off the list completely.

But the reality is, when we are coping with a constantly elevated level of stress, and when self-care is pushed aside, the effects can be devastating.

Historically, self-care has been marketed as an indulgence—images of lounging in a tub filled with bubbles or sitting on a sofa, feet up, reading a magazine while sipping tea. And while these are legitimate forms of self-care, marketing self-care as a luxury has inadvertently linked it with feelings of guilt for many humanitarians who regularly witness suffering all around them. In addition to guilt, there's a common misconception that self-care takes up a lot of time we either don't have or that could be used for something more productive. Choosing to take care of ourselves when the people around us are struggling or "pushing through" can feel selfish and maybe even lazy. But here's the thing: Self-care is not selfish or lazy. On the contrary, it's an active choice and an absolute necessity in this line of work.

It might sound melodramatic, but neglecting self-care is akin to inflicting trauma on ourselves, and the effects are exactly what one would expect from experiencing trauma—physical, mental, emotional, and even relational distress. Eventually our body, our mind, our connection to a sense of purpose, and even our relationships will give out. And when that happens, we don't just struggle to take care of ourselves, we struggle to show up for the people we're caring for and trying to serve. Once we hit that point, it can be hard to claw our way back.

It's easy to understand this cognitively and to be fully on board with the idea of prioritizing our own well-being and making time for self-care. Yet the reality is that most of us fail to follow through in our day-to-day lives.

It's not surprising, really. Humanitarians are under immense pressure to help the most vulnerable people in the world. When we take five minutes to sit in silence or to take a walk to process the suffering of a displaced person or an abuse survivor, we may have feelings of guilt and shame. When we're faced with human tragedy on a daily basis, our own needs can feel trivial and self-care seem indulgent.

But people working across the humanitarian sector face challenges that go beyond traditional workplace stressors like stress, anxiety, and burnout. We're also dealing with vicarious or secondary traumatic stress, moral injury, and compassion fatigue. On top of these workplace stressors, we may be living with chronic diseases or pain, experiencing grief, and managing family relationships or financial stress. Any one of these things taken on its own can feel overwhelming. Taken together, it can feel impossible enough to make even the most resilient among us stumble. And if you are, have, or will in the future experience the impact of these stressors, that doesn't make you weak—it makes you human.

So if we know that showing up for ourselves is absolutely essential to showing up for other people, how do we remove the stigma of self-care? How do we, as people working in mission-driven humanitarian organizations, embrace the notion that self-care is a must-have, not an indulgent nice-to-have?

It starts with a *mindset shift*. We have to stop comparing ourselves to other people and start recognizing the validity of our own experiences—then giving ourselves the time, space, *and permission* to attend to them. It's also about understanding our individual stress signatures and acknowledging that what's stressful for me might not be what's stressful to you, and vice versa. It's about letting go of stereotypical ideas of what self-care looks like and not getting caught up in a cycle of things we *should* do, feel, or experience. It's about asking ourselves what gets in the way of our self-care and proactively creating a plan to find a way around these obstacles.

I had to change my own views about self-care after I got sick while working in India. As I started learning more about what makes us flourish and thrive as humans, I realized that self-care is really about resetting our nervous system. As human beings, our survival reactions are only meant to kick in for short periods of time to protect us from imminent harm. However, for many humanitarians working in fast-paced, high-stress jobs, survival mode becomes our default way of living.

This is problematic because survival mode activates our sympathetic nervous system, also known as the body's gas pedal because it prepares the body to literally fight or flee. Think of this as our brain ringing an alarm to let our body know something is wrong, that we're in imminent danger. In response, our body releases a cascade of stress hormones—including epinephrine, which mobilizes the body to fight or flee, and cortisol, which keeps our body revved up and on high alert. All of this is great when we actually are in danger, but it's incredibly damaging when it's perpetually turned on.

Our brains have evolved since the time when our prehistoric ancestors were trying to avoid being eaten by saber-tooth tigers, but as human beings, we have an inherent negativity bias—an evolutionary survival mechanism that helped our prehistoric ancestors identify threats like poisoned berries and saber-tooth tigers so they could stay alive. The oldest part of our brain continues to scan our environment through the lens of this negativity bias. The problem is, it can't differentiate between a real threat and a perceived one, nor can it tell the difference between a threat to our body as opposed to a threat to our identity or ego. As far as your brain is concerned, that vague email from your boss asking you to "come see me" or sitting in a traffic jam on the way to catch a flight presents the same level of danger as being physically attacked.

All these perceived threats to our identity and ego have become our modern-day saber-tooth tigers, leaving us in a near-constant state of survival. In this state of ever-present stress, restorative functions within the body slow down, and if unaddressed, over time lead to inflammation in the body and chronic health conditions. Practicing self-care helps activate our parasympathetic nervous system, also known as the body's brake pedal because it helps slow things down, usher in a sense of calm, and bring us back into a mode where our body can rest and heal.

When the parasympathetic nervous system is activated, there are six areas of well-being that contribute to human flourishing. Optimal well-being in each of these areas requires self-care practices that specifically address and refill each of these buckets. Rarely are all of these buckets completely full at the same time, and that's okay. Identifying which buckets need to be topped up can help us design a more targeted approach to self-care that feels more manageable and leaves us thriving and energized. The six areas are as follows.

- *Mental*: the ability to regularly experience or engage in mental or intellectual stimulation
- *Physical*: the ability to enhance the healthy functioning of your body through nutrition, rest, and movement
- *Emotional*: the ability to connect, express, process, and reflect on a full range of emotions
- *Practical*: the ability to fulfill core aspects of your daily life
- *Social*: the ability to connect, nurture, and deepen the relationships in your life
- *Spiritual*: the ability to feel connected to something bigger than yourself and tap into your own inner wisdom

When our stress response is activated in one or more of these areas, we need to choose self-care practices that specifically address that area. For example, if I've worked more than ten hours per day nonstop for two weeks and feel depleted, taking some earned time off would be a physical act of self-care. If I'm feeling despondent or disturbed by current events, taking a break from doom scrolling through news sites or social media would be an act of emotional self-care. If I'm stressed out because my finances are out of control, creating a budget would be a practical act of self-care. If I'm feeling lonely and isolated because I'm traveling for work and far from loved ones and friends, reaching out to someone I care about would be an example of social self-care. Reading books, journaling, walking in nature, or going to a temple, mosque, or church are all forms of spiritual self-care, with the list of self-care options being limited only by your imagination.

Each person is different, so the combination of choices and practices that best support you will vary. Because of this, it's important to try different practices to identify the ones that make you feel good and regenerate your mind, body, and spirit. It's also important to keep in mind that bigger self-care practices—like getting a massage, talking to a therapist, or taking an afternoon off—are important, but they tend to happen less frequently due to a lack of time or access to the activity or the aforementioned guilt. An alternative or supplement to periodic larger acts of self-care is practicing micro self-care practices throughout the day. Some examples include the following.

- Spending a few minutes before starting your day to practice gratitude
- Taking three deep breaths between tasks or meetings
- Walking to get a cup of coffee or tea with a colleague
- Checking in with your body every two to three hours to see what it needs and taking a corresponding action

Redefining self-care and learning to integrate micro self-care practices or creating a daily self-care routine—rather than relying solely on larger, more substantial acts of self-care—is not only more realistic and manageable day-to-day, but over time it's more impactful because these little ongoing practices help you intentionally regulate your nervous system throughout the day. With the parasympathetic nervous system activated, you're no longer operating in survival mode and are able to flourish and protect yourself from stress and burnout. Over time, these practices will lead to emotional regulation—moments when our nervous systems are calm and we're able to respond rather than react. Then, from this place of regulated emotions, we can use our positions of influence and leadership to transform the organization we work within and its systems.

SET CLEAR BOUNDARIES

We'll never be able to prioritize self-care if we allow it to slide to the bottom of the list every time an urgent matter comes up at work or someone needs us to do something. This is why boundaries are essential to practicing self-care—simple, but not easy. Most of us weren't taught the benefits of boundaries as children, and now as humanitarians, honoring our limits through boundary setting can feel rude, aggressive, or selfish. But boundaries aren't any of these things; they're gifts of clarity that help us create accountability over our time and energy. They allow us to feel safe and respected both physically and emotionally. They are shields that protect us from burnout, exhaustion, and illness and allow us to flourish and thrive.

The problem is, boundaries are rarely created alone—they're almost always accompanied by pushback and guilt. People who are controlling, manipulative, abusive, or don't have healthy boundaries of their own are typically the ones who push back when we set a boundary. While we can have compassion for these individuals, it's important to remember that their reaction is about them, not you. It's not your job to make your boundary okay for them. This is of course simple in concept, but not easy and requires a lot of practice. Some ways to strengthen your boundary-setting muscles include:

- *Reframe Your Guilt*: Guilt is a product of our *shaping* stories, especially ones about having to be everything to everyone or engaging in selfless service. While guilt isn't a pleasant emotion to experience, like any other negative emotion, working through it requires us to feel it and reframe the thought associated with it. We often forget that feelings are not facts and allow our feelings to control us and our actions. Reframing the thought requires us to tap into the truth of why we need the boundary and the consequence of not having it. For example, if you're asked to work through your lunch hour every day, you might feel guilty about stepping away for a short period of time when the work you do directly impacts the life of another human. In that moment, stop to consider the consequence of dropping the boundary. By working through lunch, you're ignoring your body's need for food and your mind's need to rest, both of which can impact your concentration and judgment and could detrimentally impact the person you're trying to serve.

- *Notice the Signals*: Our bodies send us signals when we're reaching a personal limit—cues like a tight jaw, clenched fists, fluttering stomach, or a general feeling of restlessness. This discomfort is a message from our body about an arising boundary need. For example, if my lower back hurts after sitting for hours at work, it may be my body telling me I need to get up and stretch or walk for a few minutes. In the midst of a busy day, taking time to practice this little act of self-care might feel challenging or indulgent, but the consequence of not taking the time I need for myself in this moment could be back pain so bad that it becomes impossible to concentrate or sit at my desk at all, maybe even requiring time off to heal.

- *Assess Priorities, Time, and Energy*: Feeling scarcity related to our time isn't unique to humanitarians. It's an all-too-common feeling in a societal culture that often values busyness and productivity above all else. But trying to do everything, be everything, and experience everything is an express train to burnout, resentment, and for humanitarians, compassion fatigue. Making a list of our priorities and examining where we spend our time and energy can help us determine whether we need to make any adjustments to ensure that by saying *yes* to addressing someone else's needs, we're not saying *no* to our own.

- *Practice Saying No*: As a humanitarian, saying *no* when someone is in need is incredibly challenging, especially if the reason we're saying *no* is because we need, or want, to do something for ourselves. If we're not used to asserting our boundaries, we may feel compelled to provide an explanation to validate our *no*. But explanations are a courtesy, not a requirement. If you choose to explain, be sure you understand why you're explaining and that it's not for the wrong reasons.

It takes time, space, and compassion to get used to setting boundaries for ourselves, but the more we practice doing so, the easier it becomes over time to hold them for ourselves, and to respect those set by others.

BECOME A RADICALLY HUMAN LEADER

My own experiences have taught me that it is possible to work in service of others *and* be healthy, happy, connected, and joyful—the two situations aren't mutually exclusive. But creating the circumstances for this duality in mission-driven humanitarian organizations requires moral courage and radically human leadership at all levels of the organization.

Practicing radically human leadership isn't about having a particular title or position in the organization. It's about using self-awareness, self-compassion, and curiosity to notice and address the stories we tell ourselves, so we can remove barriers that often hold us back from building trust with colleagues and connecting with each other on a human-to-human level. This is often challenging, because most of us are listening to an inner monologue that's grounded in self-criticism. The narrator of our internal stories goes by a lot of names—the inner critic, negative self-talk, the inner critical coach, and my personal favorite, the itty bitty shitty committee. But whatever the name, it holds us back because it says things to us we'd never consider saying to anyone else.

It's important to understand that telling ourselves these stories is actually an evolutionary survival mechanism from a time when our prehistoric ancestors knew that being kicked out of the tribe would likely result in death. Today, our default stories, which often consist of all the mean and terrible things we'd never say to anyone else, are our way of protecting ourselves by preemptively saying what we believe others might be thinking. By saying these things to ourselves first, our brain believes it's keeping us safe and ensuring our survival. But this "protection" often ends up preventing us from taking risks, trying new things, and pushing ourselves to grow. A lifetime of this inner monologue, coupled with our *shaping* stories, has created neural pathways—deep ruts in our brains. When our stress reaction gets activated, we default into one of these pathways and into familiar patterns of reaction.

These default patterns and reactions show up in our professional lives just as much as they do in our personal ones. The challenges and pressures inherent in most leadership roles often have leaders creating stories that support the belief that leading others requires an air of control, quashing any feelings of vulnerability, and hiding behind a mask of perfectionism at work. But when leaders use the bulk of their energy to hide behind these masks, they're not just prevented from working to their full capacity, they're putting pressure on peers and staff to hide behind masks of their own. This leads to everyone denying their own vulnerability and muddling through their days without asking for the help or support they need. In contrast, mindful awareness, self-compassion, and curiosity help us create new neural pathways that allow us to remove barriers to connection in the workplace—a foundational step toward human-centered leadership.

- *Cultivate mindful awareness*: This allows us to become the best versions of ourselves—as leaders and as humans. It requires us to be brave, empathetic, vulnerable, transparent, and accountable to ourselves first by looking in the proverbial mirror to see our own humanness—our flaws, biases, judgments, and fears. By looking inward with curiosity to explore our own *shaping* and *surviving* stories, we begin to *see* how they've influenced our decision-making and perceptions, and then we can *shift* them. We begin treating our staff with more understanding and grace. We lean into curiosity rather than making assumptions. We stop glorifying perfectionism and find lessons in our mistakes. We stop micromanaging our staff and treat them like adults who know how to manage their time. We provide meaningful feedback and acknowledge that people are doing the best they can in a given situation. We have the hard conversations and hold people accountable when they're not doing their part. This new awareness also insists that we *share* our individual stories to normalize vulnerability, cultivate greater connection, and create spaces of belonging where every staff member feels seen, heard, and valued.

- *Practice self-compassion*: If mindful awareness is what allows us to see our own humanity and that of others, self-compassion is what enables us accept it. Self-compassion teaches us to take the kindness we typically reserve for others and use it on ourselves. Again, simple but not easy. When we first start looking at our *shaping* and *surviving* stories and tune in to the voice of our inner critic, it can leave us feeling a little raw and off kilter—unsettled. In addition to being kind to ourselves by intentionally changing the words of our ever-present internal monologue, or by doing something nice for ourselves, self-compassion also reminds us that the hardship we're experiencing is temporary, and we're not alone—we're a part of a larger common humanity. The more we practice self-compassion and accept that as human beings we will make mistakes, the easier it becomes to treat the people around us with compassion, too.

- *Be curious*: In my work with leaders, I often note that most people don't wake up in the morning, stretch their arms high above their head, and declare, "Today I'm going to go out into the world to be mediocre!" The truth is, most people are genuinely doing the best they can in any given moment, and while their best may be different from our own—and it may change from one moment to the next—it's more likely than not that they're doing all they can in light of their current circumstances. Curiosity can help radically human leaders look beyond surface-level staff interactions or reactions without judgment, to connect more deeply. It can help radically human leaders create bridges of trust with their staff by simply taking a breath to reset their nervous system before reacting to a challenge, or asking questions rather than making assumptions about reactions or motives. As trust builds over time, so do our feelings of safety, autonomy, and dignity as human beings. And with this trust, we can all remove the masks we're hiding behind and connect more deeply with others.

Radically human leadership allows for imperfection and the messiness of being human. It's a way of being that invites us to stay connected to the true essence of who we are so we can connect with those same parts of the people around us.

FOR LEADERS AND ORGANIZATIONS: PROVIDE A HOLISTIC, HUMAN-CENTERED DUTY OF CARE

The term *duty of care* originated in tort law and in its simplest form refers to a legal obligation on each of us to take reasonable steps to protect others from predictable harm. For example, a store has a duty of care to inform customers that the floor is wet after it's been mopped so someone doesn't fall and hurt themselves, and auditors have a duty of care to confirm financial statements of a company to ensure they're not going to experience financial harm.

Duty of care covers a wide range of issues within a workplace and often shows up in organizations in the following ways.

- Ensuring a safe work environment for all staff
- Ensuring that staff don't regularly work long hours outside of emergency situations or without being compensated
- Defining staff roles, job descriptions, and assignments clearly
- Providing sufficient training and performance feedback
- Protecting staff from bullying, harassment, and discrimination

The duty of care practiced in many mission-driven humanitarian organizations has primarily focused on the physical health and safety of their staff. For example, organizations with global missions might ensure that flights are on reputable airlines, or provide every person on the team the vaccinations and medications needed to fight potential diseases and ailments, or offer information about foods to avoid and any restrictions on movement while in another country. In healthcare, during the COVID-19 pandemic duty of care included providing medical staff access to personal protective equipment and ensuring that they were compensated for working overtime. It's true that physical health and safety of staff is critical to ensuring they're able to do their work and meet the mission; however, in humanitarian organizations, a focus on physical health and safety is not enough, especially in a post-COVID-19 world.

According to a 2022 report from the World Health Organization, the COVID-19 pandemic triggered a 25% increase in the prevalence of anxiety and depression worldwide. Globally, an estimated 12 billion workdays are lost every year due to depression and anxiety at a cost of $1 trillion US dollars per year in decreased productivity. These statistics represent the general population. However, humanitarians often experience additional demands on their minds, bodies, and spirits that are not typically experienced in non-humanitarian workplaces. Exposure to direct and secondary trauma and violence, long working hours, back-to-back deployments, moral injury, and extended periods of time away from loved ones and friends leave humanitarians more susceptible to occupational stress, trauma, and mental-health challenges. Left unaddressed, these demands will impact the bottom line of the organization through attrition, lost productivity, low morale, and a loss of institutional knowledge.

Addressing these issues requires a new, more holistic duty-of-care framework that goes beyond protecting only the physical health, safety, security, and well-being of staff. A new framework must also address the mental, emotional, spiritual, and relational aspects of staff health and well-being. To do this, I propose the framework below, which consists of four key commitments.

- Commitment 1: Normalize and address occupational mental-health challenges and trauma
- Commitment 2: Evolve from metrics-driven cultures into human-centered ones
- Commitment 3: Support rest and recovery
- Commitment 4: Foster shared purpose and commitment

COMMITMENT 1: NORMALIZE AND ADDRESS OCCUPATIONAL MENTAL-HEALTH CHALLENGES AND TRAUMA

Some might argue that people working in mission-driven fields had been operating in stress-, crisis-, and trauma-mode long before the pandemic arrived and have done fine. I'd propose that they really weren't fine. While they've survived every bad thing that's happened until now, most people in this line of work are perpetually operating in survival mode, often without realizing it. Childhood traumas and other pivotal moments that shaped their worldview created their go-to survival responses, and they aren't something to simply outgrow over time.

Operating in survival mode isn't sustainable over the course of a career. Trying to compartmentalize stress, crisis, and trauma doesn't work, and insisting that these factors don't impact the way people show up at work simply isn't true, especially as our workforce demographics begin changing and a new generation of employees who have grown up prioritizing their well-being enters the workforce. Organizations across mission-driven sectors can support humanitarians in shifting from surviving to thriving by acknowledging and normalizing occupational mental-health challenges and trauma, designing cultures of empathy and compassion, and promoting trust and psychological safety across the organization.

Become a Trauma-Informed Organization

The term *VUCA*, often used in the business world, describes this situation of constant, unpredictable change that is now the norm. VUCA stands for volatility, uncertainty, complexity, and ambiguity, and operating in a VUCA environment can destabilize people and leave them feeling anxious, unmotivated, overwhelmed, and stuck in survival mode. The humanitarian sector as a whole has always faced change, but today's challenges, exacerbated by the COVID-19 pandemic, have created a VUCA environment, the effects of which are traumatic, on top of the traumas humanitarians encounter in the course of their work every day. Becoming a trauma-informed organization requires that all levels of the organization understand what trauma is, how it shows up in your line of work, and most importantly, how to normalize and acknowledge it to remove the associated stigma.

In its simplest form, trauma is an event or experience that affects our ability to cope and function. As research on trauma has advanced over time, a distinction has emerged to divide trauma into two main categories: big-T traumas and little-t traumas. Events that fall into the big-T trauma category typically include serious injury, sexual violence, natural disaster, or life-threatening situations. They're the traumas that create a memory that delineates our lives into before the event and after the event. When they happen, these traumas often have a noticeable impact and can leave us feeling powerless. However, it's important to understand that big-T traumas are not necessarily more significant or detrimental to the person experiencing them. Research shows that repeated exposure to little-t traumas causes more emotional harm and tends to be more dysregulating for people than a single big-T traumatic event.

Little-t traumas refer to ongoing stressors like poverty, chronic abuse, discrimination, race-based traumatic stress, subtle acts of exclusion (microaggressions), misogyny, and harassment. Add to these neglect in subtler forms like constantly changing job policies, inadequate communication, and a lack of caring in workplace cultures, and it's a wonder anyone can function each day. Because people have varying levels of resilience and different interpretations of what constitutes trauma, these little-t traumas can be hard to identify and, therefore, often go unaddressed. But these little-t traumas chip away at us, ultimately impacting our ability to flourish and thrive in our day-to-day lives.

Unfortunately, without acknowledging the impact of trauma on individuals and the systems in which they work, organizations send the message that what their people are experiencing isn't as important as the work they are expected to do.

In addition to these more general forms of trauma, humanitarians are also susceptible to occupational traumas including the following.

- *Vicarious trauma*: experience of trauma symptoms that can result from repeated exposure to other people's trauma and their stories of traumatic events
- *Secondary traumatic stress*: emotional duress that results when an individual hears about the firsthand trauma experiences of another
- *Post-traumatic stress*: unprocessed trauma resulting from exposure to life-threatening or highly distressing events that lasts more than one month and affects daily functioning

- *Moral injury*: perpetrating, failing to prevent, bearing witness to, or learning about acts that transgress one's deeply held beliefs and expectations
- *Compassion fatigue*: a combination of physical, emotional, and spiritual depletion associated with caring for others who are in significant pain and physical distress
- *Burnout*: prolonged physical and psychological exhaustion related to a person's work

Becoming a trauma-informed organization takes time and radically human leaders. A few things organizations and leaders can do to get there include the following.

- *Listen and acknowledge*: A willingness to listen and acknowledge what another person is experiencing is foundational to trauma-informed leadership. This requires giving people time and opportunity to share their experiences and then validating them through active listening. Active listening includes empathizing, asking open-ended questions, and mirroring back what you've heard. This allows the person to realize you've heard them and helps foster connection. Listening and acknowledging isn't about fixing or reframing the situation. It's about giving someone the gift of presence and ensuring that they feel seen and heard.
- *Create transparency around available support*: When a person is experiencing distress or trauma as a result of something that has happened in their own life or in the workplace, they may need access to resources to support their mental, emotional, physical, or relational health and well-being. However, because of the stigma associated with this type of help, people often won't ask. Therefore, it's important to make support broadly available, and to provide information about how to access this support through a variety of platforms, including emails, text messages, flyers or posters, and during all-hands or team meetings. Ensuring that people know what support is available and providing them with the time and information they need to access it makes it more likely that they will choose the intervention that best supports their needs in a given situation.
- *Lead by example*: It's easy to read a set of talking points urging staff to practice self-care or take advantage of available support, but modeling it is far more challenging—yet also far more effective. Leaders set the tone in the organization, and if they're sending emails

at all hours of the night, working late, coming to work frustrated and angry, or regularly blaming, judging, and criticizing others, that behavior will trickle down through the organization. Leaders need to learn how to regulate and, when needed, reset their own nervous system and to model authenticity and vulnerability by asking for help. Something as simple as taking three long, deep breaths between tasks or meetings, taking a short 10-to-15-minute walk during lunch, engaging in a regular gratitude practice, or saying those three dreaded words—"I don't know"—can go a long way toward resetting the nervous system and showing your staff that you're human, just like they are.

Occupational mental-health challenges and traumas are inherent to humanitarian work. Organizations that want to retain staff, build institutional knowledge, and see sustained success in the future must create a trauma-informed culture. Organizations that fail to adapt to the health and well-being needs of their staff by acknowledging and normalizing the realities of the work will never effectively meet their mission.

Design Cultures of Empathy

I've heard the phrase "our systems are broken" too many times over the course of my career. But the truth is, our systems aren't broken. They're doing exactly what they were designed to do. People often forget that we live in a world of systems that were created by humans. If the humans are traumatized—and almost every human being has been—the systems will be, too.

Every system is built by human beings who bring their own lenses, created by lifetimes of experiences—Big-T and little-t traumas experienced firsthand and even generational traumas unwittingly passed down from one generation to the next through DNA. These experiences exert enormous influence over leaders' actions, reactions, and choices. When they set out to create new systems, their own stories influence what they're creating, which often results in systems that perpetuate a lack of diversity, equity, inclusion, and belonging. And no matter how great the mission of an organization, the systems almost always fail to prioritize workforce health and well-being, which eventually leads to high turnover, low staff morale, and a loss of institutional knowledge.

This is further exacerbated because we operate in cultures that dismiss empathy, compassion, and connection in favor of productivity and perfectionism. This not only results in mission-driven organizations valuing technical skills above relational skills, but it also creates the foundation upon which toxic workplace cultures are built. Leaders in these organizations are rarely taught how to connect on a human-to-human level, or to value that skill in others, and instead they lead from a place of fear. I've worked with many leaders over the years who refused to hold people accountable because they were afraid to have the hard conversation, or who wouldn't acknowledge when someone on their team was in pain because they were afraid to say or do the wrong thing. Fear-based leadership isn't sustainable, healthy, or effective.

When we're confronted with someone who is in pain or has experienced a trauma, we generally make assumptions, try to comfort them, try to help them fix the situation, try to fix the situation for them, or try to relate to the person by telling them about our own experience. This is also where we sometimes engage in toxic positivity—quickly reframing the situation with platitudes like "everything happens for a reason" or "this too shall pass." In mPEAK, we explain that while these statements might be an expression of wisdom and truth under other circumstances, when they're used as an automatic reaction to pain, they're actually examples of spiritual bypassing, an attempt to find a silver lining in every negative experience. While these can be natural reactions in moments of discomfort, they're not always helpful. They can instead minimize or dismiss another person's pain as we seek to avoid our own feelings of unease or awkwardness.

Empathy is the ability to put yourself in another person's shoes and share their feelings. Many leaders struggle with how to connect with and support others when they themselves are stressed out or dealing with their own trauma. In those moments, the thought of taking on another person's fear, sadness, grief, or trauma can feel overwhelming and often results in leaders simply ignoring the issue. But empathy doesn't require us to do anything extraordinary, fix anything, or say something in particular. As humans, our brains are wired to mimic both the emotions and behaviors of the people around us through mirror neurons in our brains. These mirror neurons are what give us the capacity to experience and express empathy—one of the linchpins of cultures built on connection and trust, and at the heart of radically human leadership. Through empathy, we're meeting the person where they are in a given moment, and connecting to what they might be thinking, feeling, or experiencing.

When my mom passed away, for several months my boss Jennifer would ask, "How are you?" and then give me the time to share how I felt. If I was having a bad day, she didn't try to fix it or relate by talking about herself— she simply acknowledged and validated my experience. Knowing she was taking time out of her very busy schedule to ask me how I was made me feel seen and valued. The flip side of this was a colleague who came up to me on my first day back in the office and commented on how nice it must have been for me to be able to take such a long vacation. His assumption left me feeling hurt and essentially put a wall between us, rather than creating a feeling of connection.

This is one example. However, intentionally designing cultures of empathy requires many little acts, perhaps including the following.

- Giving your full attention to people in meetings rather than being on your phone or computer
- Carving out a couple of minutes at the beginning of a meeting to get to know more about your team's lives or interests
- Taking a few minutes to provide constructive feedback to help team members grow and flourish in their work
- Acknowledging when someone seems upset or not quite like themselves

Everyone is busy, but taking a few minutes to connect through empathy can have long-lasting positive impacts for individuals and for the organization as a whole. It also lets people know they matter, and when people feel like they matter, they connect with others in the workplace over a shared feeling of purpose and meaning.

Heal Root Issues and Organizational Trauma

Trauma is an occupational reality in mission-driven humanitarian organizations: primary trauma, vicarious trauma, critical-incident stress, and moral injury, just to name a few. Just as these traumas impact individuals, there's another, somewhat pervasive, unrecognized trauma that impacts organizations across the humanitarian sector: *organizational trauma.*

Many mission-driven humanitarian organizations are (generally unwittingly) contributing to the trauma experienced by their workforce. And we aren't talking about it enough, which I understand. It can be hard for mission-driven humanitarian organizations charged with serving and protecting vulnerable human beings to get on board with the idea that existing policies or practices, or the demanding nature of the organization's work itself, might be traumatizing the organization as a whole and causing their people and culture to suffer.

Leaders across these organizations may feel resentful, wondering why their employees insist on complaining when the organization is providing wellness programs and other perks and has stated an intention to create more diversity and inclusion. But all the perks and programs and statements of intention won't have the desired impact as long as root issues continue to remain unacknowledged and unresolved within the organization. Even with the best of intentions, organizational trauma can take root.

I learned about the concept of organizational trauma from the seminal work on the topic, *Organizational Trauma and Healing*, written by two of my mentors, Pat Vivian and Shana Hormann. Their work highlights that there are many things that contribute to organizational trauma, including, but not limited to:

- A lack of transparency in organizational communication and decision-making, which leaves staff speculating or gossiping about leadership motives and choices as they relate to fulfilling the mission
- Top-down issues that don't take account of workforce health, well-being, and other needs
- Perceptions of or actual racial, social, or other inequities or unfairness in the workplace
- Outdated policies and procedures related to hiring, firing, promotions, and developmental opportunities

Each of these factors, and so many others, are like wounds to the heart of the organization, which, when left unaddressed, result in pieces of the system becoming traumatized. Collectively we're so focused on addressing the overwhelming needs of the mission that we stop noticing when things aren't right within the organization itself. Over time, the cumulative impact of not addressing these issues as they arise is that organizational trauma gets woven into the fabric of the culture, and eventually it becomes the norm. When I work with organizations to heal root issues and organizational trauma, I often share an anecdote about two young fishes swimming along. An older fish passes by and says, "Hello, boys. How's the water today?" The two fishes continue to swim in silence for a few minutes until one turns to the other and says, "What the heck is water?" Organizational trauma is the water we're swimming in without even realizing it.

That's the not-so-great news. The better news is that we can reset and redesign once-traumatized cultures, transforming them into cultures of connection and belonging where the staff—and by extension the mission—flourish. Leaders and organizations can begin healing root issues and organizational trauma through methods that include the following.

- *Figuring out where the organization is right now:* Not where leaders *think* it is, but where it really, truly is when it comes to organizational trauma. Organizations need to have the facts and understand the current lay of the land before they can devise an effective plan. It's helpful to bring in an outside consultant who specializes in organizational trauma to ensure the organization is taking the right approach.
- *Acknowledging organizational history:* This can be hard; organizational amnesia is common, especially when it comes to racial and social inequities, biases, microaggressions, and prejudice. None of us likes to think about times when we could have done better but didn't. However, acknowledging mistakes and choices of the past, or the impact of inherited policies and procedures, is an integral step to healing those forms of trauma and an absolute necessity for creating a more diverse, equitable, inclusive, and accessible organizational culture.
- *Strengthen the organization's core mission and align it with organizational values:* Engage staff to revisit the organization's core mission—not just in relation to the *people your organization serves* but in relation to the *people who serve in your organization* as well. Once the organization has solidified its mission, the staff can begin to identify and operationalize aligned core values that are then integrated into all aspects of organizational culture through annual operating plans and other messaging, training programs, and meetings.
- *Create processes that serve the people in the organization:* Healing root issues and organizational trauma ultimately moves the organization toward building a more grounded, inclusive, and connected culture. This type of culture change requires scaffolding and structure to

support new processes that will serve the people working within the organization.

- *Foster organizational spirit:* Find ways to nurture organizational spirit and foster a sense of belonging among your team. You're all working toward the same mission and experiencing many of the same challenges and stresses along the way; you truly are all in it together. So do what you can to create a sense of equity, belonging, and connection that makes everyone feel seen, heard, and valued.
- *Ensure leadership buy-in:* Designing a culture that moves away from organizational trauma and toward psychological safety starts from the top down. It's crucial to ensure that the entire leadership team is on board and understands the role they can play in supporting their people. When you have leadership buy-in—when the people at the top understand how organizational trauma impacts not just the workforce, but the bottom line—it becomes infinitely easier to introduce lasting change. So encourage all leaders to model kindness, gratitude, compassion, and healthy boundaries.

Organizational trauma is common, particularly across the humanitarian sector, but it isn't inevitable or permanent. Recognizing it and acknowledging it can be hard, but it can also be the most significant way to improve not just the lives of an organization's workforce, but of the people the organization is designed to serve, too.

COMMITMENT 2: EVOLVE FROM METRICS-DRIVEN CULTURES INTO HUMAN-CENTERED ONES

We are, as a culture, obsessed with metrics. It's understandable. After all, organizations are accountable to the people they serve, to their boards or the public, and to stakeholders. There are targets to aim for and goals to achieve. And when they're met, we know we've done a good job. They're the way we collectively judge our success.

Metrics in and of themselves aren't bad. But they become problematic when everything else—like bringing empathy and compassion to the workplace, or fostering a culture that leads to healthy, happy employees—is viewed as an added bonus, a nice-to-have.

The counterintuitive truth is that the more we focus on putting people at the center of our organizations, the more we end up hitting those benchmarks and the better we are at fulfilling our operational needs. Unfortunately, that's the opposite of the way we're taught to do it. We're taught to see humans as resources. We've come to accept that because we're all so stretched in the workplace, we have neither the time nor the energy to deal with the emotional side of being human. We're continually discouraged from stepping out of our work personas and showing our human vulnerability.

But working in this way leads to organizations that are ineffective, inefficient, and burn through staff at an alarming rate. And this is uniquely challenging for mission-driven humanitarian organizations, where the ethos is caring for others. Because humanitarians believe so passionately in the work we do, we often push ourselves beyond our limits, stringing ourselves out in the process. And if we're not supported by a human-centered culture, if we're required to constantly hide our vulnerability, and if well-being isn't the foundation upon which the culture is built, we *will* burn out.

It's worth considering whether organizations are really meeting their mission if achieving the metrics comes at the cost of the health and well-being of staff in the form of high attrition, low morale, loss of institutional knowledge, burnout, compassion fatigue, moral injury, trauma, and chronic health conditions. We all have targets to hit and operational needs to take care of, but we have people to take care of too. And when we commit to taking care of our people, when we create a human-centered organization that supports staff and protects not only their physical health but also their mental, emotional, and relational health and energy, we create a working environment in which people are willing *and* able to achieve exactly what you need them to.

When organizations shift from a metrics-focused culture to a human-centered one, they equip, empower, and encourage their staff to care for themselves as they care for others—to serve others without sacrificing themselves—sending a message that the health and well-being of their staff matters. *That their staff matters.* But there isn't a quick fix. Shifting organizational culture requires organizations to play the long game and invest time and resources into prioritizing social connection, healing root issues and organizational trauma, and creating opportunities to share stories.

Prioritize Social Connection

As human beings, we are hardwired for social connection—an evolutionary survival mechanism passed down from our prehistoric ancestors who relied on each other to meet basic needs and learned (often the hard way) that being left behind or ostracized from the group would likely result in death. Connection is a fundamental human need, as necessary to our survival as food, water, and shelter. The quality of our social connections at work—supportive interactions, a sense of belonging, and effective teamwork—improve our well-being and can protect against harmful effects of workplace stress.

Research shared in the US Surgeon General's 2023 Advisory on the Healing Effects of Social Connection and Community shows that social connection positively influences our physical, cognitive, and mental health and well-being, and it boosts our ability to flourish and thrive in our work and life. On the flip side, social isolation and loneliness have been directly correlated with premature death—as much as smoking up to 15 cigarettes a day—and poor health directly related to a number of diseases including cardiovascular disease, hypertension, and diabetes.

Prioritizing social connection and making it a foundational element of human-centered cultures is essential to belonging. Social connection strengthens mental, emotional, spiritual, and relational health and well-being and builds trust within the organization. And human-centered cultures of connection and belonging don't just happen—they're created through everyday moments of engagement grounded in gratitude, kindness, respect, and empathy. Over time, these shared values and beliefs drive individual and collective behaviors and ultimately shape organizational programs and policies. Consider the following as a few ways to cultivate social connection.

- *Start on day one*: There are few things worse than showing up for work on the first day and feeling like nobody knew you were coming. Onboarding new employees is a great opportunity to show new staff members from the start that they matter. A robust onboarding program should not only help new staff understand the technical aspects of their job and highlight key policies and procedures, it should give them a better understanding of organizational values, norms, and culture. Assigning each new staff member to a more-seasoned one as a mentor can help them build relationships and connections on day one.

- *Create a gratitude-rich environment*: Gratitude and recognition are about more than simply saying thank you or handing out awards. They're about appreciating what is valuable and meaningful for an individual or team. Expressing gratitude not only promotes social connection, but research compiled by the National Institute of Health shows that employees with high levels of gratitude have been shown to experience higher levels of well-being, engagement, and productivity. Many employee awards and recognition programs celebrate individuals who contributed to a large project or helped the organization reach a key metric. While this type of recognition can be nice, it's often limited to a small number of people, when the reality is that an organization functions and succeeds because of the work of many people. Celebrating little wins along the way can create levity in day-to-day work, while also making individuals feel seen and valued for their contributions. Fostering a gratitude-rich environment, where acknowledgment and gratitude flow freely up, down, and across the organization can be meaningful and result in positive emotions for the people receiving the praise, as well as their colleagues who witness it. A few ways to celebrate the little wins include building appreciation and praise into team meetings, sharing team success with senior leaders, creating a wall of gratitude where team members can share their thanks and appreciation with each other, and setting aside a few minutes on your calendar every week to create a consistent practice of showing gratitude and appreciation to the people around you.

- *Support work/life harmony*: Work/life *balance* implies that all things are equal, and can leave us feeling like we're failing when we can't find the balance we're looking for. Work/life harmony, on the other hand, is our ability to integrate personal and professional demands by bringing the different pieces of our lives together and making them work in the way that best supports us from one moment to the next. Supporting work/life harmony requires organizations to implement policies and strategies that allow staff to foster meaningful relationships outside of work as well as within their workplace. Longer hours don't equate to greater productivity, but extended periods of time away from family, friends, and loved ones has a proven negative impact on our quality of life outside of work. Organizations can support work/life harmony by respecting staff boundaries between personal and work time, alleviating anxiety and fear of missing work demands, and encouraging staff to rest and connect outside of work. In addition, creating predictable schedules with flexibility built into start and end times allows staff to attend to personal and family needs or emergencies that arise. Also, depending on the nature and requirements of the work, if organizations can provide staff with more autonomy over how, when, and where they work, it can help minimize work/life conflicts and build trust within the team.

Significant evidence demonstrates the link between social connection and our health, well-being, and even our risk for premature death. Given that most adults spend the majority of their waking hours at work, it's important to prioritize social connection both within and outside of the workplace.

Promote Trust and Psychological Safety Across the Organization

Creating healthy, happy, and innovative cultures grounded in connection and belonging not only requires empathy, but also requires trust and psychological safety. Trust is fundamental to our sense of safety, autonomy, and dignity as human beings. It is also an integral part of every relationship we have. When we trust someone, we feel safe to share what is important to us, including our thoughts, ideas, efforts, hopes, and concerns. When others trust us, they reciprocate in kind. It doesn't mean we always agree, just that we listen to, respect, and value what each other has to offer. In fact, trust allows us to disagree, debate, and test each other's thinking as we work together to find ideas and solutions.

Psychological safety promotes trust by creating an environment of rewarded vulnerability where people can remove the masks of fear and show up as their whole selves. Psychologically safe environments empower staff to take interpersonal risks and make mistakes—the opposite of cultures that have normalized perfectionism and blame. Empathy denotes understanding. Understanding leads to trust. And trust promotes teamwork and collaboration, as well as providing a sense of safety where people can take their masks off and connect more deeply with those around them—an empathic cascade. The bonds established through these little, everyday moments of empathy and connection in the workplace ensure that people will come together and support each other when their organization faces hardship and crisis situations.

When the pandemic first started and many organizations moved to 100% telework, some were able to manage basic logistics as they related to schedules and equipment distribution. But very few, if any, organizations understood how the resulting trauma, lack of meaningful connection, and isolation people experienced would impact their staff's mental health and well-being, and in turn, their ability to be productive.

Since those early days of uncertainty in 2020, we've learned that on a good day, our mind wanders about 50% of the time. According to David Michels, a senior executive coach specializing in global transformation and change practice, in times of high stress and crisis, mental noise reduces the ability to process information by up to 80%, on average. Attention spans shrink to just twelve minutes or less with the ability to retain no more than three main ideas. Under stress, people also have difficulty hearing, understanding, and recalling information.

I shared this information with leaders in the RAIO Daring Leaders Project just as COVID started. By the end of the year, we'd learned through program metrics that the teams with leaders who demonstrated empathy by regularly checking in, acknowledging workers' fears, and meeting them where they were emotionally formed tight bonds and supported each other through the uncertainty.

Since then, the realities of the individual and collective trauma and the grief we've experienced as a global society—both the loss of life and the loss of life as we once knew it—have started to sink in. Tack on the politicization of masking and vaccinations, the assaults on women's rights, wars and famine around the world, health and financial stressors, lack of personal and professional boundaries, renewed calls for racial and social justice, and any number of existential crises, and we've got a whole lot of people who are essentially walking powder kegs trying to navigate their daily lives without exploding—or imploding. These explosions and implosions can be minimized or avoided by fostering an environment where staff feel safe to express their opinions and are invited to engage with leaders to inform decisions that impact how they work. A few suggestions for building trust and psychological safety are as follows.

- *Normalize making mistakes*: When leaders admit that they don't know something or that they made a mistake, their vulnerability and directness shows staff that it's okay not to be perfect. In addition to owning our mistakes, it's important to forgive staff when they make mistakes. Doing this requires awareness of our desire to react, and then breathing and resetting the nervous system so we can respond with intention, focusing on the positives: the mistake was caught, it can be fixed, and a lesson can be learned from the experience. Normalizing mistakes promotes creativity and innovation by encouraging staff to take risks and think bigger when encountering a problem, rather than operating from a place of fear.

- *Create brave spaces*: Brave spaces are different from safe spaces in that they acknowledge that we're humans who come to each situation with our own wounds and scars. Brave spaces recognize our imperfections and the likelihood that we will make mistakes and hurt others, but that when we do, we will own them and work to repair the hurt and damage we may have caused. Bringing your team together and asking them what they need for this to be a brave space, where they feel safe and can show up fully with the others on the team, helps leaders and staff understand their own needs and the needs of their colleagues, allowing them to meet them where they are. Memorializing this list of operating agreements, sharing them with the team, and regularly referencing them can empower the team to compassionately hold each other accountable to the agreements and, in turn, to each other.

- *Adopt a beginner's mindset*: Many leaders believe they must have the answer to every question and the right solution for every problem. This belief and the perfectionistic tendencies it supports tends to quash creativity and innovation, because trying to be perfect closes us off to hearing other ideas that might be better in a given situation. Approaching initiatives, team processes, and meetings with curiosity and a beginner's mindset helps us remember that just because something has been done a certain way for a long time doesn't mean it can't be changed or improved upon. It also reminds the team that you're human, and it's okay for them to be, too.

Trust and psychological safety are essential for cultivating support and connection among team members and minimizing the negative impacts of adversity and hardship on staff and the organization as a whole.

Create Opportunities to Share Stories

I sometimes wonder if my desire to alleviate the pain and suffering of people in need would have been as strong—as visceral—had it not been for the issues with mental health, displacement, and violence I grew up witnessing, experiencing, and surviving. I also wonder how much less shame I might have carried or how much faster I might have healed in the face of compassion fatigue, vicarious trauma, moral injury, and burnout had I known I was not alone in my suffering.

When I work with leaders, I often talk about how compassion, curiosity, empathy, and openness are some of the greatest tools we have in our leadership toolbox. In fact, they're some of the greatest tools we have as humans just trying to get through life as best we can. They also are the foundation for creating connection and belonging for ourselves and with the people around us.

The Industrial Revolution is credited with making our workplaces more efficient and standardized; for me, though, the lasting legacy of that time period has been the loss of our ability to show up and be human in professional spaces. We've instead been conditioned to believe that we have to bifurcate our lives into the personal and the professional, and while the professional often bleeds into the personal, we do everything we can to ensure the personal never bleeds into the professional.

But this bifurcated existence isn't sustainable. We're all whole human beings, and regardless of how well we think we can compartmentalize our lives, we simply can't leave pieces of ourselves at the door when we come into work, especially in this age of remote work where the lines between the personal and the professional are more blurred than ever.

What if there was a way to allow us to be whole at all times, including in the workplace?

Turns out, there is: *sharing* our stories.

Our need to share stories is inherent to being human. Storytelling is yet another evolutionary survival mechanism that allows us to make meaning of what's happening in our life at any given moment and to discern between friend and foe, danger and safety. Our stories help us understand who we are as individuals and our role in the world. They influence and build the lenses through which we see and experience the circumstances and people around us.

Yet storytelling isn't practiced or promoted across much of the humanitarian field. I had to search for answers in silence and navigate unnecessary shame because there were no spaces where I felt safe and empowered enough to say, "Last week, while I was interviewing an applicant, I couldn't stop crying, and I'm worried that something is wrong with me." And truly, without the memory of Wade, my first boss at the Colorado Attorney General's office, and his wisdom about the impact of our work on our mental health and his decision to address it (see chapter 13), I don't know where I would be today.

But what if my organization had acknowledged the occupational realities of this line of work and created opportunities for me to gather with colleagues to share and explore our stories together in community? To recognize that we are not alone in our humanity? To find lessons and grow through our trauma together? What if I'd had access to brave spaces where, even for a few minutes, my colleagues and I could have set aside the armor we carried around all day and bonded over shared interests or sought comfort and support in the face of challenge? I know it would have taken away much of the shame I carried for years, believing there was something wrong with me. It would have helped me better prioritize my health and well-being, allowing me to be more present and connected to my work and enhancing my ability to meet my organization's mission.

Story-healing circles are a form of storytelling rooted in the *healing circles* widely used among Native Americans, First Nations people of Canada, and indigenous peoples, and are a powerful tool for addressing and healing occupational traumas through storytelling. Story-healing circles don't require much preparation and allow us to share our life experiences at work and support perspective taking—the act of perceiving a situation or understanding a concept from an alternative point of view—as well as practice empathy, cultural humility, listening, courage, vulnerability, and healing. A story-healing circle is a small group of individuals coming together, in person or virtually, to share stories focused on a common theme. Regardless of the theme or topic, the act of each person sharing their story allows for a rich and complex shared experience to emerge, creating a feeling of common humanity and allowing people to see similarities and differences in their experiences. Story-healing circles can be light and playful or deep and serious, depending on the intentions and desired outcomes for the group.

Here are a few low-, medium-, and high-lift suggestions for integrating story-healing circles into day-to-day operations in the workplace.

- *Three-Minute Story-Healing Circles (low lift)*: Take three minutes at the beginning of a meeting to give team members an opportunity to answer a simple prompt like "what I'm grateful for today" or "the highlight of my weekend" or "the project I'm most excited about." This is an easy way for people to bond and connect before jumping into the substance of the meeting. This type of story-healing circle has the leader invite the team to divide up into groups of three and gives each person one minute to respond to the prompt. Once the three minutes are up, you can debrief with the full group by asking if anything stood out in the conversation or how people feel after the interaction. This type of story-healing circle can be done in person, virtually, or in a hybrid situation.

- *Coffee Chats (medium lift)*: In chapter 17, I mention that my RAIO Thrive team created coffee chats to cultivate connection and address the fear, anxiety, and social isolation people were feeling in the early days of the pandemic. These chats were virtual story-healing circles that lasted between thirty and forty-five minutes and were limited to no more than twelve people and a facilitator to ensure that everyone who wanted to would have a chance to speak. We initially selected themes like anxiety, grief, and navigating uncertainty because these were issues with which we knew the workforce was struggling. As new issues arose—a potential furlough, the murder of George Floyd, the challenges of homeschooling children—we created corresponding chats. We also polled the workforce to get their input about topics they wanted to discuss. Within months of starting, we were offering eight to ten different coffee chats each week, facilitated by various levels of leaders. What made these chats particularly effective is that they were open to the entire workforce, which meant supervisors from our offices in Chicago and Boston might be in a chat with staff from our offices in Los Angeles, New York, Houston, and Miami— allowing people to get to know their colleagues from across the organization. In addition, by engaging senior leaders as facilitators, we gave our staff unique opportunities to get to know their leaders and vice versa on a human-to-human level.

- *Post-incident or -deployment debriefings (high lift)*: These types of story-healing circles generally take place after a crucial incident such as the death of a colleague or a traumatic national or global event like 9/11, or after staff return from being deployed to other locations. These story-healing circles can be anywhere from one to three hours in duration and ideally should be limited to ten to twelve people to make it more comfortable for sharing experiences. These types of story-healing circles should always have a facilitator who is trained or certified to facilitate the topic at hand and is comfortable running a small group.

It's important to remember that integrating story-healing circles into the culture of an organization takes time, especially since we've been conditioned for so long to keep our thoughts and emotions to ourselves. Part of this process is helping staff and leaders understand that vulnerability doesn't require us to share our whole life's story, just our humanity. In leading my team, vulnerability looked like explaining my regrets about my early leadership experiences and micromanagement. It looked like asking for help as I navigated my grief after my mom passed away. It looked like admitting I didn't have all the answers and being open, curious, and not threatened when members of my team had suggestions or solutions for problems we were trying to solve.

When writing this book, being vulnerable didn't require me to share all the details of my life, but rather, it was about sharing those thoughts, actions, and experiences that provided context for my experiences at work and with my career or that seemed relevant and might help readers connect more deeply with their own personal and professional experiences. In a similar vein, story-healing circles create vulnerability through shared experiences in our work and its impact. Organizations can start with lower-lift story-healing circles and work their way up, the important factor being consistency—in terms of how often circles are offered, how long they last, and how they're facilitated. For this reason, it's important to have trained facilitators who understand the intentions of the circle and who can keep circle participants on track, ensuring that everyone has equal space and attention.

COMMITMENT 3: SUPPORT REST AND RECOVERY

As more people considered the fragility of life in the aftermath of the initial waves of COVID-19, they began to reevaluate their values and definitions of success, leading to movements like the Great Resignation and quiet quitting. These were coping strategies to help individuals make meaning out of the trauma they had experienced. They craved a slower pace of life, greater work/life harmony, and to forge deeper connections with the people around them.

In response, many organizations launched corporate well-being programs, arranged for organization-wide self-care days or weeks, created awards and recognition programs, and instituted gratitude weeks or months. While these are all nice gestures, on their own they're not enough—and likely never will be—because they don't actually address or heal root issues or build self-awareness. Healing root issues and building self-awareness requires organizations to integrate recovery into the daily workflow, to stop viewing exhaustion as a badge of honor, and most importantly, to normalize rest and recovery and make it a part of the culture.

Staff health and well-being is bigger than any one program or initiative. It's an acknowledgement of the occupational realities of mission-driven humanitarian work *and* must be a value that's integrated into the fabric of organizational culture. Organizations can begin this process of integration by creating conditions for work and recovery to coexist, cultivating a workplace culture that values restorative care, and promoting rest rather than normalizing burnout.

Create Conditions for Work and Recovery to Peacefully Coexist

As human beings, we inherently know that rest and recovery are necessary for optimal performance at work. But organizations rarely think to build recovery time into the workday, especially since it feels counter to the culture of busyness we're conditioned to uphold and carry on. Beyond higher levels of productivity, research noted in *Forbes* magazine has shown that taking breaks from work can increase job satisfaction, creativity, mental health, and well-being among staff. This doesn't refer to just vacation days, sick days, and mental-health days, but regular breaks during the day. While organizations may argue that these types of efforts negatively impact the bottom line, research shows that making long-term investments in workforce health and well-being supports retention and the development of institutional knowledge, and positively impacts recruitment of new staff.

I personally noticed the impact of taking breaks every time I was posted abroad at a US embassy. There was a clear distinction between American staff and locally employed staff—people from the country who were hired to work in that particular embassy. Both groups worked hard and met their metrics and targets, but unlike the Americans, who often worked long hours, had use-or-lose paid time off left at the end of the year, and regularly skipped breaks, local staff had seamlessly made work/life harmony a way of life. Work was a place they came to for a set number of hours, during which they used their breaks to connect with colleagues over coffee or lunch. Rarely did I see anyone eating at their desks or working late. Local staff used their weekends and vacation days to disconnect from work, connect with family and friends, and recharge. Later, when I led the Thrive team, I made a point of encouraging my team members to find ways to incorporate recovery into their workday. I found that people who were exhausted and burned out when assigned to work for my team became more energized and engaged with their colleagues and the work within a matter of weeks.

While these actions and behaviors may be a natural way of life in some cultures, they can be learned and adopted within all humanitarian organizations. The following are some suggestions for doing so.

- *Proactively encourage support and recovery options*: Many organizations *reactively* offer support to staff after they're already stressed out, burned out, or struggling with occupational mental-health challenges. Proactively encouraging support and recovery options from day one clearly conveys to staff that their health and well-being are important. But taking the extra step of helping them create a plan for integrating recovery practices into their workday is the difference between nice words and meaningful action. Things like one-on-one or group coaching sessions or story-healing circles focused on topics like mindset, nutrition, movement, and recovery are great ways for staff to come together and support each other as they work to navigate these issues. In addition, mindfulness apps or websites can provide breathwork and meditation breaks that last anywhere from one to thirty minutes and can help staff reset their nervous system in the midst of a busy workday. Taking the time to help staff figure out how best to incorporate these types of routines into their daily workflow helps integrate work/life harmony and create happier, healthier, and more engaged employees.

- *Empower staff to take microbreaks*: Many organizations build in 15-minute breaks and half-hour lunch breaks. However, in cultures where everything is deemed to be urgent, breaks are often ignored by staff who feel pressured to keep working. Microbreaks are defined as any brief activity that helps to break up the monotony of physically or mentally draining tasks. These breaks work because they're a form of psychological detachment—you mentally disengage from work-based tasks and allow your brain to recover. In addition, empowering staff to choose how to recover based on their needs helps foster self-awareness of mind/body reactions and needs, allows individuals a sense of autonomy and agency over aspects of their workday, and builds trust because their workday isn't being micromanaged. Typically, microbreaks consist of short activities that last anywhere from a few seconds to several minutes and result in boosted attention spans, lower stress levels, and reduced fatigue. Microbreaks can include stretching for two minutes at your desk; watching a short, funny video; walking to the window and focusing on something outside; taking a short walk around the building; listening to ocean or nature sounds for one minute; leaning back in your chair and staring at the ceiling; or closing your eyes and taking three deep breaths between tasks or meetings.

- *Model good habits*: Working in the humanitarian sector is demanding, fast-paced work that requires creativity, productivity, and the ability to navigate new challenges on a regular basis. Any one of these things on their own can be difficult—taken together, they can feel like a backpack full of rocks that humanitarians must carry around every day. As humans, we need a lot of energy to process information, create strategies, and find new ways to handle various challenges. As much as we'd like to believe we're infallible, the truth is, there isn't an endless energy supply. Energy reserves must be continuously replenished, and the best way to do this is to take breaks. Leaders who talk to their teams about the importance of taking breaks but regularly work through lunch, work late, and work on weekends send a conflicting message that can leave staff uncomfortable or unwilling to take their own breaks for fear of being seen as weak or unable to handle the demands of the work. However, leaders who regularly take a few minutes to take a walk, grab a coffee, or close their eyes and breathe, and who ensure that they're not available at all times help to normalize the need for recovery, making it more likely that their team members will follow suit. As counterintuitive as it sounds, an entire team taking time to slow down for moments throughout the day has the capacity to improve productivity, engagement, and the overall quality of their work.

Cultivate Workplace Cultures That Value Restorative Care

Sleep and rest are not only essential to work, they're a necessity for good physical and mental health and directly impact our quality of life. But we live and operate in cultures of busyness, where we're chronically exhausted and on the verge of burnout.

Mission-driven humanitarian organizations that regularly include early or late shifts, ask employees to work overtime, or hold work events in the evenings or weekends make it more likely that their employees aren't able to adequately restore their energy reserves. In addition, these workplace cultures often have heavy workloads and limited flexibility, which can also contribute to poor employee sleep. Over the long term, this not only impacts performance and productivity, but can exacerbate problems like racism, discrimination, and bullying because of the impact of sleep deprivation on mental health and cognitive functioning. Normalizing the value of sleep and rest not only protects staff health and well-being, it also makes it more likely that the organization will be able to effectively meet its mission. Some things organizations can do to promote the value of restorative care include the following.

- *Educate employees about the importance of sleep*: Sleep is one of the most underrated tools for enhancing our health and well-being. A lack of sleep can affect every aspect of our life, including health and safety, job effectiveness and productivity, and our mood and mental health. When we're sleepy or overtired, we move more slowly, our attention drifts more easily, and we can suffer from headaches or brain fog. As a result, accidents, injuries, poor decision-making and judgment, and mistakes are more likely. We've been taught that eight hours of sleep is enough, but the reality is that everyone has different sleep needs, which depend on individual health issues, neurodiversity needs, family dynamics, and living accommodations. Holding regular workshops about the importance of sleep, the ways it impacts job performance and health, and how to engage in good sleep hygiene can help staff better understand how vital sleep is to their well-being and provide them with tools to improve their sleep.

- *Work with staff to assess and adjust workloads*: Workloads are often determined by people at higher levels in the organization who are removed from the day-to-day realities of what it takes to meet determined metrics. Inviting staff to share their thoughts and experiences about managing current workloads supports their needs as well as mission needs. First, it empowers staff with a sense of agency and ownership over their work and fosters trust with management, while also supporting greater work/life harmony. Second, it ensures that mission needs are being met by creating realistic workload metrics that staff are likely able to meet. Though many organizations have traditionally used a top-down approach, working hand-in-hand with staff and adjusting to meet their needs makes it far more likely that mission metrics will not only be met, but the needs of the organization as a whole will be better supported through retention and the development of institutional knowledge as more employees stay with the organization for longer periods of time.

Stop Normalizing Burnout and Promote Rest

Prioritizing work over rest and normalizing burnout is fairly common in mission-driven humanitarian organizations. If we're exhausted or burned out, it means we've given everything we have to others—our family, loved ones, friends, and the people we serve. We've left nothing for ourselves. Most of us have moved through our careers wearing our exhaustion as a badge of honor—a way to show the world that we're dependable, capable, and strong, that we're worthy of being humanitarians. This isn't a sustainable existence, and the problem is perpetuated every time organizations celebrate or reward selflessness to the point of depletion while choosing not to address any of the fundamental issues that led to this state in the first place. Every time the organization institutes "mandatory overtime," or looks the other way when staff work beyond their allotted hours without compensation, or maintain unrealistic workloads, they send the message that meeting the mission, even at the cost of the health and well-being, is more important than everything else.

Resting is about restoring our energy reserves, and just as we might target our self-care practices to address the part of ourselves that is feeling depleted, understanding which area of our life is in need of rest can go a long way toward generating more energy and supporting our health and well-being. Educating staff about the different types of rest and promoting ways to practice micro-resting opportunities during the workday are ways to support them in their efforts to integrate resting into their day-to-day lives. This benefits staff, the organization, and the people you're working to serve. Being overworked and exhausted, as well as rest and sleep deprived should not be a state to which we aspire. It saps our ability to be fully present with others and holds us back from developing high-quality connections and deep and meaningful relationships. It prevents us from getting the rest our minds and bodies need to effectively function, which not only impacts our health and well-being, but our accuracy, productivity, endurance, and performance over the long term. Rather than making exhaustion a status symbol, or a measure of success or worthiness, mission-driven humanitarian organizations have an opportunity to proactively create conditions to avoid staff burnout and exhaustion.

COMMITMENT 4: FOSTER SHARED PURPOSE AND COMMITMENT

If our work is *what* we do, the meaning is *why* we do it, and the purpose is the *intention* that drives us. In the midst of the stress, adversity, and challenges that often accompany humanitarian work, the weight of bureaucracy, burnout, and trauma can sometimes become so heavy and all-consuming that we lose our connection to why we chose to serve in the first place. This lack of meaning and purpose can leave use feeling like we're flailing around, confused and alone. And if unaddressed, it can lead humanitarians to walk away from work they have loved and felt fulfilled by until now.

Fostering shared purpose and commitment is an opportunity for mission-driven humanitarian organizations to empower staff to co-create organizational vision and goals, and to foster social connection by encouraging staff to approach colleagues with curiosity, an open mind, and a desire to learn from each other. It is a pathway to the heart of flourishing, where we know that we matter, that our work matters; where we feel respected and valued and connected to a sense of purpose and meaning in our work. Most of the things highlighted in the three previous commitments also contribute to fostering shared purpose and commitment, but additional ones organizations may want to consider include offering developmental training, coaching, and mentoring and providing ongoing meaningful feedback.

Offer Developmental Training, Coaching, and Mentoring

While some organizations offer limited upward mobility, believing that this will keep staff in their positions for the rest of their careers isn't necessarily realistic. Organizations that support their staff by providing opportunities for growth are more likely to have staff remain with the organization, even if they move within it. Investing in developmental training, coaching, and mentoring not only builds staff members' emotional intelligence and relational skills, but it allows organizations to create a deep bench of new leaders who can step up, and step into, positions as people pause, retire, or move on to other opportunities. Or these can simply be a way to allow people to take breaks without the work suffering—a necessity in humanitarian organizations. A few ways organizations can be intentional in their approach include the following.

- *Use human-centered design to identify training needs*: Developmental training comes in a variety of forms—everything from formal workshops and training programs to shadowing opportunities and temporary assignments in other positions or locations. The best way to determine what kind of developmental training would support the needs of your workforce is to engage staff through a survey or listening sessions to hear directly from them about how the organization can support their development. In my former workplace, we began using a process called human-centered design—an approach to problem-solving that puts the needs of people at the heart of the process—to engage staff on a variety of issues. Using this process empowered staff to engage on topics that were important to them and identify potential solutions that they, as the people doing the work and experiencing the challenges, were uniquely qualified to offer. Each potential solution was tested and iterated upon until it was ready to be implemented. Through this process, staff solutions included a job-exchange program between different offices, so people could learn new skills and more about how other offices were doing similar work, as well as a comprehensive program grounded in our organizational values to onboard new staff.

- *Offer more than one type of mentoring program*: Mentoring is a one-on-one relationship that enables people to learn and grow from others. Typically, mentoring programs pair new leaders with more senior leaders. However, mentoring shouldn't be reserved only for people going through leadership programs since it's also been shown to support personal and career development, build diversity, support a culture of learning, reduce training costs, and improve productivity. In addition to formal leadership mentoring, organizations can offer peer mentoring and group mentoring. In my former organization, we also offered speed mentoring, through which staff had the opportunity to meet with eight to ten different mentors for ten minutes each. This allowed them to learn more about different leadership styles and career paths, and it was also fun. By offering more than one type of mentoring program, organizations can support more staff as they develop and grow.

- *Facilitate access to coaching*: While coaching and mentoring are similar, there are some key differences that make it important to offer both options within an organization. Mentors tend to provide guidance and advice based on their expertise and knowledge of doing the work. Coaching is a co-active partnership between coach and client where the coach asks deep, meaningful questions to help the client tap into their own strengths and knowledge as they navigate roadblocks that stand between them and their goals. Unlike mentors, which can come from within the workforce or leadership ranks, coaches working with organizations have typically gone through some kind of a training or certification process that qualifies them to serve in the role. Coaching requires organizations to train individuals within the organization or hire coaches from the outside.

Another way organizations can facilitate access to coaching is to subsidize the cost for staff through personal-development funds or other available funding.

Provide Ongoing and Meaningful Feedback

Feedback is one of the biggest challenges leaders encounter in their careers, and also one of the major contributors of stress. For staff, feedback is often implicitly (or explicitly in some cases) associated with criticism, which can make giving it uncomfortable and receiving it disheartening. Competing priorities coupled with a lack of confidence when it comes to having crucial conversations means that many leaders and organizations only provide feedback once or twice per year. This lack of ongoing communication can leave leaders and their teams feeling anxious, stressed out, and in some cases, resentful.

When I work with leaders, I encourage them to think about feedback as an ongoing, two-way conversation that not only provides staff with opportunities for growth, but also acknowledges and celebrates the wins along the way. A mindset shift about feedback can lead to improved feedback discussion and foster deeper connection and well-being for all. It also helps to create brave cultures where honest and productive feedback is based on the premise of "clear is kind" and where grace and compassion are woven into the process to create more meaningful interactions. A few feedback suggestions for leaders include the following.

- *Have ongoing performance conversations*: The key word here is *conversation*. Performance discussions should never be one-sided, nor should they happen only one or two times per year. Having regular one-on-one sessions with team members—asking them what's going well and what challenges they're encountering—creates an opportunity to correct behavior that needs correcting, while celebrating the things that are going well. Conversations don't need to be long, and they can be at a frequency that feels supportive. Inviting staff to help you create a schedule that works for everyone not only provides some autonomy and agency around feedback, but it contributes to psychological safety and ensures there won't be any surprises at the end of the year.
- *Acknowledge limiting factors*: There's nothing more frustrating than getting feedback that ignores the reality of what staff are

encountering in their day-to-day lives. Acknowledging challenges like demanding workloads, lack of equipment or training, changing policies, lack of clear guidance, and interpersonal issues, in addition to things like anxiety, overwhelm, and exhaustion, recognizes the humanity of the employee and fosters deeper connection.

- *Normalize sympathetic joy across the organization*: Sympathetic joy is a way to replace negative feelings like envy or jealousy toward another with positive feelings of happiness for them. Practicing sympathetic joy invites us to look for what shines about another person or causes them to glow. It also encourages us to notice where they have more energy and excitement, perhaps because they're using their strengths. The key to sympathetic joy is that it's sincere and nonjudgmental. Practicing sympathetic joy taps into the mirror neurons in our brain, creating a cascading effect. That way, when we witness others being their best, we increase our own odds of feeling more positivity. With each person we encounter throughout the day, we get the benefit of someone else's success. Think of it as a type of vicarious joy for other people's happiness. Making sympathetic joy an organizational value or norm fosters connection and community as people learn to support one another rather than seeing each other as competitors, and it leads to celebrating the little wins along the way.

Fostering open, two-way dialogue and creating tethers of joy between staff members makes people want to commit to the work *and* to the organization. It also nurtures creativity and innovation and ensures that the organization and its staff are showing up as the best versions of themselves as they work to serve others and meet the mission.

IT'S TIME TO CHOOSE SERVICE WITHOUT SACRIFICE

I spent almost two decades working in a fast-paced, high-stress organization where the work we did directly impacted the lives of people in dire situations. I know from experience how challenging it can be to take a break, eat lunch, or even get to the bathroom in these environments. I also understand the guilt associated with taking any time—let alone during the workday—to practice self-care when people are counting on us to get the work done. I acknowledge all of this because I recognize that proposing a duty of care grounded in social connection and asking organizations to carve out time during the workday for staff to engage in self-care may seem radical, or simply unrealistic in light of workloads and real-world demands.

But here's what I also know to be true as a humanitarian: the work never ends, and at the end of the day everyone—and I mean everyone—is replaceable. We have to choose to prioritize our health and well-being as individuals and as organizations. This is why I felt hopeful in October 2022 when the Surgeon General of the United States, Vivek Murthy, announced a new framework for workplace mental health and well-being, which promotes thriving over merely surviving.

The framework, which consists of five pillars—psychological safety, connection and belonging, work/life harmony, mattering at work, and opportunities for growth—were the same guiding principles of RAIO Thrive—the holistic well-being program I launched in my organization in 2017, the RAIO Daring Leaders Project I launched in 2020, and the duty-of-care framework I've introduced in this book. My hope is that as more programs like RAIO Thrive and the Surgeon General's initiative begin to show up in mission-driven organizations, the idea of thriving rather than merely surviving will begin to integrate into the fabric of the organizational culture I left behind, and into organizational cultures across the humanitarian sector as a whole.

As heartbreaking as the COVID-19 pandemic was, as individuals, it presented us with space to pause, reflect, and reset. For some people, it was an opportunity to slow down and spend more time with family and loved ones. For others, it exacerbated anxiety, fear, and loneliness. What we know for sure is that it changed many people profoundly and led them to reassess their values and priorities. It led them to crave greater and more meaningful connection to those around them and in their work, and it helped them recognize their own strength and new paths and possibilities for their life. It left many people in a different head space and a different heart space than before the pandemic started.

With this as the new starting line, mission-driven humanitarian organizations have a unique opportunity to pause, reflect, reset, and begin the process of rewriting the narrative of service before self—a chance to recognize and honor the humans at the heart of your humanitarian workforce by extending to your staff the ethos of care and compassion typically reserved for the people you serve. This is an opportunity to move from merely surviving to thriving as an organization by acknowledging the occupational stressors and traumas that impact humanitarians and working with staff to address and heal root issues within the organization. It's a moment to reimagine the concept of a duty of care that protects the whole human by promoting social connection and sharing stories, as well as elevating staff health and well-being to the same level as other decision factors, making it a cornerstone of shifting organizational culture and meeting the mission.

Unfortunately, many organizations still don't understand this. For every two steps forward we see through initiatives like the ones released by the Surgeon General, large organizations take one step back, as evidenced by the Office of Personnel Management (OPM) Director Kiran Ahuja's release of a memo for *Advancing Future of the Workforce Policies and Practices to Support Mission Delivery* in March 2023 in response to the COVID-19 pandemic. The memo laid out a vision and strategy to create a workforce that is "inclusive, agile, and engaged, with the right skills to enable mission delivery." And yet, not one of the five key priority areas addressed the mental health and well-being needs of the workforce, nor was staff health or well-being mentioned anywhere in the memo. Given that OPM essentially serves at the US federal government's human-resources arm and sets the tone for human resources government wide, its failure to prioritize staff mental health and well-being was not just a missed opportunity, but also short-sighted, given the new generation of workers entering the federal workforce for whom protection of their mental health and well-being is non-negotiable.

Leaders play a key role in shifting organizational culture because they set the tone and drive change. Modeling radically human leadership through self-awareness, self-compassion, and curiosity allows for deeper connection and fosters psychological safety in the workplace. Acknowledging the trauma people are experiencing through empathy and creating opportunities for staff to gather bravely and vulnerably to share their stories not only makes people feel seen, but it helps to remove the shame and stigma associated with many of the occupational mental-health challenges and trauma humanitarians may experience at different points in their career.

The more people are able to connect on a human-to-human level, the easier it becomes to weave feelings of connection and belonging into the fabric of organizational culture.

But none of this is possible without each of us taking time to do the work first. Our organizations change when the people within them change. Working through lunch, or not taking breaks or time off are choices, just as much as intentionally making time to take a walk or connect with friends or engage in a hobby is a choice. Prioritizing self-care and engaging in a regular mindfulness practice can help us more easily notice, name, and navigate through challenging situations. As much as I believe organizations owe staff a duty of care that protects them as whole human beings, I also believe that each one of us has a responsibility to care for ourselves, too. It can't be one or the other—it must be both together.

All it takes is a few brave, human-centered leaders to create significant shifts in organizations, and my hope is that sharing my story will help others in mission-driven spaces find the courage to share their own, that the stories of my personal experiences with violence, displacement, mental illness, and other trauma will serve as mirrors for your own experiences, encouraging compassion and removing some of the stigma and shame that often travel hand in hand with these challenges. I hope the stories of burnout, compassion fatigue, vicarious trauma, and moral injury I've shared will create an awareness for leaders in mission-driven organizations and spark discussions about a duty of care in your organization. I hope intentionally making changes and engaging in new self-care practices for ourselves and within our organizations will help more individuals advocate for their own health and well-being, and that together we'll rewrite the narrative of service before self and shift our collective expectations about what it means to be a humanitarian.

My greatest wish is that you begin to create awareness and practice self-compassion to heal your stories and move toward being happier and healthier, so you can live your life to the fullest and continue to show up to do the important work this world needs you to do, now more than ever.

YOU DON'T NEED TO DO IT ALONE

Turning the tide and healing occupational trauma across the humanitarian sector isn't something any one person can do. It's a story we must write together. Yet at the same time, each of us must make a choice to prioritize our own health and well-being. If you would like support in making these important shifts, please visit www.rootsintheclouds.com to learn more about how we can begin to work together to change the narrative of *service before self* to *service without sacrifice*.

DEFINITIONS, NOTES, AND RESOURCES

I n the pages that follow you'll find citations for books, articles, and videos that have contributed to my healing and to my knowledge base so I could write this book. I've included them here as additional resources that might help you in your own healing journey, along with definitions and background information about historical events noted in the book to provide additional context.

DEFINITIONS

ASYLUM: a form of protection that allows an individual to remain in another country instead of being removed (deported) to a country where they fear persecution or harm

ASYLEE: a noncitizen in the United States who is found to be unable or unwilling to return to their country of nationality, or to seek the protection of that country, because of persecution or a well-founded fear of persecution

BURNOUT: prolonged physical and psychological exhaustion related to a person's work

COMPASSION FATIGUE: loss of the ability to nurture

DACA: On June 15, 2012, President Obama announced the Deferred Action for Childhood Arrivals via executive action as a way to protect people who were brought to the US without citizenship or residency as children.

DHS: an acronym for the Department of Homeland Security, which was established in 2002, combining 22 different federal departments and agencies—including US Citizenship and Immigration Services—into a unified, integrated Cabinet agency

DUTY OF CARE: a holistic framework for staff well-being that addresses their mental, emotional, spiritual, relational, and physical health and well-being

GUJARATI: the language and people who come from the state of Gujarat in India

HUMANITARIAN: anyone working to alleviate the pain and suffering of others

INDIAN GIVER: a derogatory term to describe a person who gives something to another and then takes it back or expects an equivalent in return

INDIAN STANDARD TIME: technically defined as the time zone observed throughout India, but used colloquially as a cultural reference about how Indian people are always running late

MICROAGGRESSIONS: a statement, action, or incident regarded as an instance of indirect, subtle, or unintentional discrimination against members of under-served groups and populations

MINDFUL AWARENESS: the act of noticing what is happening as it happens

MINDFUL PERFORMANCE: the quality of presence that emerges when one lets go of striving for an outcome and trusts the wisdom and talent available in the moment

MINDFULNESS: the awareness that arises from paying attention on purpose in the present moment, non-judgmentally

MISSION-DRIVEN: making policies, processes, communications, and decisions that align with an organization's core values and further its defined mission

MORAL INJURY: perpetrating, failing to prevent, bearing witness to, or learning about acts that transgress one's deeply held moral values, beliefs, and expectations

*m***PEAK:** an acronym for Mindful Performance Enhancement, Awareness & Knowledge, a mindful-performance course created by Pete Kirchmer with the UC San Diego Center for Mindfulness

MUSLIM BAN: a series of Trump administration executive orders starting in January 2017 that prohibited travel and refugee resettlement from select predominantly Muslim countries

NGO: non-governmental organization

OTHERING: to view or treat a person or group of people as intrinsically different from and alien to oneself

PSYCHOLOGICAL SAFETY: a belief held by members of a team that they won't be punished or humiliated for taking risks, expressing their ideas, asking questions, voicing concerns, or making mistakes in the workplace

PTSD: an acronym for post-traumatic stress disorder, which is defined as a range of reactions a person might experience in the aftermath of trauma

RAIO: an acronym for the Refugee, Asylum and International Operations directorate—an operational arm within US Citizenship and Immigration Services, Department of Homeland Security

RDLP: an acronym for the RAIO Daring Leaders Project, a leadership-development program based in mindfulness and positive psychology that I developed for the Refugee, Asylum and International Operations directorate

REFUGEE: a person who has been forced to leave their country in order to escape war, persecution, or natural disaster

SECONDARY TRAUMATIC STRESS: the emotional duress that arises when a person hears the firsthand trauma experiences of another

SELF-COMPASSION: the act of turning kindness toward ourselves

USCIS: an acronym for US Citizenship and Immigration Services; during the Great Depression in 1933, President Franklin Roosevelt ordered the consolidation of federal immigration and naturalization functions into the Immigration and Nationality Service (INS), which oversaw the immigration process, enforcement, and border-patrol activities until Congress passed the Homeland Security Act of 2002. On March 1, 2003, USCIS assumed responsibility for immigration services by focusing exclusively on the administration of benefits applications. The Homeland Security Act created Immigration and Customs Enforcement (ICE) and Customs and Border Protection (CBP) to oversee immigration enforcement and border security.

VICARIOUS TRAUMA: the experience of trauma symptoms after being repeatedly exposed to other people's trauma and their stories of traumatic events

VUCA: an acronym coined in 1987 to describe or reflect on the volatility, uncertainty, complexity, and ambiguity of general conditions or situations

NOTES AND RESOURCES

AUTHOR'S NOTE

Daniel J. Siegel, *The Developing Mind: Toward a Neurobiology of Interpersonal Experience,* 3rd Edition (New York, The Guilford Press, 2020).

David Treleaven, *Trauma-Sensitive Mindfulness* (New York, London, W.W. Norton & Company, 2018).

"Ensō." Wikipedia, January 30, 2023. https://en.wikipedia.org/wiki/Ens%C5%8D.

A NOTE ABOUT READING THIS BOOK

Pete Kirchmer, *mPEAK Coach's Practicum,* Sessions 3, 5 (San Diego, Mindfulness Based Health, 2020).

INTRODUCTION

Integrating palliative care and symptom relief into the response to humanitarian emergencies and crises: a WHO guide. Geneva: World Health Organization; 2018. Licence: CC BY-NC-SA 3.0 IGO.

Charles R. Figley, *Caring for the Military,* 1st Edition (New York, Routledge, 2016).

PART ONE – SHAPING

Pete Kirchmer, *mPEAK Coach's Practicum,* Session 3 (San Diego, Mindfulness Based Health, 2020).

Chapter 1 – The History We Carry Within Us (Generational Trauma)

Mark Wolynn, *It Didn't Start with You: How Inherited Family Trauma Shapes Who we Are and How to End the Cycle* (New York, Penguin Books, 2016).

Yashvantrai Sheth, interviews by Dimple Dhabalia, December 2003, April 2022.

Meghan Garrity, "50 years ago, Uganda ordered its entire Asian population to leave: A new data set explores mass expulsions around the world," *The Washington Post*, August 4, 2022, https://www.washingtonpost.com/politics/2022/08/04/uganda-idi-amin-asians-1992/.

Chapter 2 – The Moments that Split Us (Othering and Identity Trauma)
Lakshmi Gandhi, "The History Behind the Phrase 'Don't Be an Indian Giver'," National Public Radio, September 2, 2013, https://www.npr.org/sections/codeswitch/2013/09/02/217295339/the-history-behind-the-phrase-dont-be-an-indian-giver.

Tiffany Jana, Michael Baran, *Subtle Acts of Exclusion: How to Understand, Identify, and Stop Microaggressions* (Oakland, Barrett-Koehler Publishers, 2020).

PART TWO – SURVIVING
Pete Kirchmer, *mPEAK Coach's Practicum,* Session 5 (San Diego, Mindfulness Based Health, 2020).

PART THREE – SEEING
Pete Kirchmer, *mPEAK Coach's Practicum,* Session 5 (San Diego, Mindfulness Based Health, 2020).

Bassel van der Kolk, MD, *The Body Keeps the Score* (New York, Penguin Books, 2015).

Elizabeth A. Stanley, PhD, *Widen the Window: Training Your Brain and Body to Thrive During Stress and Recover from Trauma* (New York, Avery, 2019).

Chapter 10 – A Painful Lesson (Burnout)
Michael Drayton, *Anti-burnout: How to Create a Psychologically Safe and High-performance Organization* (New York, Routledge, 2021).

Alessandra Pigni, *The Idealist's Survival Kit: 75 Simple Ways to Avoid Burnout* (Berkeley, Parallax Press, 2016).

Liz Sly and Ahmed Ramadan, "Insurgents seize Iraqi city of Mosul as security forces flee," *The Washington Post*, June 10, 2014, https://www.washingtonpost.com/world/insurgents-seize-iraqi-city-of-mosul-as-troops-flee/2014/06/10/21061e87-8fcd-4ed3-bc94-0e309af0a674_story.html.

Chapter 11 – A Conflicted Oath (Moral Injury)

"Muslim Travel Ban," *Immigration History*, https://immigrationhistory.org/item/muslim-travel-ban/.

Executive Order 13769, *Protecting the Nation from Foreign Terrorist Entry into the United States*, https://www.federalregister.gov/documents/2017/02/01/2017-02281/protecting-the-nation-from-foreign-terrorist-entry-into-the-united-states.

"A.C.L.U. Complaint on Trump Immigration Order," *The New York Times*, January 28, 2017, https://www.nytimes.com/interactive/2017/01/28/us/politics/ACLU-Complaint.html.

Chapter 13 – A Shared Anguish (Vicarious Trauma and Compassion Fatigue)

Thomas Patrick Melady, Margaret Badum Melady, *Uganda: The Asian Exiles* (Maryknoll, Orbis Books, 1976).

Dharam P. Ghai, *Portrait of a Minority: Asians in East Africa* (Nairobi, Oxford University Press, 1965).

Mahmood Mamdani, *From Citizen to Refugee: Uganda Asians Come to Britain,* 2nd Edition (Oxford, Pambazuka Press, 2011).

"Stopping Rape as a Weapon of War in Congo," *Human Rights Watch*, September 18, 2009, https://www.hrw.org/news/2009/09/18/stopping-rape-weapon-war-congo.

Jean Hatzfield, *Machete Season: The Killers in Rwanda Speak* (New York, Farrar, Straus and Giroux, 2005).

Charles R. Figley, *Traumatization and comfort: Close relationships may be hazardous to your health.* Keynote presentation at the conference, Families and Close Relationships: Individuals in Social Interaction; February 1982, Lubbock, Texas: Texas Tech University.

Laurie Anne Pearlman, Lisa McKay, *Understanding & Addressing Vicarious Trauma,* Online Training Module Four (Pasadena, The Headington Institute, 2008).

Lucinda Hardwick, "Kindness can be cruel: experiencing trauma by proxy," *The Guardian*, April 22, 2014, https://www.theguardian.com/global-development-professionals-network/2014/apr/22/vicarious-trauma-humanitarian-workers.

PART FOUR – SHIFTING

David Orenstein, "MIT scientists discover fundamental rule of brain plasticity," *MIT News*, June 22, 2018, https://news.mit.edu/2018/mit-scientists-discover-fundamental-rule-of-brain-plasticity-0622.

Chapter 14 – From Disconnection to New Purpose (Connection)
Vivek H. Murthy, 19th Surgeon General of the United States, *Together: The Healing Power of Connection* (New York, Harper Wave, 2020).

Chapter 16 – From Perfectionism to Human-Centered Leadership (Curiosity and Empathy)
Katherine Manning, *The Empathetic Workplace: 5 Steps to a Compassionate, Calm, and Confident Response to Trauma on the Job* (Nashville, Harper Collins Leadership, 2021).

Chapter 17– From Shattered to Sharing (Vulnerability)
Brené Brown, *Dare to Lead: Daring Greatly and Rising Strong at Work* (New York, Random House, 2018).

PART 5 – SHARING

Chapter 19 – Becoming Whole (Healing Through Story)
Pete Kirchmer, *mPEAK Coach's Practicum,* Session 1 (San Diego, Mindfulness Based Health, 2020).

PART 6 – SERVICE WITHOUT SACRIFICE: A HUMANITARIAN MANIFESTO

FOR INDIVIDUALS
Jon Kabat-Zinn, *Wherever you go, there you are: Mindfulness meditation in everyday life* (New York, Hachette Books, 1994).

Locating Yourself – A Key to Conscious Leadership, https://conscious.is/video/locating-yourself-a-key-to-conscious-leadership.

Carol S. Dweck, PhD, *Mindset: The New Psychology of Success, How We Can Learn to Fulfill Our Potential* (New York, Random House Publishing Group, 2007).

Caren Osten Gerszberg, "Why Your Outbreath is Connected to Your Well-Being," *Mindful Magazine Online*, September 9, 2021, https://www.mindful.org/why-your-breath-is-connected-to-your-well-being/.

Dimple Dhabalia, "Why Radically Important Leadership is More Important Than Ever," Medium.com, November 15, 2021, https://dimpledhabalia.medium.com/why-radically-human-leadership-is-more-important-than-ever-1cefee1da4df.

FOR LEADERS AND ORGANIZATIONS

COMMITMENT 1

Become a Trauma-Informed Organization

"Managing in a VUCA World: Thriving in Turbulent Times," *Mind Tools,* https://www.mindtools.com/asnydwg/managing-in-a-vuca-world.

Bruce D. Perry, MD, PhD, Oprah Winfrey, *What Happened to You? Conversations on Trauma, Resilience and Healing* (New York, Flatiron Books, 2021).

Paul Conti, MD, *Trauma: The Invisible Epidemic: How Trauma Works and How We Can Heal From It* (Boulder, CO, Sounds True, 2021).

Thomas Hübl, *Healing Collective Trauma: A Process for Integrating Our Intergenerational and Cultural Wounds* (Boulder, CO, Sounds True, 2020).

Design Cultures of Empathy

Pete Kirchmer, *mPEAK Coach's Practicum,* Session 5 (San Diego, Mindfulness Based Health, 2020).

Heal Root Issues and Organizational Trauma

Pat Vivian and Shana Hormann, *Organizational Trauma and Healing*, (North Charleston, SC, CreateSpace, 2013).

COMMITMENT 2

Prioritize Social Connection

Our Epidemic of Loneliness and Isolation—The U.S. Surgeon General's Advisory on the Healing Effects of Social Connection and Community, 2023, https://www.hhs.gov/sites/default/files/surgeon-general-social-connection-advisory.pdf.

Annamaria D Fabio, Letizia Palazzeschi, Ornella Bucci, "Gratitude in Organizations: A Contribution for Healthy Organizational Contexts," *Frontiers in Psychology*, November 17, 2017, https://www.ncbi.nlm.nih.gov/pmc/articles/PMC5699179/.

Eric Mosley, Derek Irvine, *Making Work Human: How Human-Centered Companies are Changing the Future of Work and the World* (McGraw-Hill, 2020).

Sarah Green Carmichael, "The Research is Clear: Long Hours Backfire for People and for Companies," *Harvard Business Review*, August 19, 2015, https://hbr.org/2015/08/the-research-is-clear-long-hours-backfire-for-people-and-for-companies.

Jodi Clarke, MA, LPC/MHSP, "How Constantly Being Busy Affects Your Well-Being," *Very Well Mind*, May 23, 2022, https://www.verywellmind.com/how-the-glorification-of-busyness-impacts-our-well-being-4175360.

Promote Trust and Psychological Safety Across the Organization

Amy C. Edmondson, *The Fearless Organization: Creating Psychological Safety in the Workplace for Learning, Innovation, and Growth* (Hoboken, John Wiley & Sons, Inc., 2019).

David Michels, "Learning to Lead During Times of Crisis," *Forbes Online*, April 14, 2022, https://www.forbes.com/sites/davidmichels/2022/04/14/learning-to-lead-during-times-of-crisis/?sh=65690753241a.

Beth Strano, "Untitled Poem by Beth Strano," *Facing History & Ourselves,* April 22, 2022, https://www.facinghistory.org/resource-library/untitled-poem-beth-strano.

Anne Iversen, "How to Develop a Beginner's Mindset: A Critical Trat In Business Today," *Forbes Online*, April 21, 2021, https://www.forbes.com/sites/forbeshumanresourcescouncil/2021/04/21/how-to-develop-a-beginners-mindset-a-critical-trait-in-business-today/?sh=14d6c66b65a0.

Create Opportunities to Share Stories

David JP Phillips, "The Magical Science of Storytelling," November 12, 2015, Stockholm, Sweden, TEDx Stockholm, https://www.youtube.com/watch?v=Nj-hdQMa3uA.

Annie Brewster, *The Healing Power of Storytelling: Using Personal Narrative to Navigate Illness, Trauma, and Loss* (Berkley, North Atlantic Books, 2022).

Angus Fletcher, *Wonderworks: Literary Invention and the Science of Stories* (New York, Simon & Schuster, 2021).

The Moth, Meg Bowles, Catherine Burns, Jennifer Hixon, Sarah Austin Jenness, Kate Tellers, *How to Tell a Story: The Essential Guide to Memorable Storytelling from the Moth* (New York, Crown, 2022).

COMMITMENT 3

Create Conditions for Work and Recovery to Peacefully Coexist

Garen Staglin, "Building Recovery Time Into The Workflow," *Forbes Online*, November 22, 2021, https://www.forbes.com/sites/onemind/2021/11/22/building-recovery-time-into-the-workflow/?sh=26f14afd7abe.

Cultivate Workplace Cultures That Value Restorative Care

Arianna Huffington, *The Sleep Revolution: Transforming Your Life, One Night at a Time* (New York, Harmony Books, 2016).

Tom Rath, *Eat Move Sleep: How Small Choices Lead to Big Changes* (San Francisco, Missionday, 2013).

Saundra Dalton-Smith, MD, "The 7 types of rest that every person needs," *ideas.ted.com*, January 6, 2021, https://ideas.ted.com/the-7-types-of-rest-that-every-person-needs/.

COMMITMENT 4

Offer Developmental Training, Coaching, and Mentoring

An Introduction to Design Thinking – PROCESS GUIDE, Institute of Design at Stanford, https://web.stanford.edu/~mshanks/MichaelShanks/files/509554.pdf.

Provide Ongoing and Meaningful Feedback

Jeremy Adam Smith, "What Is Sympathetic Joy and How Can You Feel More of It?" *Greater Good Magazine*, March 1, 2022, https://greatergood.berkeley.edu/article/item/what_is_sympathetic_joy_and_how_can_you_feel_more_of_it.

IT'S TIME TO CHOOSE SERVICE WITHOUT SACRIFICE

The U.S. Surgeon General's Framework for Workplace Mental Health and Well-Being, October 2022, https://www.hhs.gov/sites/default/files/workplace-mental-health-well-being.pdf.

Kiran A. Ahuja, *Memorandum for Heads of Executive Agencies and Departments: Advancing Future of the Workforce Policies and Practices to Support Mission Delivery*, March 7, 2023, https://chcoc.gov/content/advancing-future-workforce-policies-and-practices-support-mission-delivery.

Mark C. Perna, "5 Non-Negotiables for Gen Z Workers in 2023—And Why They Matter," *Forbes Online*, January 10, 2023, https://www.forbes.com/sites/markcperna/2023/01/10/5-non-negotiables-for-gen-z-workers-in-2023-and-why-they-matter/?sh=44505dbe1442.

ACKNOWLEDGMENTS

I'd like to begin by acknowledging God and my Guru for removing obstacles from my path as I moved through the journey of writing and putting this book out into the world. For giving me strength to reach into the depths of my soul to find, and share, moments of my life that have been locked away for decades. For filling me with the courage to share my experiences for the benefit of others. For guiding me with care and compassion at each and every step. And for trusting me to be the vessel through which you shared your wisdom. Thank you for sharing pieces of you to make me the woman I am today. I'm deeply humbled and grateful to serve through you.

I'd like to acknowledge all the ancestors who came before me, especially the long line of brave and resolute women who, from one generation to the next, refused to be kept down or silenced. I hope voicing my truth through the stories in this book releases and heals the patriarchal energy and generational trauma of banishment and abandonment experienced by so many women in my lineage. Thank you for sharing pieces of yourselves to make me the woman I am today. I love you and am deeply humbled and grateful to know I come from a long line of female warriors.

I'd like to acknowledge my mom and dad, for the love, guidance, and values you instilled in me. It took me a long time to understand how each piece of wisdom you shared was a gift that would stay with me forever. I know that though you've both left this world, you continue to stand on each side of me, guiding me, supporting me, and loving me as only you two could. Thank you for sharing pieces of yourselves to make me the woman I am today. I'm deeply humbled and grateful to be your daughter.

Mom, I'd like to acknowledge you for your tenacity, determination, and grace in the face of adversity and hardship. You were the strongest, most beautiful person I've ever known, and though I'm grateful for the time I got to spend with you, I wish every day that you could have stayed longer. I often travel back in my mind to our last months together—laughing, talking, exploring, watching Hindi movies, taking pictures, cooking, eating, and serving others until the end. It's like your soul knew I'd need these memories to sustain me after you were gone. But the memory that makes my heart swell, fills my eyes with tears, and for which I'm most grateful, is that morning in May, just two months before you left this world, when you held my face between your hands, looked me in the eyes and said, "I want you to know I love you and I am so proud of you." The tenderness and care with which you shared your love with me that morning is something I continue to feel to this day. Your love was endless and made me feel safe. I hope the stories I've shared in this book make you proud and release some of the pain you carried within you for so long. I love you and am deeply humbled and grateful to have called you Momma.

Dad, I'd like to acknowledge you for having the courage and perseverance to break away from what was known and comfortable to start a new life, on your terms, half-way around the world. I can't imagine what it must have been like for you to bear your pain in silence for so many years as you battled the demons within. I know the dreams you envisioned didn't always become reality, but I take comfort in knowing that we three women in your life loved you fiercely and made you proud. With each passing year, I see more of you in me—your creativity, passion, laughter, your round face, and your ability to fill up a room and connect deeply with the people around you. I hope the stories I've shared here help the world recognize your humanity and bring you peace wherever you are. I love you and am deeply humbled and grateful to have called you Dad.

Kajal, my beautiful, big-hearted sister, I'd like to acknowledge you for your humor, spirituality, and ability to see the forest when I get stuck in the trees. You are the most thoughtful and heartfelt human I've ever known. You are a gifted healer and your deep intuition allows you to see people at their very core. Your desire to care for others knows no bounds, and I can't imagine having survived all the challenges we've experienced in this lifetime without you. You are my most loving protector, and you make me laugh and tap into the silly side of me that I'm often too afraid to show to others with ease. You are my best friend and confidant, and I love you more than words can express. Thank you for designing the beautiful cover of this book—it means a lot to me that a part of you is memorialized in what I've created. Thank you for sharing pieces of yourself to make me the woman I am today. I'm deeply humbled and grateful to call you my sister.

Yashvantrai Sheth, or as I know you, Yashu mama, I'd like to acknowledge you for being a quiet but steadfast presence in my life that has always been there to protect and stand with me through the many moments of sorrow and joy. Thank you for so generously sharing and trusting me to tell your story. My earliest memories on this earth include flashes of you—making gathiya in the kitchen on Sundays when everyone gathered to watch the Denver Broncos in our living room, playing with your dog Simba in the backyard, going to Cherry Creek Dam to have sunflower seeds and watch the sunset. You're one of the most kindhearted people I've ever known, and one of the few who truly lives without expectation and whose love is unconditional. You're a poet who lives life on his own terms, without regret, taking the time to listen to birdsongs and see beauty all around you—a trait I believe I've inherited from you. I love you. Thank you for sharing pieces of yourself to make me the woman I am today. I'm deeply humbled and grateful to call you my uncle.

I'd like to acknowledge my mom's family for protecting us and being a safe haven during the many storms we encountered over the course of our lives. I hold memories of summers in Toronto, all of us packed into Faversham Court peeling lychees, folding mithai boxes, and laughing—always laughing. Saying thank you doesn't seem like enough to convey my gratitude for all that you are and all that you've done for us. Thank you for sharing pieces of yourselves to make me the woman I am today. I love you and am deeply humbled and grateful to be a member of this family.

I'd like to acknowledge Wade Livingston, my first boss and mentor who understood the concept of work/life harmony long before it was a thing. Thank you for modeling healthy service, and for understanding and acknowledging the toll that this work takes on our minds and bodies, and making those of us on your team understand and acknowledge it, too. Without the seeds you planted all those years ago, none of this would have happened. I am deeply humbled and grateful to have called you my boss, mentor, and a friend.

I'd like to acknowledge Dr. Ali Safayan, MD. You're not only an extraordinary functional health practitioner, but one of the most thoughtful and generous people I've ever met. In an age when many doctors don't take the time to get to know their patients, and choose to prescribe pharmaceuticals to address surface conditions, you regularly sit with each patient for as long as it takes, and work with us to identify and address root issues. Thank you for the patience and care with which you've always treated me, and for helping me see what I was doing to my body by not prioritizing my own health and well-being. I am deeply humbled and grateful to have you by my side on the path of my healing journey.

I'd like to acknowledge my colleagues and mentors at US Citizenship and Immigration Services who are in the midst of some of the greatest challenges you've ever faced. Yet you continue getting up each morning and showing up to serve. Your dedication to service inspires me every day, and drives my desire to change the system so you can keep doing the work you love, without losing yourself in the process. I care about each of you and am deeply humbled and grateful to have served alongside you for almost two decades.

I'd like to acknowledge all the humanitarians and you, the readers, regardless of the sector, who continue to serve the world's most vulnerable people. Thank you for taking the time to read my words. I hope you saw pieces of yourself in my stories and that they inspire you to move toward healing your own story, if you need to. I don't know if you need to hear this, but I want to say it because it doesn't get said enough: though there may struggles along the way, your work touches the souls of the people you serve and stays with them long after you part ways. Thank you for the work you do. I'm deeply humbled and grateful to be able to serve you in the same way.

I'd like to acknowledge all the writers in my writing group who supported me through each breakthrough, and each breakdown, as I uncovered long-buried stories from the dark corners of my brain and heart and got them on to the page. These include Amanda Johnson, Aaron Johnson, Alyssa Coehlo, Valorie Thomas, Lori Geisey, Lisa Boone, and special thanks to Meridith Merchant—my soul traveler—who, in addition to witnessing my book coming to life, was there for me during some of the darkest and most challenging moments of the process. Thank you. I'm deeply humbled and grateful to have been part of such an extraordinary group of writers.

I'd like to acknowledge my beta readers: Nadia Daúd, Kris Lantheaume, Shana Hormann—thank you for the time and thoughtful feedback you provided on early drafts of this book. And a special thanks to Melissa Coleman, Dawn McKeever, and Debbie DeVoe for your love and support when it felt like things were falling apart, and for reading and re-reading multiple versions of this book and providing detailed feedback that helped me refine my message and move me closer to where I needed to be. Thank you to my editor, Jessica Royer Ocken, who stepped into the process and navigated the pages of my manuscript with patience, ease, and the eye of a hawk, asked thoughtful questions, and guided me with love and tenderness. Thank you all for taking the time and sharing your knowledge and expertise to help me make this book the very best that it could be. I love you and am deeply humbled and grateful to have you in my life.

To all my incredible friends—and there are too many to name here—thank you for your love, support, friendship, and thought-provoking chats which sparked new ideas and made this book richer. To anyone I may have inadvertently forgotten, or for new soul-travelers who I met after this book went to press, and therefore didn't get your name in these acknowledgments—please forgive me. I love you all and am deeply humbled and grateful to call you my friends.

Finally, thank you for choosing to read this book. Regardless of where your path leads you, I want you to know that I will be your most ardent supporter and advocate. My greatest wish is for you to be happy, healthy, and able to experience joy as you savor the little moments of everyday life. May you continue to serve others with grace and dignity, and may we work together to change the narrative of service above self once and for all.

I am deeply humbled and grateful to walk alongside you on this journey.

With so much gratitude,

ABOUT THE AUTHOR

D IMPLE DHABALIA is the founder of Roots in the Clouds, a boutique consulting firm specializing in using the power of story to heal individual and organizational trauma and moral injury. She is also a writer, podcaster, coach, and facilitator, who brings over twenty years of experience working at the intersection of leadership, mindfulness, and storytelling.

Her path to becoming a thought leader in this field was a circuitous one, unfolding over the course of almost two decades of living, working, and traveling in more than 40 countries, serving the most vulnerable people in the world. With both the empowering and challenging experiences from her career as a catalyst, Dimple launched Roots in the Clouds in 2021 with the personal mission of transforming mission-driven sectors by building human-centered cultures that are able to meet mission needs *and* create psychologically safe spaces of empathy, connection, well-being and belonging for staff.

Today Dimple's work supports a holistic approach to addressing individual and organizational trauma and moral injury. She creates brave spaces for emerging and seasoned leaders to use the power of stories to preserve their own humanity as they work to preserve it for others.

Dimple is an International Coaching Federation-accredited coach, certified in Applied Positive Psychology (CAPP), and is a certified *Mindful* Performance Enhancement, Awareness, and Knowledge (*m*PEAK) facilitator. She has a JD from the University of Denver, College of Law, and a BA in Institutions and Policies and a Politics Philosophy and Economics degree from William Jewell College and Oxford University.

INDEX